"*Just Babies* is exactly the combination of penetrating insight, cutting-edge science, and elegant prose that millions of readers have come to expect from one of psychology's best writers and sharpest minds."
—DANIEL GILBERT, Edgar Pierce Professor of Psychology, Harvard University; author of *Stumbling on Happiness*

"Paul Bloom is a scientist who knows how to tell a fascinating and charming story. As a new parent, I found *Just Babies* not only full of insights into my son's developing moral sense but also a great pleasure to read."
—JOSHUA FOER, author of *Moonwalking with Einstein*

"*Just Babies* is a vital contribution to the scientific study of morality that fills in a major gap in our understanding of human nature, and as a bonus it's a riveting read!"
—MICHAEL SHERMER, publisher of *Skeptic* magazine; author of *The Science of Good and Evil*

"Paul Bloom is one of the best psychologist-writers today. In *Just Babies* he combines hard data with charming anecdote and incisive analysis to explore one of the most profound questions that's ever confronted mankind: how we become moral beings. He makes an erudite and impassioned case for the primacy of deliberation and reason in our lives—a truth given short shrift in pop psychology."
—SALLY SATEL, M.D., coauthor of *Brainwashed*

JUST BABIES

THE ORIGINS

OF

GOOD AND EVIL

PAUL BLOOM

CROWN PUBLISHERS / NEW YORK

Library of Congress Cataloging-in-Publication Data
Bloom, Paul, 1963–
    Just babies : the origins of good and evil /
    Paul Bloom.
        pages cm
    1. Ethics—Psychological aspects. 2. Good and evil.
    3. Values. 4. Child development. I. Title.
    BJ45.B56   2013
    155.4'1825—dc23   2013012697

ISBN 978-0-307-88684-2
eISBN 978-0-307-88686-6

Printed in the United States of America

Jacket design by Christopher Brand
Jacket photography by Chris Frazer Smith (wristband);
Masterfile/royalty free (arms)

10 9 8 7 6 5 4 3 2 1

First Edition

Dedicated to Elaine Reiser and Murray Reiser,

for their love and support

Man was destined for society. His morality, therefore, was to be formed to this object. He was endowed with a sense of right and wrong merely relative to this. This sense is as much a part of his nature, as the sense of hearing, seeing, feeling; it is the true foundation of morality. . . . The moral sense, or conscience, is as much a part of man as his leg or arm. It is given to all human beings in a stronger or weaker degree, as force of members is given them in a greater or less degree. It may be strengthened by exercise, as may any particular limb of the body.

—THOMAS JEFFERSON, 1787

CONTENTS

Preface   1

1   THE MORAL LIFE OF BABIES   7

2   EMPATHY AND COMPASSION   33

3   FAIRNESS, STATUS, AND PUNISHMENT   59

4   OTHERS   101

5   BODIES   131

6   FAMILY MATTERS   159

7   HOW TO BE GOOD   187

Acknowledgments   219

Notes   223

Index   265

JUST BABIES

PREFACE

In 2005, a writer living in Dallas heard that an acquaintance of hers was suffering from kidney disease. Without a transplant, Sally Satel would soon be on dialysis, tethered to a machine to filter her blood for three days a week. After doing some research and talking with her husband, Virginia Postrel flew to Washington, D.C., and had her right kidney transplanted into Sally's body. Kidney transplants typically occur between family members, but Virginia and Sally were not even close friends. Still, Virginia said that she felt empathy for Sally's situation and liked the idea of being able to help in a straightforward way. Others go even further: they log on to sites such as matchingdonors.com and arrange to donate their kidneys and other organs to complete strangers.

Some people see this sort of altruism as evidence of a moral code implanted by God. Among them are prominent scientists like Francis Collins, the head of the National

Institutes of Health, who argues that such acts of selfless-ness prove that our moral judgments and moral actions cannot be fully explained by the forces of biological evolu-tion. They demand a theological explanation.

Along with this transcendent kindness, though, there is appalling cruelty. I read in the newspaper this morning about a man whose girlfriend broke off their relationship; he later stalked her and threw acid at her face. I remember, as a child, first hearing about the Holocaust, of gas cham-bers and sadistic doctors and children being turned into soap and lampshades. If our wondrous kindness is evidence for God, is our capacity for great evil proof of the Devil?

Then there are the more mundane acts of kindness and cruelty. For myself, it's the bad things that I remember the most. Some of the choices I have made in the past still make me squirm. (If this is not true of you, then you are a much better person than I am—or much worse.) Some were honest mistakes based on what I thought was right at the time. But in other instances, I knew the right thing to do but chose to do something else. As Yoda might have put it, Strong is the Power of the Dark Side. Still, while I admit that I retain both of my kidneys, I have sacrificed to help others and taken risks for causes that I felt were right. In all of these regards, I am perfectly typical.

Morality fascinates us. The stories we enjoy the most, whether fictional (as in novels, television shows, and mov-ies) or real (as in journalism and historical accounts), are tales of good and evil. We want the good guys to be rewarded—and we really want to see the bad guys suffer.

Our appetite for punishment can go to extremes. In England a few years ago, a cat was found trapped in a garbage bin after having been lost for many hours. The owner discovered what had happened by viewing footage from a security camera overlooking the street. A middle-aged woman had picked up the cat, looked around, opened up the bin, and tossed it in. Then she had closed up the bin and walked away. The owner posted this video on Facebook, and the woman, Mary Bale, was quickly identified. Now, it's not hard to see why Bale's action would be upsetting to the cat owner (and to the cat, for that matter), but thousands of people were powerfully affected by what they saw. They wanted her blood. Someone created a Facebook page called "Death to Mary Bale," and she had to be put under police protection. Indeed, people have been murdered by mobs that believe them to be guilty of immoral acts—including acts that others believe to be morally acceptable, such as having sex without being married.

How can we best understand our moral natures? Many would agree with Collins that this is a question of theology, while others believe that morality is best understood through the insights of novelists, poets, and playwrights. Some prefer to approach morality from a philosophical perspective, looking not at what people think and how people act but at questions of normative ethics (roughly, how one should act) and metaethics (roughly, the nature of right and wrong).

Then there is science. We can explore our moral natures using the same methods that we use to study other aspects of our mental life, such as language or perception or memory. We can look at moral reasoning across societies or explore how people differ within a single society—liberals versus conservatives in the United States, for instance. We can examine unusual cases, such as cold-blooded psychopaths. We might ask whether creatures such as chimpanzees have anything that we can view as morality, and we can look toward evolutionary biology to explore how a moral sense might have evolved. Social psychologists can explore how features of the environment encourage kindness or cruelty, and neuroscientists can look at the parts of the brain that are involved in moral reasoning.

I will touch upon all of this in the pages that follow. But I am a developmental psychologist, so I am largely interested in exploring morality by looking at its origins in babies and young children. I will argue that contemporary developmental research tells us something striking about our moral lives. It shows that Thomas Jefferson was right when he wrote in a letter to his friend Peter Carr: "The moral sense, or conscience, is as much a part of man as his leg or arm. It is given to all human beings in a stronger or weaker degree, as force of members is given them in a greater or less degree."

Jefferson's view that we have an ingrained moral sense was shared by some of the Enlightenment philosophers of his period, including Adam Smith. While in Edinburgh, the summer before completing this book, I found myself entranced by *The Theory of the Moral Sentiments*. Most know Smith through his more famous text, *An Inquiry into the Nature and Causes of the Wealth of Nations,* but Smith himself thought his first book was the better one. The work is finely written and thoughtful and generous, with sharp insights into the relationship between imagination and empathy, the limits of compassion, our urge to punish others' wrongdoing, and much else. It is exhilarating to look at contemporary scientific findings through Smith's eyes, and I will be quoting him to a potentially embarrassing degree, like an undergraduate who has read just one book.

Much of this current book describes how developmental psychology, supported by evolutionary biology and cultural anthropology, favors the view of Jefferson and Smith that some aspects of morality come naturally to us. Our natural endowments include:

- a moral sense—some capacity to distinguish between kind and cruel actions
- empathy and compassion—suffering at the pain of those around us and the wish to make this pain go away
- a rudimentary sense of fairness—a tendency to favor equal divisions of resources
- a rudimentary sense of justice—a desire to see good actions rewarded and bad actions punished

Our innate goodness is limited, however, sometimes tragically so. Thomas Hobbes, in 1651, argued that man "in the state of nature" is wicked and self-interested, and I will go on to explore the ways in which Hobbes was right.

We are by nature indifferent, even hostile, to strangers; we are prone toward parochialism and bigotry. Some of our instinctive emotional responses, most notably disgust, spur us to do terrible things, including acts of genocide.

In the penultimate chapter, I show how an appreciation of the moral natures of babies can ground a new perspective on the moral psychology of adults, one that takes seriously our natural propensity to divide the world into family versus friends versus strangers. And I end by exploring how we have come to transcend the morality we are born with—how our imagination, our compassion, and especially our intelligence give rise to moral insight and moral progress and make us more than just babies.

1

THE MORAL LIFE
OF BABIES

The one-year-old decided to take justice into his own hands. He had just watched a puppet show with three characters. The puppet in the middle rolled a ball to the puppet on the right, who passed it right back to him. It then rolled the ball to the puppet on the left, who ran away with it. At the end of the show, the "nice" puppet and the "naughty" puppet were brought down from the stage and set before the boy. A treat was placed in front of each of them, and the boy was invited to take one of the treats away. As predicted, and like most toddlers in this experiment, he took it from the "naughty" one—the one who had run away with the ball. But this wasn't enough. The boy then leaned over and smacked this puppet on the head.

Throughout this book, I will suggest that experiments like these show that some aspects of morality come naturally to us—and others do not. We have a moral sense that enables us to judge others and that guides our compassion and condemnation. We are naturally kind to others, at least some of the time. But we possess ugly instincts as well, and these can metastasize into evil. The Reverend Thomas Martin wasn't entirely wrong when he wrote in the nineteenth century about the "native depravity" of children and concluded that "we bring with us into the world a nature replete with evil propensities."

I am aware that the idea that babies are moral creatures sounds ridiculous to some, so I will begin by being clear about precisely what I am saying.

By *babies,* I really do mean babies—"mewling and puking in the nurse's arms," as Shakespeare put it. Now there are babies and there are babies. I won't be talking much about babies before the age of about three months, mostly because of lack of experimental data—it's difficult to study their minds using the methods we have available. Without such data, I would be cautious about claiming that such tiny creatures really do have a moral life. After all, even if some of morality comes naturally to us, many natural traits don't emerge right away—think of freckles and wisdom teeth and underarm hair. The brain, like the rest of the body, takes time to grow, so I am not arguing that morality is present at birth. What I am proposing, though, is that certain moral foundations are not acquired through learning. They do not come from the mother's knee, or from school or church; they are instead the products of biological evolution.

What about "morality"? Even moral philosophers don't agree about what morality really is, and many nonphilosophers don't like to use the word at all. When I've told people what this book is about, more than one has responded with "I don't believe in morality." Someone once told me—and I'm not sure that she was joking—that morality is nothing more than rules about whom you can and can't have sex with.

Arguments about terminology are boring; people can use words however they please. But what I mean by *morality*— what I am interested in exploring, whatever one calls it— includes a lot more than restrictions on sexual behavior. Here is a simple example:

> *A car full of teenagers drives slowly past an elderly woman waiting at a bus stop. One of the teenagers leans out the window and slaps the woman, knocking her down. They drive away laughing.*

Unless you are a psychopath, you will feel that the teenagers did something wrong. And it is a certain type of wrong. It isn't a social gaffe like going around with your shirt inside out or a factual mistake like thinking that the sun revolves around the earth. It isn't a violation of an arbitrary rule, such as moving a pawn three spaces forward in a chess game. And it isn't a mistake in taste, like believing that the *Matrix* sequels were as good as the original.

As a moral violation, it connects to certain emotions and desires. You might feel sympathy for the woman and anger at the teenagers; you might want to see them punished. They should feel bad about what they did; at the very least, they owe the woman an apology. If you were to suddenly remember that one of the teenagers was you, many years ago, you might feel guilt or shame.

Hitting someone is a very basic moral violation. Indeed, the philosopher and legal scholar John Mikhail has suggested that the act of intentionally striking someone without their permission—*battery* is the legal term—has a special immediate badness that all humans respond to. Here is a good candidate for a moral rule that transcends space and time: If you punch someone in the face, you'd better have a damn good reason for it.

There are other, less direct, moral violations. The teenagers might have thrown a brick at the woman. Or they might have purposefully sideswiped her car, damaging it; this would harm her even if she wasn't there to witness it. They might have killed her dog. They might have gotten roaring drunk and hit her with their car by mistake—this would be wrong even if they had no malicious intent, because they should have known better.

Some wrongs can be done without any physical contact at all—they could have shouted a racist insult at her, e-mailed her a death threat, spread vicious gossip about her, blackmailed her, posted obscene pictures of her on the Internet, and so on. Sitting alone at my computer writing this late at night, I'm impressed by the number of terrible and illegal things I could do without leaving my desk— each of us now lives just a few keystrokes away from a felony.

One can even be immoral by doing nothing at all. Surely parents who choose not to feed their children have done something wrong; most of us would feel the same about someone who let a dog or cat starve to death.

The law sometimes diverges from common sense in this regard. Consider the case of two young men—Jeremy Strohmeyer and David Cash Jr.—who walked into a Nevada casino in 1988. Strohmeyer followed a seven-year-old girl into the women's restroom and molested and murdered her. The wrongness of Strohmeyer's act is obvious from both a moral and a legal perspective. But what about Cash, who was with Strohmeyer in the restroom, halfheartedly tried to get him to stop, and then gave up and went for a walk? As he later said, he wasn't going "to lose sleep over somebody else's problems."

Strohmeyer went to prison, but Cash didn't, since it was not illegal in Nevada to fail to stop a crime from happening. Still, there was a sense on the part of many that he had done something wrong. There were demonstrations against him at his university and demands that he be expelled. (Indeed, legislators changed the law in Nevada in response to this very case, bringing it more in line with public sentiment.) Cash is now being stalked on the Internet; people report on his whereabouts, hoping to ruin his prospects for getting a job and finding friends, wishing to destroy his life, even though they were personally unaffected by his failure to act. This illustrates how much moral transgressions matter to us. We don't merely observe that Cash is a bad guy; some of us are motivated to make him suffer.

For other types of moral wrongs, the issue of harm is not as clear-cut. Think about:

- bestiality (without causing the animal any pain)
- breaking a promise to a dead person
- defacing the national flag
- sexual contact with a sleeping child (but the child is unharmed and never learns about it)
- incest between consenting adult siblings
- consensual cannibalism (Person A wishes to be eaten by Person B after he dies, and Person B obliges)

Now, some of these activities may actually be harmful—for example, incest, even between consenting adults, could lead to psychological damage. But in many of these cases, it's clear that nobody, in a concrete sense, is actually worse off. Still, for many people, these activities give rise to the same reactions that would be elicited by an act such as physical assault—anger at the perpetrators, a desire for them to be punished, and so on.

The examples on this list might seem exotic or contrived, but we can easily come up with victimless acts that provoke the same type of moral outrage in the real world. In some places consensual homosexual relations are viewed as evil, and in some countries they are punishable by death. (So, yes, morality *is* sometimes about whom you are allowed to sleep with.) In some societies, premarital sex is thought to stain the honor of the woman's family, so much so that a father may feel obliged to rectify the situation by murdering his own daughter. In the United States and Europe, we have laws against prostitution, drug usage, euthanasia, the marriage of adult siblings, and the selling of body organs. Such restrictions are sometimes justified in terms of harm, but often they have their roots in a gut feeling that such actions are just plain wrong; they violate human dignity, perhaps. Any theory of moral psychology has to explain how these intuitions work and where they come from.

Not all morality has to do with wrongness. Morality also encompasses questions of rightness, as nicely illustrated by a study of spontaneous helping in toddlers, designed by the psychologists Felix Warneken and Michael Tomasello. In one condition of the study, the toddler is in a room with his or her mother present. An adult walks in, his arms full, and tries to open a closet door. Nobody looks at the child or prompts him or her or asks for help. Still, about half do help—they will spontaneously stand up, wobble over, and open the door for the adult.

This is a small example for a small individual, but we see this kindness writ large when people donate time, money, or even blood to help others, sometimes strangers. This behavior too is seen as moral; it inspires emotions like pride and gratitude, and we describe it as good and ethical.

The scope of morality, then, is broad, encompassing both the harsh, judgmental elements and the softer, altruistic elements, including, as Adam Smith put it, "generosity, humanity, kindness, compassion, mutual friendship and esteem, all the social and benevolent affections."

SOME moral customs and beliefs are plainly learned, because they vary across cultures. Anyone who travels or even who reads broadly will be aware of moral differences. Herodotus made this point 2,500 years ago in a passage of his *Histories,* starting with the observation that "everyone without exception believes his own native customs, and the religion he was brought up in, to be the best." He then recounts a story about Darius, king of Persia:

> *He summoned the Greeks who happened to be present at his court, and asked them what they would take to eat the dead bodies of their fathers. They replied that they would not do it for any money in the world. Later, in the presence of the Greeks, and through an interpreter, so that they could understand what was said, he asked some Indians of the tribe called Callatiae, who do in fact eat their parents' dead bodies, what they would take to burn them. They uttered a cry of horror and forbade him to mention such a dreadful thing. One can see by this what custom can do.*

It is easy to think of moral beliefs that are peculiar to our own culture and time. For example, probably just about all the readers of this book believe that it's wrong to hate someone solely because of the color of his or her skin. But this is a modern insight; for most of human history, nobody saw anything wrong with racism. My favorite summary of contemporary moral differences comes from the cultural anthropologist Richard Shweder, who provides a long list of things that are considered by different societies to be neutral, laudable, or appalling:

masturbation, homosexuality, sexual abstinence, po-
lygamy, abortion, circumcision, corporal punishment,
capital punishment, Islam, Christianity, Judaism,
capitalism, democracy, flag burning, miniskirts, long
hair, no hair, alcohol consumption, meat eating, medi-
cal inoculations, atheism, idol worship, divorce, widow
marriage, arranged marriage, romantic love marriage,
parents and children sleeping in the same bed, parents
and children not sleeping in the same bed, women being
allowed to work, women not being allowed to work.

But while the excerpts from Herodotus and Shweder illustrate diversity, they also hint at universals. Ethnographic reports often ignore what humans share, in part because of the tendency of anthropologists to exaggerate how exotic other people are (something that the anthropologist Maurice Bloch has described as "professional malpractice") and in part because, from an anthropological perspective, there isn't anything interesting to say about universals; it would be like reading in a travel guide that the people you will encounter have noses, drink water, and age over time. It is all too obvious to be worth noting. By the same token, we take for granted that people everywhere have a natural disapproval toward actions such as lying, breaking a promise, and murder. Herodotus doesn't talk about people who don't care what you do with dead bodies; Shweder doesn't describe people who are indifferent about incest. Such people don't exist.

If you think of evolution solely in terms of "survival of

the fittest" or "nature red in tooth and claw," then such universals cannot be part of our natures. Since Darwin, though, we've come to see that evolution is far more subtle than a Malthusian struggle for existence. We now understand how the amoral force of natural selection might have instilled within us some of the foundation for moral thought and moral action.

Actually, one aspect of morality, kindness to kin, has long been a no-brainer from an evolutionary point of view. The purest case here is a parent and a child: one doesn't have to do sophisticated evolutionary modeling to see that the genes of parents who care for their children are more likely to spread through the population than those of parents who abandon or eat their children.

There are other kinship bonds as well, though, such as between siblings and cousins, and while these might be weaker, the difference is of degree, not kind. The story goes that the evolutionary biologist J. B. S. Haldane was once asked if he would give his life to save his drowning brother and he responded that he wouldn't—but he would happily do so for two brothers or eight cousins. Since he shared, on average, half of his genes with each brother and one-eighth of his genes with each cousin, this was the proper strategy from the genes' perspective. Haldane was being clever when he answered by making reference to these calculations— few people are consciously motivated by an explicit desire to preserve their genes—but these are the sorts of calculations that explain our normal motivations and desires. It turns out, then, that there is no hard-and-fast difference, as far as the genes are concerned, between an individual and its blood relatives. In this way, selfish genes can create altruistic animals, animals that love others just as they love themselves.

We are also capable of acting kindly and generously toward those who are not blood relatives. At first, the evolutionary origin of this might seem obvious: clearly, we thrive by working together—in hunting, gathering, child care, and so on—and our social sentiments make this coordination possible. Adam Smith pointed this out long before Darwin: "All the members of human society stand in need of each others assistance, and are likewise exposed to mutual injuries. Where the necessary assistance is reciprocally afforded from love, from gratitude, from friendship, and esteem, the society flourishes and is happy." And so it is to everyone's benefit to care about those around us.

But there is a wrinkle here; for society to flourish in this way, individuals have to refrain from taking advantage of others. A bad actor in a community of good people is the snake in the garden; it's what the evolutionary biologist Richard Dawkins calls "subversion from within." Such a snake would do best of all, reaping the benefits of cooperation without paying the costs. Now, it's true that the world as a whole would be worse off if the demonic genes proliferated, but this is the problem, not the solution—natural selection is insensitive to considerations about "the world as a whole." We need to explain what kept demonic genes from taking over the population, leaving us with a world of psychopaths.

Darwin's theory was that cooperative traits could prevail if societies containing individuals who worked together peacefully would tend to defeat other societies with less cooperative members—in other words, natural selection operating at the group, rather than individual, level. Writing of a hypothetical conflict between two imaginary tribes, Darwin wrote: "If the one tribe included . . . courageous, sympathetic and faithful members who were always ready to warn each other of danger, to aid and defend each other, this tribe would without doubt succeed best and conquer the other." An alternative theory, more consistent with individual-level natural selection, is that the good guys might punish the bad guys. That is, even without such conflict between groups, altruism could evolve if individuals were drawn to reward and interact with kind individuals and to punish—or at least shun—cheaters, thieves, thugs, free riders, and the like.

Other moral universals are harder to explain from an evolutionary perspective. Why are we so obsessed with the morality of sex? Why are we so quick to make moral distinctions on the basis of superficial physical features such as skin color? And how can we explain the emergence of moral notions such as equal rights for all? These are the topics of later chapters.

We should take seriously, then, the idea that we possess an innate and universal morality. But we can't know if this is true until we study the minds of babies.

Such research is hard; it is notoriously difficult to know

what is going on inside of a baby's head. When my sons were babies, I would stare at them and wonder what, precisely, stared back. They were like my dog, only more fascinating. (Now they are teenagers, wonderful in many ways, but a lot less professionally interesting—I know what it's like to be a teenager.) The developmental psychologist John Flavell once said that he would give up all his degrees and honors for just five minutes inside the head of a two-year-old. I would give up a month of my life for those five minutes— and I'd give up six months for five minutes as an infant.

Part of the problem is that we don't remember. The comedian Louis C.K. once compared a baby's brain to an Etch A Sketch that you shake at the end of every day. Memories don't stick; even young children don't remember their babyhood. The psychologist Charles Fernyhough describes asking his three-year-old daughter what it was like to be a baby. Trying to be helpful, she says: "You know what? . . . When I were a little baby, it was very sunny."

Babies are even harder to study than rats and pigeons, which can at least run mazes or peck at levers. When my colleague and collaborator Karen Wynn is giving a public talk about conducting research with baby subjects, she puts up a picture of a slug for comparison.

You might think that psychologists scan babies' brains, and, indeed, some researchers have made a promising start at this. But the brain-imaging methods designed for use with adults often are not suitable for babies because they are too dangerous or because the subjects must remain awake but still for a long period of time. Certain special techniques, such as near-infrared spectroscopy, can be more easily used with babies, and might lead to important discoveries in the future. But at this point, the data they yield—about changes in blood oxygenation in parts of the brain—tell us little about the specifics of mental life. If you want to know *where* in the baby's brain some cognitive process is taking place, these methods are the cat's pajamas. But they are typically too insensitive to answer more precise questions about how babies think and what they know.

Fortunately, we have better methods. In the 1980s, psychologists began making use of one of the few behaviors that young babies can control: the movement of their eyes. These really are windows into the baby's soul. How long babies stare at an object or a person—their "looking time"—can tell you a lot about their understanding.

One specific looking-time method is *habituation*. Like adults, if babies see the same thing over and over again, they'll get bored and look away. Boredom—or "habituation"—is a response to sameness, so this method reveals what babies see as similar and as different. Suppose you were interested in whether babies can tell dogs from cats. Show them pictures of cats over and over again, until they get bored with cats. Then show them a picture of a dog. If they perk up, they can detect a difference; if they are still bored, then they can't—for them, cat, cat, dog is the same as cat, cat, cat.

More generally, looking-time methods can help assess what someone finds to be new, interesting, or unexpected. Such methods are particularly well suited for babies. The psychologist Alison Gopnik points out that adult attention can be captured by external events—we will instinctively turn if someone calls our name, say—but we usually have control over what to attend to. By sheer will, we can choose to think about our left foot, visualize what we had for breakfast, and so on. But babies are largely at the mercy of the environment. The part of the brain responsible for inhibition and control, the prefrontal cortex, is among the last to develop. Gopnik compares baby consciousness to that of an adult dumped into the middle of a foreign city, totally overwhelmed, constantly turning to see new things, struggling to make sense of it all. Things are even worse for a baby, actually, because even the most stressed-out adult can choose to think of something else: we can look forward to getting back to the hotel; imagine how we would describe our trip to friends; fantasize, daydream, or pray. The baby just *is,* trapped in the here and now. No wonder babies are often so fussy. Luckily for researchers, their lack of internal control means that they are vulnerable to our methods.

Looking-time studies are difficult to construct, in part because one has to be careful to make sure that babies are responding to the right thing. For example, many studies find that babies distinguish two objects from three objects. If you bore the babies by showing them a series of pictures of two objects—two dogs, two chairs, two shoes, et cetera—and then show them a picture of three objects, they will look longer, suggesting that they can tell the difference between two and three. But a skeptic will point out that two objects typically take up less space than three, so perhaps babies are responding to the space that the objects fill up—less versus more. One can try to address this by contrasting two bigger objects and three smaller objects, so that they fill up the same overall space, but the skeptic can then worry that babies are responding, not to the number of objects, but to big objects versus small objects. It turns out to be exquisitely complicated to design a study that isolates just the relevant variable—but it can be done.

The development of looking-time methods set off a revolution in how we think about the minds of babies. The first studies to use this method focused on early knowledge of physical objects—a baby's "naive physics." Psychologists showed babies magic tricks, events that seemed to violate some law of the universe: you remove the supports from beneath a block and it floats in midair, unsupported; an object disappears and then reappears in another location; a box is placed behind a screen, and the screen falls backward into empty space. If babies expect the world to work in accordance with the principles of physics, they should find these outcomes surprising. And their looking times show that they do—babies look longer at such scenes than at scenes that are identical in all regards except that they don't violate physical laws. A vast body of research now suggests that—contrary to what legions of psychology undergraduates were taught for decades—babies think of objects largely as adults do, as connected masses that move as units, that are solid and subject to gravity, and that move in continuous paths through space and time.

In a classic study, Karen Wynn found that babies can also do rudimentary math with objects. The demonstration is simple. Show a baby an empty stage. Raise a screen in the middle of the stage. Put a Mickey Mouse doll behind the screen. Then put another Mickey Mouse doll behind the screen. Now drop the screen. Adults expect two dolls, and so do five-month-olds; if the screen drops to reveal one or three dolls, the babies look longer than they do if the screen drops to reveal two.

Experimenters have also used these methods to explore babies' expectations about people—their "naive psychology," as opposed to their "naive physics." We've long known that babies respond in a special way to other people. They are drawn to them. They like the sound of human voices, particularly those they are familiar with; they like the look of human faces. And they are disturbed when interactions don't go the way they expect. Here's how to freak out a baby: sit across from the baby, engage with him or her, and then suddenly become still. If this goes on for more than a few seconds, with you looking all corpselike, the baby will become upset. In one study, two-month-olds were seated across from a TV screen displaying their mother. When the mother interacted with the babies by means of real-time videoconferencing, babies enjoyed it. But when there was a time delay of a few seconds, the babies became agitated.

The psychologist Amanda Woodward designed a looking-time study to demonstrate that babies know that individuals have goals. First, a baby was placed in front of two objects and watched a hand reach for one of these objects. Then experimenters reversed the objects' locations. Babies expected that when the hand reached again, it should go for the same object, not the same location. This expectation was special to hands; if they saw a metal claw reaching for the object, the result went away.

In another set of studies, the psychologists Kristine Onishi and Renee Baillargeon showed that fifteen-month-olds can anticipate a person's behavior on the basis of his or her false belief. Babies watched as an adult looked at an object in one box, then observed the object move to another box while the adult's eyes were covered. Later on, they expected the adult to reach into the original box, not the box that actually contained the object. This is a sophisticated psychological inference, the sort of rich understanding of other minds that most psychologists used to believe only four- and five-year-olds were capable of.

Early in life, then, we are social animals, with a foundational appreciation of the minds of others.

THE study that got me started doing research into the moral life of babies wasn't designed to look at morality at all. It was intended to explore the sophistication of babies' social understanding. My colleagues and I were interested in whether babies could accurately predict how individuals would respond to someone who was either kind or cruel to them. In particular, we asked whether babies understand that individuals tend to approach those who have helped them and avoid those who have harmed them.

This is a good place to note that all of the baby studies I have been involved in are carried out in the Yale Infant

Cognition Center, which is run by my colleague (and wife) Karen Wynn. These experiments are always done in collaboration with Karen and her team of undergraduate students, graduate students, and postdoctoral fellows.

Before I get into our findings, I'll give you a general sense of how this research takes place at the lab. A typical experiment takes about fifteen minutes and begins with the parent carrying his or her baby into a small testing room. Most of the time the parent sits on a chair with the baby on his or her lap, though sometimes the baby is strapped into a high chair with the parent standing behind. At this point, some of the babies are either sleeping or too fussy to continue; on average this kind of study ends up losing about a quarter of the participants. Just as critics describe much of experimental psychology as the study of the American college undergraduate who wants beer money, there's some truth to the claim that a lot of developmental psychology is the study of the interested and alert baby.

In our initial study, led by a then–postdoctoral fellow, Valerie Kuhlmeier, we needed to show babies nice and nasty interactions. The most obvious nasty interaction is one individual hitting another, but we worried that some parents—and possibly the Yale Human Subjects Committee—wouldn't be comfortable with having the babies watch violent interactions. We decided, then, to draw upon previous work by the psychologists David Premack and Ann Premack, who showed babies animated movies where one object either helped another squeeze through a gap or blocked another from getting through a gap. Their findings suggested that the babies viewed the helping acts as positive and the hindering acts as negative.

Based on this research, we created animations in which geometrical figures helped or hindered one another. For example, a red ball was shown trying to go up a hill. In some instances, a yellow square went behind the ball and gently nudged it up the hill (helping); in others, a green triangle went in front of it and pushed it down (hindering). Next the babies saw movies in which the ball either approached the square or approached the triangle. This allowed us to explore their expectations about how the ball would act in the presence of these characters.

We found that nine- and twelve-month-olds look longer when the ball approaches the character that hindered it, not the one that helped it. This effect was robust when the animated characters had eyes, making them look more like people, which supports the notion that these were bona fide social judgments on the part of the babies. (If the individuals had no eyes, the looking-time patterns flipped for the twelve-month-olds, and the effect disappeared for nine-month-olds—they looked at each scenario for the same amount of time.) This understanding seems to emerge at some point between six and nine months: a later study, using three-dimensional characters with faces, replicated the finding with a new sample of ten-month-olds but found no effect for six-month-olds.

These studies explore babies' expectations about how characters would act toward the helper and the hinderer, but they don't tell us what babies themselves think about the helper and the hinderer. Do they have a preference? From an adult perspective, the helper is a mensch and the hinderer is a jerk. In a series of experiments led by then–graduate student Kiley Hamlin, we asked whether babies have the same impression.

Our first set of studies used three-dimensional geo-metrical objects manipulated like puppets instead of ani-mations. (It might seem odd that we used objects instead of real people, but babies and toddlers are often unwilling to approach adult strangers.) And instead of using looking-time measures, which are ideal for exploring babies' expec-tations, we adopted reaching measures, which are better for determining what babies themselves prefer. The scenarios were the same as those used in the previous experiment: a ball was either helped up a hill or pushed down the hill. Then the experimenter placed the helper and the hinderer on a tray to see which one the baby would reach for.

(Some experimental details: to ensure that the babies were responding to the actual scenario, and not just to the colors and shapes of the different objects, we systematically varied who was the helper and who was the hinderer—for instance, half the babies got the red square as the helper; half got the red square as the hinderer. Another concern was unconscious cueing: if the adults around the baby knew who the good guys and bad guys were, they might somehow convey this information. To get around this problem, the experimenter holding out the characters didn't see the pup-pet show and so didn't know the "right" answer; also, the baby's mother closed her eyes at the moment of choice.)

As we predicted, six- and ten-month-old infants over-whelmingly preferred the helpful individual to the hindering individual. This wasn't a subtle statistical trend; just about all of the babies reached for the good guy.

Such a result is open to three interpretations. Babies might be drawn to the helpful individual, they might be repelled by the hindering individual, or both. To explore this, we introduced a new character that neither helped nor hindered. We found that, given a choice, infants preferred a helpful character to this neutral one and preferred this neutral character to one who hindered, indicating that babies were both drawn to the nice guy and repelled by the mean guy. Again, these results were not subtle; babies almost always showed this pattern of response.

We then followed this up with a pair of studies looking at three-month-olds. Now, babies at that age really are sluglike; they can't control their reaching well enough to be tested with our usual method. But we noticed something with the older babies that gave us a clue as to how to proceed. Upon analyzing the video clips, we found that they didn't just reach for the helping character; they also looked toward the helping character. This suggested that for the younger babies we could use their direction of looking as a proxy for preference. When we showed the babies the two characters simultaneously, the effect was robust: the three-month-olds clearly preferred to look at the good guys.

In a second study introducing the neutral character, we got an interesting pattern of success and failure. Like the six- and ten-month-olds, the younger babies looked longer at a neutral character than at a hinderer. But they did not favor the helper over the neutral character. This is consistent with a "negativity bias" so often found in adults and children: sensitivity to badness (in this case, the hinderer) is more powerful and emerges earlier than sensitivity to goodness (the helper).

Our initial helper/hinderer studies were published in the journal *Nature* and generated a lot of discussion, both enthusiastic and skeptical. Our more critical colleagues worried that maybe babies weren't actually responding to the goodness/badness of the interaction but rather to some nonsocial aspect of the scene. We worried about the same thing ourselves, and our experiments had certain features that we hoped would exclude this possibility. We tested babies in other scenarios in which the "climber" was replaced with an inanimate block that didn't move on its own. The helper and hinderer went through the very same physical movements, but now they weren't actually helping or hindering. The substitution caused the babies' preference to disappear, which suggests that babies were indeed responding to the social interactions, not merely the movements.

Also, in a project led by Mariko Yamaguchi, then an undergraduate in Karen's lab, the research team retested the children who had been tested years ago in the original studies led by Valerie Kuhlmeier, where they had predicted the behavior of a ball who was either helped or hindered. It turned out that their performance on the original helper/hinderer experiment (but not their performance on other tasks) was related to their social reasoning skills as four-year-olds. This too suggests that the helper/hinderer experiments really do tap babies' social understanding.

Still, it was important to see whether the same results would ensue if we moved away from the original helper/hinderer scenarios, so Kiley and Karen created different sets of morality plays to show the babies. In one of these, an individual struggled to lift the lid on a box. On alternating trials, one puppet would grab the lid and open it all the way, and another puppet would jump on the box and slam it shut. In another scenario, an individual would play with a ball, and the ball would roll away. Similarly, one puppet would roll the ball back, and another puppet would grab it and run away. In both situations, five-month-olds preferred the good guy—the one who helped to open the box, the one who rolled the ball back—to the bad guy.

THESE experiments suggest that babies have a general appreciation of good and bad behavior, one that spans a range of interactions, including those that the babies most likely have never seen before. Now, we certainly haven't proven that the understanding that guides the babies' choices actually counts as moral. But the baby responses do have certain signature properties of adult moral judgments. They are disinterested judgments, concerning behaviors that don't affect the babies themselves. And they are judgments about behaviors that adults would describe as good or bad. Indeed, when we showed the very same scenes to toddlers and asked them, "Who was nice? Who was good?" and "Who was mean? Who was bad?" they responded as

adults would, identifying the helper as nice and the hinderer as mean.

I think that we are finding in babies what philosophers
in the Scottish Enlightenment described as a moral sense.
This is not the same as an impulse to do good and avoid
doing evil. Rather, it is the capacity to make certain types
of judgments—to distinguish between good and bad, kindness and cruelty. Adam Smith, though himself skeptical of
its existence, describes the moral sense as "somewhat analogous to the external senses. As the bodies around us, by
affecting these in a certain manner, appear to possess the
different qualities of sound, taste, odour, colour; so the various affections of the human mind, by touching this particular faculty in a certain manner, appear to possess the
different qualities of amiable and odious, of virtuous and
vicious, of right and wrong."

I think that we naturally possess a moral sense, and I'm
going to return to this point over and over in the pages that
follow. But morality involves much more than a capacity
to make certain distinctions. It entails certain feelings and
motivations, such as a desire to help others in need, compassion for those in pain, anger toward the cruel, and guilt
and pride about our own shameful and kind actions. We
have considered so far the head; what about the heart?

2

EMPATHY AND
COMPASSION

People could not be moral without the capacity to tell right from wrong. But if we want to explain where moral actions come from—why we sometimes behave kindly and altruistically, instead of cruelly and selfishly— this moral sense is not enough.

To see why, imagine a perfect—perfectly rotten— psychopath. He is blessed with high intelligence, good social skills, and some of the same motivations that normal people possess, such as hunger, lust, and curiosity. But he lacks a normal response to the suffering of others and is missing as well feelings such as gratitude and shame. Because of some unhappy combination of genes, parenting, and idiosyn- cratic personal experience, he is without moral sentiments.

Our psychopath need not be a moral imbecile. He could possess the simple capacities we talked about in the last chapter. Even as a baby psychopath, he might prefer an individual who helps someone up a hill over someone who pushes the character down. And as he grows up, he will learn the rules and conventions of his society. Our psychopath knows that it is "right" to rescue a lost child and "wrong" to sexually assault a woman while she is unconscious. But he doesn't feel any of the associated moral emotions, so his appreciation of right and wrong is similar to that of someone blind from birth who can state that grass is "green" and that the sky is "blue"—factually correct knowledge without the usual experiences that go with it.

Imagine trying to convince your psychopath to be kind to other people. You might tell him that he needs to repress selfish impulses for the sake of others. You could throw some philosophy at him, presenting the view of utilitarian philosophers that we should act to increase the sum total of human happiness, or going on about Immanuel Kant's categorical imperative, or John Rawls's veil of ignorance, or Adam Smith's impartial spectator. You might try a strategy that parents often use with their children and ask him how he would feel if someone behaved toward him as he often behaves toward others.

He could respond to all of this that he simply doesn't care about increasing the amount of human happiness and has no interest in the categorical imperative, or any of the rest of it. He appreciates the logical equivalence between him harming another individual and another individual harming him—he's not an idiot, after all. But, still, none of this motivates him to treat people with kindness.

Real psychopaths give answers that are much the same. The psychologist William Damon recounts a *New York*

Times interview of a thirteen-year-old mugger who viciously attacked elderly victims, including a blind woman. He showed no remorse for his actions, commenting that it made sense to target blind people because they couldn't identify him later. When the mugger was asked about the pain he had caused the woman, the reporter wrote, "The boy was surprised at the question and responded: 'What do I care? I'm not her.'" Ted Bundy was puzzled about all the fuss over the murders he committed: "I mean, there are so many people." The serial killer Gary Gilmore summed up the attitude of someone without moral feelings: "I was always capable of murder. . . . I can become totally devoid of feelings of others, unemotional. I know I'm doing something grossly fucking wrong. I can still go ahead and do it."

Or consider this interview with Peter Woodcock, who had raped and murdered three children as a teenager. After decades in a psychiatric facility, he was given a three-hour pass to wander the grounds unsupervised. During this period he invited another patient, a close friend of his, to join him in the woods, and then killed him with a hatchet.

> *Interviewer:* What was going through your mind at the time? This was someone you loved.
> *Woodcock:* Curiosity, actually. And an anger. Because he had rebuffed all my advances.
> *Interviewer:* And why did you feel someone should die as a result of your curiosity?
> *Woodcock:* I just wanted to know what it would feel like to kill somebody.

Interviewer: But you'd already killed three people.

Woodcock: Yes, but that was years and years and years
    and years ago.

CONTRAST these disturbing portraits with the moral sentiments that arise during a normal childhood. Some illustrative examples are reported by Charles Darwin in "A
Biographical Sketch of an Infant," published in 1877 in the
prestigious philosophy journal *Mind.* Darwin had read an
article about child development in the same journal, and
this motivated him to look over the notes he had collected
thirty-seven years earlier when observing the development
of his son William, a boy that he proudly described as "a
prodigy of beauty & intellect."

The diaries first recorded physical reactions ("sneezing,
hiccuping, yawning, stretching, and of course sucking and
screaming were well performed by my infant"), but reports
of what Darwin described as "the moral emotions" soon
followed. By the first half year of his life, William responded
to the perceived suffering of others: "With respect to the
allied feeling of sympathy, this was clearly shown at six
months and eleven days by his melancholy face, with the
corners of his mouth well depressed, when his nurse pretended to cry." Much later on, Darwin noted William's
satisfaction at his own kind actions: "When 2 years and 3
months old, he gave his last bit of gingerbread to his little
sister, and then cried out with high self-approbation 'Oh
kind Doddy, kind Doddy.' " Four months after that were the

first hints of guilt and shame: "I met him coming out of the dining room with his eyes unnaturally bright, and an odd unnatural or affected manner, so that I went into the room to see who was there, and found that he had been taking pounded sugar, which he had been told not to do. As he had never been in any way punished, his odd manner certainly was not due to fear, and I suppose it was pleasurable excitement struggling with conscience."

Two weeks later, Darwin wrote, "I met him coming out of the same room, and he was eyeing his pinafore which he had carefully rolled up; and again his manner was so odd that I determined to see what was within his pinafore, notwithstanding that he said there was nothing and repeatedly commanded me to 'go away,' and I found it stained with pickle-juice; so that here was carefully planned deceit."

We see in young William the battle between good and evil that typifies everyday life. Normal people often behave quite badly if they believe that they won't be held accountable for their actions, and we can all use some occasional reining in when faced with pounded sugar, pickles, and other temptations. But it's clear as well that conscience emerges at an early age to help us resist those urges. Indeed, in many instances, we don't need the threat of punishment to be good, because acting selfishly or cruelly can be inherently unpleasant. One example of this comes from a study in the 1930s that asked questions such as "How much money would it take for you to strangle a cat with your bare hands?" The average answer was $10,000—about $155,000 in today's dollars. The same individuals required only half as much money to agree to have one of their front teeth pulled out.

But a psychopath would do it for much less. Indeed, if he felt like strangling a cat, he might do so for free—so long as there was nobody watching, because he would probably be smart enough to know that this would upset people and that the resulting ostracism and punishment would get in the way of other goals that he wished to pursue. The repugnance that normal people have toward cat strangling just wouldn't be there.

Now, many novels, movies, and television shows portray psychopaths as better than the rest of us in certain regards—intimidating, charming, and successful, like the cannibal psychiatrist Hannibal Lecter or the lovable serial killer Dexter Morgan. Some psychologists and sociologists believe that psychopathy can be an asset in business and politics and that, as a result, psychopathic traits are over-represented among successful people.

This would be a puzzle if it were so. If our moral feelings evolved through natural selection, then it shouldn't be the case that one would flourish without them. And, in fact, the successful psychopath is probably the exception. Psychopaths have certain deficits. Some of these are subtle. The psychologist Abigail Marsh and her colleagues find that psychopaths are markedly insensitive to the expression of fear. Normal people recognize fear and treat it as a distress cue, but psychopaths have problems seeing it, let alone responding to it appropriately. Marsh recounts an anecdote about a psychopath who was being tested with a series of pictures and who failed over and over again to recognize fearful expressions, until finally she figured it out: "That's the look people get right before I stab them."

Other deficits run deeper. The overall lack of moral sentiments—and specifically, the lack of regard for others—might turn out to be the psychopath's downfall. We non-psychopaths are constantly assessing one another, looking for kindness and shame and the like, using this information to decide whom to trust, whom to affiliate with. The psychopath has to pretend to be one of us. But this is difficult. It's hard to force yourself to comply with moral rules just through a rational appreciation of what you are expected to do. If you feel like strangling the cat, it's a struggle to hold back just because you know that it is frowned upon. Without a normal allotment of shame and guilt, psychopaths succumb to bad impulses, doing terrible things out of malice, greed, and simple boredom. And sooner or later, they get caught. While psychopaths can be successful in the short term, they tend to fail in the long term and often end up in prison or worse.

LET's take a closer look at what separates psychopaths from the rest of us. There are many symptoms of psychopathy, including pathological lying and lack of remorse or guilt, but the core deficit is indifference toward the suffering of other people. Psychopaths lack compassion.

To understand how compassion works for all of us non-psychopaths, it's important to distinguish it from empathy.

Now, some contemporary researchers use the terms interchangeably, but there is a big difference between caring about a person (compassion) and putting yourself in the person's shoes (empathy).

Adam Smith didn't use the word *empathy*—it was coined in 1909, based on the German *Einfühlung,* meaning "feeling-into"—but he described it well: "We enter as it were into [another's] body, and become in some measure the same person with him." Empathy is a powerful, often irresistible, impulse. One squirms while watching a comedian embarrass herself on stage; it's hard to keep calm next to someone who is agitated; laughter is infectious, and so are tears. A moviegoer sees James Bond struck in the testicles in *Casino Royale* and tenses in a mirrored reaction to his pain. (My bet is that this scene is particularly unpleasant for those viewers who themselves have testicles.) Describing his childhood, John Updike wrote: "My grandmother would have choking fits at the kitchen table, and my own throat would feel narrow in sympathy."

Empathy leads to joy in the joy of others. Our reaction to another person's pleasure is complicated and can be tainted by jealousy—why is she having so much more fun than I am? But still, contagion of pleasure plainly exists. Look up the video on YouTube called *Hahaha,* in which a man makes odd sounds ("Plong! Floop!") off camera while a baby in a high chair laughs hysterically in reaction. Or check out *Baby Laughing Hysterically at Ripping Paper,* which has had over 58 million views, making it more popular than sneezing pandas and farting cats. The appeal of the videos lies in the pleasure of the babies; it leaps, as if by magic, from their heads into ours.

Adam Smith provides another example: "When we have read a book or poem so often that we can no longer find any amusement in reading it by ourselves, we can still take pleasure in reading it to a companion. To him it has all the graces of novelty; we enter into the surprise and admiration which it naturally excites in him. . . . We consider all the ideas which it presents rather in the light in which they appear to him . . . and we are amused by sympathy with his amusement." Smith has just explained one of the greatest pleasures of the Internet: the forwarding of jokes, pictures of adorable animals, blog posts, videos, and so on. His analysis also captures one of the joys of being a parent—one gets to have certain pleasurable experiences, such as going to the zoo and eating ice cream, for the first time all over again.

There is a popular neural theory for how empathy works—mirror neurons. Originally found in the brains of rhesus macaques, these cells fire both when a monkey watches another animal act and when the monkey itself performs the same action. They are blind to the difference between self and other, and they exist in other primates, including, most likely, humans.

The discovery of these neurons has caused quite a stir, with one prominent neuroscientist comparing it to the discovery of DNA. Scientists are integrating mirror neurons into theories of language acquisition, autism, and social behavior, and these cells have caught the public's attention in the same way that neural networks did several years ago: when people discuss any interesting aspect of mental life, it's a given that someone will eventually suggest that it can all be explained by mirror neurons.

This brings us to a simple theory of compassion: X sees Y in pain; X feels pain through the power of mirror neurons; and X wants Y's pain to go away, because, by doing so, X's pain will go away. Empathy, driven by mirror neurons, dissolves the boundaries between people; someone else's pain becomes your pain; self-interest transforms into compassion. Such a theory has the promise of being reductionist in the best sense: a puzzling and important phenomenon— our caring for others—is explained in terms of a more foundational psychological mechanism—empathy—which is in turn explained by a specific mechanism in the brain.

THERE'S a lot to be said for such an elegant and clean theory. But then again, as Einstein once put it, "Everything should be as simple as possible—but no simpler."

To start with, it is by now clear that the initial claims about mirror neurons are significantly overblown. Mirror neurons can't be sufficient for capacities such as language and complex social reasoning, because macaques, who possess these neurons, don't have language and complex social reasoning. They can't even be sufficient for the imitation of others' behavior, because macaques don't imitate other macaques. Mirror neurons are in parts of the brain that are distinct from those areas involved in empathy, and many psychologists and neuroscientists think that they most likely don't have a social function at all but rather are specialized for the learning of motor movements—though even here there is controversy.

In any case, mirror neurons are the least interesting part of the theory. We have the capacity for empathy, and this has to emerge somehow from our brains—if not through mirror neurons, then through some other mechanism. The interesting question isn't about neuroanatomy or neurophysiology; it's about the role of empathy in a broader theory of moral psychology.

I am too much of an adaptationist to think that a capacity as rich as empathy exists as a freak biological accident. It most likely has a function, and the most plausible candidate here is that it motivates us to care about others. Hunger drives us to seek out food; lust inspires sexual behavior; anger leads to aggression in the face of some sort of threat—and empathy exists to motivate compassion and altruism.

Still, the link between empathy (in the sense of mirroring another's feelings) and compassion (in the sense of feeling and acting kindly toward another) is more nuanced than many people believe.

First, although empathy can be automatic and unconscious—a crying person can affect your mood, even if you're not aware that this is happening and would rather it didn't—we often choose whether to empathize with another person. I can hear about the tortures suffered by a political prisoner and, through an act of will, start to imagine (to an infinitely smaller degree, of course) what it is like to be him. I can watch someone on stage receiving an award and choose to feel her nervousness and her pride. So when empathy is present, it may be the product of a moral choice, not the cause of it.

Empathy is also influenced by what one thinks of the other person. In one study, male participants engaged in a financial interaction with a stranger in which they were either rewarded or double-crossed. Then they watched that stranger get a mild electrical shock. If the stranger who was nice got shocked, the participants showed a neural response consistent with empathy—indeed the same part of their brain lit up at the sight as when they themselves got shocked. But when the stranger who was nasty got shocked, there was no empathy; parts of the brain associated with reward and pleasure lit up instead. (Women, on the other hand, were less discriminating, or just plain kinder—they showed an empathetic response regardless of how the stranger had treated them.)

Second, empathy is not needed to motivate compassion. To see this, consider an example from the philosopher Peter Singer of an obviously good act. You are walking past a lake and see a small child struggling in the water. The lake is just a few feet deep, but she is drowning. Her parents are nowhere to be seen. If you are like most people, you would wade in, even if you ruined your shoes in the process, and pull the child out. (Philosophers seem to be fond of examples with drowning children: about two thousand years ago, the Chinese scholar Mencius wrote, "No man is devoid of a heart sensitive to the suffering of others. . . . Suppose a man were, all of a sudden, to see a young child on the verge of falling into a well. He would certainly be moved to compassion.")

It is conceivable, I suppose, that empathy could lead to compassion, followed by action: you see that the girl is terrified and gasping for air, you feel the same way, you want to make your own experience of drowning go away, and this motivates you to rescue her. But this is not what normally happens. Most likely, you would splash in without ever vicariously experiencing the terror of drowning. As the psychologist Steven Pinker points out, "If a child has been frightened by a barking dog and is howling in terror, my sympathetic response is not to howl in terror with her, but to comfort and protect her."

Third, just as you can have compassion without empathy, you can have empathy without compassion. You might feel the person's pain and wish to stop feeling it—but choose to solve the problem by distancing yourself from that person instead of alleviating his or her suffering. You might walk away from the lake. A real-world case, described by the philosopher Jonathan Glover, was the response of a woman who lived near the death camps in Nazi Germany and bore witness to prisoners taking several hours to die after being shot. She was sufficiently upset to write a letter: "One is often an unwilling witness to such outrages. I am anyway sickly and such a sight makes such a demand on my nerves that in the long run I cannot bear this. I request that it be arranged that such inhuman deeds be discontinued, or else be done where one does not see it."

She was empathetic enough that it hurt her to see these

people being murdered. And she wasn't entirely insensitive to the savagery of these acts, describing them as "outrages" and "inhuman deeds." But still, she could live with these murders taking place, so long as they were being done out of sight. This is an extreme case, but it shouldn't be that incomprehensible to us. Even otherwise good people sometimes turn away when faced with depictions of pain and suffering in faraway lands, or when passing a homeless person on a city street.

In other cases, you feel the pain of another person—empathy is at full steam—but instead of compassion, it stirs a feeling that has no single word in English but a perfect one in German: *schadenfreude.* You enjoy the suffering of others and want it to keep on going or to get worse. Sadism is an extreme example of this, but some schadenfreude is normal. I might delight at the thought of my rival getting his comeuppance, imagining what he is feeling and enjoying the experience.

I've talked so far about how empathy and compassion are different; it's clear as well that compassion is not the same as *morality.* Imagine a criminal who begs a police officer to release him. The officer may feel compassion but shouldn't succumb, because there are other moral principles that should be honored. As a less dramatic example, a failing student might approach me and plead for a better grade. I might feel compassion for the student, but it wouldn't be fair to the rest of the class for me to acquiesce.

We can see the occasional clash between compassion and morality in the lab. Experiments by the psychologist C.

Daniel Batson and his colleagues find that being asked to adopt someone else's perspective makes participants more likely to favor that person over others. For example, they are more prone to move a suffering girl ahead of everyone else on a waiting list for a lifesaving procedure. This is compassionate, but it's not moral, since this sort of decision should be based on objective and fair procedures, not on who inspires the most intense emotional reaction. Part of being a good person, then, involves overriding one's compassion, not cultivating it.

WHILE compassion isn't the same as morality and sometimes clashes with it, still, it's necessary. There would be no morality if we didn't care for others.

From the first moments of life, we relate to other people. No baby is an island. Even newborns respond to other people's expressions: if an experimenter sticks out his tongue at a baby, the baby tends to razz him back. Since the baby has never looked in a mirror, she has to know instinctively that the adult's tongue corresponds to that thing in her own mouth that she has never seen. This mimicry may exist to create a bond between the baby and the surrounding adults, so that their feelings become tethered to one another. Indeed, parents and babies frequently mirror one another's expressions, often unconsciously.

Babies also respond to the pain of others. Remember how young William Darwin showed "sympathy" at six months of age, making a "melancholy face" when his nurse pretended to cry. Even a few days after birth, the sound of crying is unpleasant for babies; it tends to make them cry themselves. This isn't a dumb response to noise. Babies cry more at the sound of another baby's cry than their own, and they don't cry as much when they hear a computer-generated noise at the same volume, or when they hear the cries of a chimpanzee infant. Other creatures also find it unpleasant when members of their species are in distress. Hungry rhesus monkeys avoid pulling a lever to get food if doing so will give another monkey a painful electric shock. Rats will press a bar to lower another rat that is suspended in midair or to release a rat that is trapped in a tank full of water; and, like monkeys, they will stop pressing a bar that provides food if that action shocks another rat.

These behaviors might reflect compassion. But a more cynical explanation is that monkeys and rats—and perhaps humans as well—have evolved to find the distress of others unpleasant, without feeling anything like genuine concern for the individuals who are suffering. They experience empathy, perhaps, but not compassion.

Still, when we look at how babies and young children act, we see something more. They don't just turn away from the person in pain. They try to make the other person feel better. Developmental psychologists have long observed that one-year-olds will pat and stroke others in distress. The psychologist Carolyn Zahn-Waxler and her colleagues found that when young children see the people around them acting as if they are in pain (such as the child's mother banging her knee, or an experimenter getting her finger caught in a clipboard), they often respond by soothing. Girls are more likely to soothe than boys, which meshes with a broader body of research suggesting greater empathy and compassion, on average, in females. And you can see similar behavior in other primates; according to the primatologist Frans de Waal, a chimpanzee—but not a monkey—will put its arm around the victim of an attack and pat her or groom her.

Now, babies' and toddlers' attempts at soothing are far from perfect. They are not as frequent as they could be— toddlers soothe less than older children, who soothe less than adults. And toddlers sometimes respond to the pain of others by getting upset and soothing *themselves,* not the individual in pain. Empathetic suffering is unpleasant, and sometimes this unpleasantness is overwhelming. This is true for rats as well. In one study where rats had the chance to press a bar to stop another rat from experiencing pain-ful electric shocks, many of the rats didn't press the bar but instead "retreated to the corner of their box farthest from the distressed, squeaking, and dancing animal and crouched there, motionless."

Toddlers also sometimes respond egocentrically to oth-ers' pain, meaning that their behavior reflects how they themselves would wish to be treated. For instance, the psy-chologist Martin Hoffman describes a fourteen-month-old bringing a crying friend over to his own mother, not the friend's mother. Hoffman argues that this confusion arises because children haven't developed the cognitive sophis-tication needed to take another's perspective. But actually people of all ages can be self-centered when responding to others' distress. While I was sitting next to my wife in a restaurant the other day, she mentioned how thirsty she was. I politely handed over my beer. She looked at me. After a moment, I figured it out. She hates beer. *I* like beer.

A DIFFERENT manifestation of compassion that shows up in toddlers is helping. Over the last several decades there have been many anecdotes and studies showing spontaneous helping. In 1942, a researcher said of his son: "Very thoughtful nowadays. When I came in this morning, he said, 'Daddy want slippers' and ran off to get them." In 1966, a psychologist wrote about an eighteen-month-old who "works alongside me in the garden, manages to rake or use a trowel fairly well. . . . In the house, she helps push the vacuum or mop . . . [and] anticipates her father's needs in dressing or in building a fire in the fireplace." And another psychologist working in the early eighties described turning her lab into a messy home, with a table that needed to be set, an unmade bed, books and cards on the floor, laundry that needed to be folded, and so on. The majority of children (between eighteen and thirty months old) that she brought into the lab enthusiastically helped her clean, saying things like: "I help you, I hold that little lightbulb."

More recently, as mentioned in the last chapter, psychologists have found that toddlers help adults who are struggling to pick up an object that is out of reach or to open a door while their arms are full. The toddlers do so without any prompting from the adults, not even eye contact. This behavior is impressive, because helping—like

soothing—poses certain challenges. The toddler has to figure out that something is wrong, know what to do to make
it better, and be motivated to actually go to the effort of
helping.

Now, a skeptic will point out that we don't know *why*
this helping occurs. After all, adults often help without
being motivated by compassion. Someone stumbles toward
a closed door, arms full of books, and you leap up to open
it before they say something. This might be motivated not
by kindness so much as by habit, like automatically saying
"Bless you" when someone sneezes. Or perhaps toddlers just
enjoy the act of helping without caring about the person
being helped. If an adult is reaching for something beyond
her reach, and the child hands it over, the motivation might
be the rewarding click of a problem being solved. Or perhaps their helpful acts are performed not in pursuit of
the adults' happiness but for the adults' approval. When
children try to help, we find them adorable. Maybe this
is the point—maybe their helping is an adaptive behavior
designed to endear them to their caretakers, analogous to
their physical charms such as big eyes and round cheeks.

But researchers have evidence that suggests that helping—at least by older children—really is motivated by
genuine care for others. My colleagues Alia Martin and
Kristina Olson conducted an experiment in which an adult
played with a three-year-old and asked him or her to hand
over certain objects for certain tasks. For example, the adult
had a pitcher of water next to her and asked the child, "Can
you hand me the cup so that I can pour the water?" When

the object requested was suitable—an unbroken cup, for example—children usually handed it over. But sometimes the object requested was unsuited for the task, such as a cup with a crack in it. Martin and Olson found that children often ignored the requested item and reached for a suitable one, such as an intact cup in another part of the room. So the children weren't just dumbly complying with the adult; they wanted to actually help her complete the task.

Also, if children are really helping with the interests of someone else in mind, then they should be choosy about whom to help. The psychologist Amrisha Vaish and her colleagues found that three-year-olds were more likely to help someone who had previously helped someone else and less likely to help someone who had been cruel to another person. The psychologists Kristen Dunfield and Valerie Kuhlmeier got similar results when they conducted a study with twenty-one-month-olds. The toddlers sat across from two experimenters, each of whom held out a toy, seemingly offering to hand it over. Neither toy got to the toddler, however, because one of the experimenters was teasing and refused to release it, while the other experimenter tried to give it to the child but dropped it. Later on, when toddlers got their own toy to hand over to an experimenter, they tended to give it to the one who had made an effort, not the one who had teased them.

SHARING is a further manifestation of compassion and altruism. Children begin to spontaneously share in the second half of their first year of life, and the degree of sharing shoots up in the year that follows. They share with family and friends, hardly at all with strangers.

Some scientists, and some parents, worry that children don't share enough and wonder if this reflects some moral immaturity on their part. But this might be unfair. When a two-year-old is uncomfortable handing over his toys to a child he has just met in a psychologist's laboratory, is this really so different from an adult's unwillingness to hand over her car keys to a stranger?

So it's not surprising that experiments that look for sharing in young children find tenuous results. The psychologist Celia Brownell and her colleagues adapted an experimental method originally designed to explore altruism in chimpanzees. The researchers placed the child between two levers and offered her the choice to pull one. One lever delivered a treat to the child and a treat to an experimenter sitting on the other side of her. The second lever gave the child one treat but gave nothing to the person on the other side.

When the recipient on the other side was silent, both the eighteen-month-olds and the twenty-five-month-olds pulled the levers at random, making no attempt to give the treat to the adult. When the experimenter said, "I like crackers. I want a cracker," the twenty-five-month-olds helped, although the younger children still behaved randomly.

In their paper, the researchers focused on the bright side: two-year-olds "voluntarily share valued resources with unrelated individuals when there is no cost to them for doing so." This is indeed impressive, but I'm intrigued that neither group of children would share without prompting, even in a situation where they had nothing to lose. My guess is that this was because they were dealing with a strange adult across the table. If it were their parent or grandparent, say, the children would be a lot kinder.

This last point is worth stressing, and we'll return to it repeatedly throughout the rest of the book—before about the age of four, children show little spontaneous kindness toward strange adults. Now, some of the studies we just discussed do find kind behavior—such as helping—toward adults who aren't friends or family, but keep in mind that the adults in these studies aren't actually *that* strange. Before the typical study begins, the child (along with his or her mother or father) typically interacts with the adult experimenter as part of a "warm-up" session, where they engage in friendly reciprocal activities like rolling a ball back and forth. This makes a difference. The psychologists Rodolfo Cortez Barragan and Carol Dweck find if you don't have this sort of reciprocal interaction—just a friendly greeting by the adult and warm thanks for agreeing to participate— the extent of later helping by the children drops by about half. My bet is if there were no prior positive interaction at all—if the adult were a true stranger at the moment that he needed help—then there would be little or no spontaneous kindness on the part of the child.

So FAR we have explored people's responses to, and actions toward, others. But moral beings judge themselves as well. We feel proud of our good acts and guilty for our bad ones; and these moral feelings help us to decide what we should and shouldn't do in the future. For adults, at least, psychologists have found an intimate connection between judging others and judging ourselves. If you tend to empathize with someone, you are also likely to feel guilty for harming him or her. If you are the sort of person who is high in empathy, you are likely to be the type who is prone to guilt.

Self-evaluation in babies is difficult to study, and we know little about its development. It is easy enough to construct a situation in which we show babies a good guy and a bad guy and explore how they respond to these characters. It is harder (though perhaps not impossible) to construct a situation in which we get the babies themselves to behave in different ways and look at their responses to their own goodness or badness.

Still, we can observe signs of self-evaluation early on. Babies and young children often show signs of pride, as in the story of William's delight when he gave his gingerbread to his little sister. And there is guilt. Babies in the first year of life show distress when they harm others, and this becomes more frequent as they age.

In 1935, the psychologist Charlotte Buhler reported a clever experiment on the elicitation of guilt in children. An adult and a child were placed in a room together, and the adult forbade the child to touch a toy that was within his reach. Then the adult turned away and left the room for a moment. The researchers found that all of the one- and two-year-olds "understand the prohibition as cancelled at the moment that the contact with the adult is broken, and play with the toy." But when the adult suddenly returns, 60 percent of the sixteen-month-olds and 100 percent of the eighteen-month-olds "show the greatest embarrassment, blush, and turn to the adult with a frightened expression." The twenty-one-month-olds "attempted to make good what happened by returning the toy quickly to its place." The fear showed by the children might have been devoid of moral content, but the embarrassment—the blushing!— shows that something else was going on as well. Such reflexive displays of guilt were replaced with explicit acts of moral self-justification as the children got older: the two-year-olds in the study attempted to "motivate the disobedience, for example, by claiming the toy as their own."

As we have seen, babies are sensitive to the good and bad acts of others long before they are capable of doing anything good or bad themselves. It seems likely, then, that the "moral sense" is first extended to others and then at some later point in development turns inward. At this point, children come to see themselves as moral agents, and this recognition manifests itself through guilt, shame, and pride.

WE'VE seen certain limitations on children's empathy and compassion, but this should not distract us from how impressive it is to find such moral behavior and sentiments in creatures so young. Samuel Johnson said it best (in a very different context): "It's like a dog's walking on his hind legs. It is not done well; but you are surprised to find it done at all."

But our natural compassion would have been no surprise to Darwin, or to many of the scientists, philosophers, and theologians who preceded him. It was a conclusion eloquently expressed by one of the heroes of this book. Adam Smith is best known for his 1776 work, *The Wealth of Nations,* which makes the case that prosperity can emerge from the interactions of selfish agents. But he never believed that people were wholly self-interested beings; he was exquisitely sensitive to the psychological pull of compassion. In *The Theory of Moral Sentiments,* he begins with three sentences that make the point with eloquence and force:

> *How selfish soever man may be supposed, there are evidently some principles in his nature, which interest him in the fortune of others, and render their happiness necessary to him, though he derives nothing from it except the pleasure of seeing it. Of this kind is pity or compassion, the emotion which we feel for the misery of others, when we either see it, or are made to conceive it in a very lively manner. That we often derive sorrow from the sorrow of others, is a matter of fact too obvious to require any instances to prove it; for this sentiment, like all the other original passions of human nature, is by no means confined to the virtuous and humane, though they perhaps may feel it with the most exquisite sensibility.*

3

FAIRNESS, STATUS, AND PUNISHMENT

The comedian Louis C.K. has a routine in which he talks about his daughter's understanding of fairness. He begins, "My five-year-old, the other day, one of her toys broke, and she demanded that I break her sister's toy to make it fair." This would make the sisters *equal,* but the joke is that something here doesn't feel right: "And I did. I was like crying. And I look at her. She's got this creepy smile on her face."

Other intuitions about fairness are simpler. Imagine you have two toys and two children, and you give both toys to one child. If the other child is old enough to speak, she will object. She might say, "That's not fair!" and she'd be correct. An even split would maximize the overall happiness of the children—give each child one toy and they're both happy; divide them unevenly, and the child who gets nothing is miserable, her sadness outweighing the extra pleasure of the child who gets two. But more to the point, it's just wrong to establish an inequity when you don't have to.

Things quickly get more complicated. Questions about equality and fairness are among the most pressing moral issues in the real world. For instance, most everyone agrees that a just society promotes equality among its citizens, but blood is spilled over what sort of equality is morally preferable: equality of opportunity or equality of outcome. Is it fair for the most productive people to possess more than everyone else, so long as they had equal opportunities to start with? Is it fair for a government to take money from the rich to give to the poor—and does the answer change if the goal of such redistribution is not to help the poor in a tangible sense but just to make people more equal, as in Louis C.K.'s story of breaking his other daughter's toy?

The psychologist William Damon, in a series of influential studies in the 1970s, used interviews to explore what children think about fairness. He found that they focus on equality of outcome and ignore other considerations. As an illustration, consider this snippet from one of his studies (children are being asked about an uneven division of pennies):

Experimenter: Do you think anyone should get more than anyone else?

Anita (seven years, four months): No, because it's not fair. Somebody has thirty-five cents and somebody has one penny. That's not fair.

Experimenter: Clara said she made more things than everybody else and she should get more money.

Anita: No. She shouldn't because it's not fair for her

to get more money, like a dollar, and they get only
about one cent.

Experimenter: Should she get a little more?

Anita: No. People should get the same amount of
money because it's not fair.

You see the same equality bias in younger children. The
psychologists Kristina Olson and Elizabeth Spelke asked
three-year-olds to help a doll allocate resources (such as
stickers and candy bars) between two characters who were
said to be related to the doll in different ways: sometimes
they were a sibling and a friend to the doll; at other times,
a sibling and a stranger, or a friend and a stranger. Olson
and Spelke found that when the three-year-olds received an
even number of resources to distribute, they almost always
wanted the doll to give the same amount to the two characters, regardless of who they were.

The equality bias is strong. Olson and another researcher,
Alex Shaw, told children between the ages of six and eight
a story about "Mark" and "Dan," who had cleaned up their
room and were to be rewarded with erasers: "I don't know
how many erasers to give them; can you help me with that?
Great. You get to decide how many erasers Mark and Dan
will get. We have these five erasers. We have one for Mark,
one for Dan, one for Mark, and one for Dan. Uh oh! We
have one left over."

When researchers asked, "Should I give [the leftover
eraser] to Dan or should I throw it away?" the children almost always wanted to throw it away. The same finding held

when researchers emphasized that neither Mark nor Dan would know about the extra eraser, so there could be no gloating or envy. Even here, the children wanted equality so much that they would destroy something in order to get it.

I wonder if adults would do the same. Imagine being given five one-hundred-dollar bills, to be placed into two envelopes, with each envelope to be sent to a different person. There's no way to make things equal, but still, would you really put the fifth bill into a shredder? The children in the Shaw and Olson studies seem to care about equality a little bit too much, and one might wonder if this single-minded focus was due to their experiences outside the home. After all, the preschools and day cares where American psychologists get most of their subjects are typically institutions in which norms of equality are constantly beaten into children's heads; these are communities where every child gets a prize and everyone is above average.

This sort of experience probably has some influence. But a series of recent studies shows that an equality bias emerges long before schools and day cares have a chance to shape children's preferences.

In one of these studies, the psychologists Alessandra Geraci and Luca Surian showed ten- and sixteen-month-olds puppet shows in which a lion and a bear each distributed two multicolor disks to a donkey and a cow. The lion (or the bear, on alternate trials) gave each animal one disk, and the bear (or the lion) gave one animal two disks and the other nothing. The children were then shown the lion and the bear and asked, "Which one is the good one?

Please show me the good one." The ten-month-olds chose randomly, but the sixteen-month-olds preferred the fair divider.

The psychologists Marco Schmidt and Jessica Sommerville did a similar study with fifteen-month-olds, using actual people instead of toy animals but, again, showing a fair division and an unfair division. They found that the fifteen-month-olds looked longer at the unfair division, suggesting that they found it surprising. (A control study ruled out the possibility that toddlers just look longer at asymmetric displays.)

Other research suggests that children can sometimes override their focus on equality. In an experiment by psychologists Stephanie Sloane, Renee Baillargeon, and David Premack, nineteen-month-olds observed as two individuals playing with toys were told by a third party to start cleaning up. When both individuals cleaned up, the toddlers expected the experimenter to later reward them equally, looking longer if she didn't. But when one character did all the work and the other was a slacker who continued to play, babies looked longer when the experimenter rewarded both characters, presumably because they didn't expect equal reward for unequal effort.

Also, when given an uneven number of resources to distribute, children are smart about what to do with the extra resources. As mentioned above, six- to eight-year-olds would rather toss away a fifth eraser than have an unequal division between two characters who cleaned a room. But if you just add one sentence—"Dan did more work than

Mark"—almost all children change their answers. Instead of throwing away the eraser, they want to hand it over to Dan. Remember also the experiment in which children got to distribute resources through a doll and, when there was an even number of resources, tended to distribute them equally. The same researchers found that if there was an odd number of resources and children weren't given the option of throwing one away, three-year-olds would have the doll give more to siblings and friends than to strangers; give more to someone who had previously given the doll something than to someone who hadn't; and give more to someone who was generous to a third person than to someone who wasn't.

Young children don't know everything. Some experiments that I've done with the psychologists Koleen McCrink and Laurie Santos find that older children and adults think about relative generosity in terms of proportion—an individual with three items who gives away two is "nicer" than someone with ten items who gives away three—while young children focus only on absolute amount. And other studies find that our understanding of the factors that can justify inequality—such as luck, effort, and skill—develops even through adolescence.

What we do see at all ages, though, is an overall bias toward equality. Children expect equality, prefer those who divide resources equally, and are strongly biased to divide resources equally themselves. This fits well with a certain picture of human nature, which is that we are born with some sort of fairness instinct: we are natural-born egalitarians. As the primatologist Frans de Waal puts it: "Robin Hood had it right. Humanity's deepest wish is to spread the wealth."

WE DO seem to want to spread the wealth when it comes to other individuals. But I don't think that the Robin Hood theory is right when we ourselves are involved. Instead, we seek relative advantage; we are motivated not by a desire for equality but by selfish concerns about our own wealth and status. This can be seen in the lifestyles of small-scale societies, in laboratory studies with Western adults, and, most of all, in the choices made by young children when they themselves have something to lose.

Let's look at societies first. For much of recorded history, we've lived in conditions of profound inequality. Aleksandr Solzhenitsyn tells an unnerving story of what a truly nonegalitarian society looks like, from the Russia of the last century:

A district party conference was underway in Moscow Province. It was presided over by a new secretary of the District Party Committee, replacing one recently arrested. At the conclusion of the conference, a tribute to Comrade Stalin was called for. Of course, everyone stood up (just as everyone had leaped to his feet during the conference at every mention of his name). The small hall echoed with "stormy applause, rising to an ovation."

For three minutes, four minutes, five minutes, the

"stormy applause rising to an ovation" continued. But palms were getting sore and raised arms were already aching. And the older people were panting from exhaustion. It was becoming insufferably silly even to those who really adored Stalin. . . .

Then, after eleven minutes, the director of the paper factory assumed a business-like expression and sat down in his seat. And, oh, a miracle took place! Where had the universal, uninhibited, indescribable enthusiasm gone? To a man, everyone else stopped dead and sat down. They had been saved! The squirrel had been smart enough to jump off his revolving wheel.

That, however, was how they discovered who the independent people were. And that was how they went about eliminating them. That same night the factory director was arrested. They easily pasted ten years on him on the pretext of something quite different. But after he had signed the Form 206, the final document of the interrogation, his interrogator reminded him:

"Don't ever be the first to stop applauding!"

A more modern example comes from North Korea, where, in 2011, citizens were imprisoned after Kim Jong-il's funeral for not mourning in a convincing enough fashion.

Much of recorded history tells of societies led by Stalins, and this might reveal something about the nature of our psychology. Perhaps *Homo sapiens* is a hierarchical species, just like some of the great apes that we study. We are wired for dominance and submission—evolutionarily prepared to live in groups with a strong leader (an "alpha male" or "Big Man") and everyone else below him. If so, then we would expect to see these social structures in contemporary small-scale societies, since, in important regards, they live as all of us lived about ten thousand years ago, before agriculture, the domestication of animals, and modern technology.

In 1999, the anthropologist Christopher Boehm addressed this issue in *Hierarchy in the Forest,* which reviewed the lifestyles of dozens of small-scale human groups. Perhaps surprisingly, he found that they are egalitarian. Material inequality is kept to a minimum; goods are distributed to everyone. The old and sick are cared for. There are leaders, but their power is kept in check; and the social structure is flexible and nonhierarchical. It looks less like Stalin's Russia and more like Occupy Wall Street.

I don't want to romanticize the hunter-gatherer lifestyle—I wouldn't want to live in a world without novels and antibiotics. And they aren't *that* nice to one another, anyway. They are egalitarian when it comes to relationships between adult males but hierarchical otherwise: parents dominate their children and husbands control their wives. Also, *egalitarian* doesn't mean *pacifist.* Hunter-gatherer societies are hyperviolent—there's violence against women, violence between men competing for mates, and violence against rival groups. For these reasons, most people reading this book are better off than the average member of a contemporary hunter-gatherer tribe. Still, a very low-status person in a modern society—an elderly homeless man living on the streets of Manhattan, say, or a teenage prostitute in São Paulo—might well be better off as a member of such a tribe, where at least there would be community, sustenance, and respect.

It looks so far that the anthropological evidence supports the Robin Hood theory, that humans are naturally imbued with some deeply ingrained preference for fairness and that this leads to equality in our "natural" social structures. But actually, Boehm argues the opposite. He observes that the egalitarian lifestyles of hunter-gatherers exist because the individuals care a lot about status. Individuals in these societies end up roughly equal because everyone is struggling to ensure that nobody gets too much power over him or her. This is invisible-hand egalitarianism. Think about three children and a pie. One way that they can all get equal shares is if they all care about equality and agree that everyone should get the same. But the other way to get an equal division—the more human way, I think—is that each child is careful to ensure that he or she doesn't get less than anyone else.

This strategy can work, in the pie example and the real world, only if individuals are able to defend their rights and protect their status. In the societies that Boehm describes, tribe members use criticism and ridicule to bring down those who they think are too big for their britches. As Natalie Angier put it: "Among the !Kung bushmen of the Kalahari in Africa, a successful hunter who may be inclined to swagger is kept in check by his compatriots through a ritualized game called 'insulting the meat.' You asked us out here to help you carry that pitiful carcass? What is it, some kind of rabbit?"

There is also behind-the-back gossip and open mockery. Boehm cites a scholar who writes: "Among the Hadza . . . when a would-be 'chief' tried to persuade other Hadza to work for him, people openly made it clear that his efforts amused them." (This was how graduate students treated me when I started as an assistant professor.) And there are more serious penalties. Wannabe Stalins can be abandoned by their group, a fate that is akin to a death sentence. Or they can just be straight-out whacked. When a Baruya man tries to take his neighbors' livestock and have sex with their wives, he is murdered. When a leader becomes "very quarrelsome and strong in magic," his tribesmen respond by handing him over to a "vengeance party" from another tribe.

The egalitarian lifestyle of the hunter-gatherers, then, emerges from people jockeying for position, caring for themselves and those they love, and being willing to work together to protect themselves from being dominated. As Boehm puts it, "Individuals who otherwise would be subordinated are clever enough to form a large and united political coalition. . . . Because the united subordinates are constantly putting down the more assertive alpha types in their midst, egalitarianism is in effect a bizarre type of political hierarchy: the weak combine forces to actively dominate the strong."

Sadly, the sort of egalitarianism that Boehm describes has come to an end for most of us. Populations grew, agriculture emerged, animals were domesticated, and new technologies were invented. Because of this, the available sanctions by the weak became less effective and the countermeasures by the powerful become deadlier. If we live in a small hunter-gatherer society, and an alpha male is asserting control, then we can laugh at him or ignore him. We can hold meetings, and if enough of us are unhappy, we can beat him up or kill him. But none of this works in societies where interactions are no longer face to face and where individuals or small groups of elites can accumulate grossly disproportionate resources, both material and social. An ambitious hunter-gatherer might have a gang of friends with rocks and spears; Stalin had an army and a secret police, gulags and rifles and thumbscrews. In the modern world, an ambitious and cruel leader driven by status hunger can form a group that dominates a population a thousand times larger. It is no longer so easy for the weak to gang up to dominate the strong (although some have argued that the Internet—being decentralized and somewhat anonymous—is helping to even the score).

LET's turn now to adults within our own society. Over the last few decades, researchers in the field of behavioral economics have designed clever and simple games to explore just how kind, fair, and egalitarian we really are.

The first of these is known as the Ultimatum Game. The idea is simple. The participant walks into the lab and is randomly chosen to be either the "proposer" or the "recipient." If she is chosen to be the proposer, she is given some sum of money, say $10, and has the option of giving any fraction of this money to the recipient. The recipient, in turn, has just two options—to accept the offer or to reject it. Importantly, if the offer is rejected, neither person keeps any money, and the proposer is aware of this rule before she makes her offer. The experiment is typically conducted anonymously, as a one-shot game—the proposer and the recipient are in different rooms, don't know who the other is, and will never encounter each other again.

Assuming that both participants are perfectly rational actors who care only about money, the proposer should give as little as possible. And the recipient should accept this offer, because $1 is better than nothing, and turning it down can't lead to a better offer in the future, since the game is played only once. But this rarely happens. The proposer typically offers half or a little less than half of the amount.

This could conceivably reflect a Robin Hood impulse on the part of the proposer: a belief that an equal split is the right thing to do. But an obvious alternative is that proposers are acting out of self-interest, as they believe that miserly offers will be rejected. And they are right to believe this: in the lab, recipients do reject low offers, giving up a profit so that a stingy proposer gets nothing.

While turning down low offers is, in some sense, a mistake (the recipient walks away with nothing), the Ultimatum Game turns out to be one of those paradoxical situations in which it pays to be irrational, or at least to be thought of as irrational by others. If I were a selfish individual and knew that I was playing a one-shot Ultimatum

Game with an emotionless robot, then, as proposer, I would offer the minimum, because I would know it would be accepted. But if I was dealing with a normal person, I would worry that I would have a low offer rejected out of spite. And so I would hand over more money.

(According to the behavioral economist Dan Ariely, when students in economics classes are put in the position of the proposer, they often offer the minimum, and this works out fine for them because they are playing with other economics students, who accept the minimum. It's only when these rational proposers play with noneconomists that they are in for an unpleasant surprise.)

The recipient's rejection of a low offer also makes sense when we realize that our minds were not adapted for one-shot anonymous interactions. We evolved in a world in which we engaged in repeated interactions with a relatively small number of other individuals. So we are wired to respond to the lowball offer as if it were the first of many, even if we know, consciously, that it isn't. The rejection, then, is a corrective "Screw you, buddy" that would make perfect sense if you were going to play the same person multiple times. And the psychological state that motivates this rejection is outrage toward the person making the offer. You can see this in the recipients' faces, which contort into looks of contempt or disgust, and in their brains, where the areas associated with anger become more active. In one study, where recipients were allowed to send anonymous messages to the proposers who lowballed them, typical messages included "Should not have been greedy. Oh well, you make nothing"; "Dude, that's kinda greedy"; "Thanks For Nothing"; and "You suck."

What, precisely, is so annoying about being lowballed? The philosopher Shaun Nichols spells out the logic here: "If Jim is told to divide a good with Bill, and Jim elects to defy the [norm of equal division], giving Bill a tenth of the good, what is Jim's justification? Since the good was a windfall, Jim can hardly claim that he earned the greater share. Given the presence of an equal-division norm, it will be natural to think that Jim is treating Bill as inferior." Now, knowing this, Jim might refrain from making the low offer through the exercise of empathy—he might cringe at the thought of what it would feel like to be Bill, to be insulted in this manner, and this might motivate him to offer a fair division. But Jim might also refrain for a more selfish reason: If Bill is angry enough, he can retaliate and leave Jim with nothing.

Individuals' behavior in the Ultimatum Game, then, provides no support for the Robin Hood theory. But now consider the Dictator Game. First thought up by the psychologist Daniel Kahneman and his colleagues, this is just like the Ultimatum Game except that it removes the stage where the recipients get to make a choice. The participants get sums of money and can give however much they want to anonymous strangers. And that's it—they keep what they choose to keep.

Plainly, a self-interested agent would give nothing. But this is not what people do. There have been more than a hundred published studies on dictator games, and it turns out that most people do give, and the average gift is between

20 and 30 percent. Some studies find even greater generosity, reporting that many people give half or just a bit less than half.

Unlike in the Ultimatum Game, this generosity cannot be explained as due to fear of retaliation. So one interpretation of these findings is the Robin Hood analysis—the dictator hands over the money out of a sense of fairness. That is, the person who gets to make the choice has managed to put aside her particular position in the world and is considering the optimal solution from the position of an uninvolved bystander. Since there is no reason for the dictator to get more than the other person, she is driven to split the windfall evenly (though, because of human frailty, she might keep a bit extra for herself).

Now, I'm not the first to point that there's something odd about this interpretation. While it's true that some people believe in the egalitarian principle that the best world is one where resources are evenly divided, we don't, as a rule, feel compelled to give away half of our money to the person standing next to us. We are often generous, but not in this sort of indiscriminate way. This is true even when the money comes as a windfall. Suppose you find twenty dollars on the sidewalk. Do you immediately hand over ten dollars to the next person who walks by, on the logic that it was just luck that it was you who found it and not he? Likely not.

So why are people so nice in these laboratory experiments? A different sort of explanation is social pressure. The participants know that they are in a study that is looking at kindness and fairness. The situation is typically framed so that one can act on a continuum of generosity, and the worst thing is to give nothing. The finding that most people give something might largely be explained by the fact that nobody wants to look like an ass.

To see the effects of an audience, just imagine, as one researcher suggested, playing the Dictator Game on national television, with all your family and friends watching. Wouldn't this make you more generous? It is not surprising that laboratory studies find that the more observable one's choice is, the more one gives. Even pictures of eyes on the wall or on the computer screen make people kinder, presumably because they trigger thoughts of being watched. The idea here was nicely expressed by Tom Lehrer, in his song about the Boy Scouts: "Be careful not to do / Your good deeds when there's no one watching you."

While the standard Dictator scenario is supposed to be anonymous, still, participants might not believe experimenters' assurances that this is so. And they're *right* to be suspicious; sometimes they are being lied to. Furthermore, the motivation to make a good impression on others might be operative even when one consciously believes that there is no audience.

This might all seem picky. If people give generously, what difference does it make if this generosity is motivated by worries about how others will see them? It turns out, though, that a pure egalitarian impulse is one thing and the desire to look good is quite another. Two clever sets of experiments make this point.

In the first, the psychologist Jason Dana and his colleagues tweaked the standard Dictator Game. They set up the basic game with $10, but now some participants could choose between playing the regular game or taking $9 and leaving the game. They were told that if they chose this second option, the recipient would never learn that he or she was ever in a Dictator Game.

A selfish individual, just in it for the money, would agree to play the game and keep the whole $10 for the maximum gain. A generous individual, on the other hand, would agree to play and give away some chunk of the $10. Neither would opt out for $9, because this option would give the player less than $10 (and so doesn't make sense from a selfish perspective) and would give the other person nothing (and so doesn't make sense from a generous perspective).

Still, over a third of participants chose to take the $9. This is likely because they wanted the money but didn't want to be put in a position where they would feel pressured to give a substantial amount of it away. The analogy here is walking down a street where a beggar is waiting. If you were cold-blooded, you would walk by and do nothing; if you were generous, you would walk by and hand over some money. But if you didn't want to be put in a position of feeling obliged to give, you might take a third option: you might cross the street to avoid the beggar altogether.

The second set of experiments was done by the economist John List. He started with a game where the dictator was given $10 and the recipient was given $5. As usual, the dictator could give as much of his money to the other person as he wanted. In this simple condition, the average gift was $1.33, a sensibly generous amount.

A second group of participants were told that they could give as much as they wanted—but they could also take $1 from the other person. Now, the average gift dropped to 33 cents. And a third group were told that they could give as much as they wanted but could also take as much as they wanted, up to the whole $5. Now, they *took* on average $2.48, and very few gave anything.

We should stop and marvel at how weird this is. If the standard explanation of giving in the Dictator Game is correct—that it reflects an impulse to share the wealth—it shouldn't matter if someone adds the option of taking. But suppose now that the giving is motivated, at least in part, by a desire to look good. Now the option of taking makes a difference, because the worst possible option is no longer giving nothing, it's taking away all of the other person's money. The participant might think: A real jerk would leave this person with nothing. I don't want to look like a jerk—I'll just take a little. Taken together, these studies suggest that the behavior in the Dictator Game is influenced by factors that have little to do with altruistic and egalitarian motives and much to do with *looking* altruistic and egalitarian.

THE economist Ernst Fehr and his colleagues were among the first to explore how children behave when faced with economic games. They tested Swiss children, from three to eight years old, and instead of money, they used candies. In the experiments I'll discuss here, the children were told that their decisions would affect children that they didn't know who came from the same playschool, kindergarten, or school.

One of the games was a variant of the Dictator Game: each child was given two candies and had the option of either keeping one and giving the other away or of keeping both. In this condition, the seven- and eight-year-olds were generous—about half of them gave away a candy. But the younger children were greedy—only about 20 percent of the five- and six-year-olds gave away a candy, and only about 10 percent of the three- and four-year-olds did so. This selfishness on the part of young children fits with more recent research on the Dictator Game in different countries—including America, Europe, China, Peru, Brazil, and Fiji—that finds that young children are much less likely than older children or adults to give away what they have to a stranger.

One might conclude that young children don't care at all about equality when they themselves are involved. But perhaps this is unfair. Maybe the youngest children have the same equity/kindness/fairness impulse as the older ones, but they have less self-control and so, unlike the older children, they cannot overcome their self-interest. Their appetite overwhelms their altruism.

To test this theory, Fehr and colleagues developed another game—the Prosocial Game—that avoids this conflict between altruism and self-control. Here the child gets a candy no matter what; the choice is whether to give the other individual a candy as well. This allows children to be altruistic (and fair, and egalitarian) at no cost to themselves.

The seven- and eight-year-olds did as one would expect: about 80 percent gave away a candy. For the younger children, however, only about half did. That is, about half of the children in the younger age groups chose not to give away a candy to a stranger—even if it cost them *nothing*.

Other studies explore children's emotional reactions to fair and unfair distributions that they themselves are affected by. The psychologist Vanessa LoBue and her colleagues tested three-, four-, and five-year-olds in preschools and did so up close and personal—unlike the studies so far, this one didn't have children deal with anonymous strangers. Instead, the experimenters would pair up two children from the same class. The children played together with blocks in a quiet room for five minutes and then they put the blocks away. An adult came in to tell them that since they had helped to clean up, they were going to get stickers. In full view of both the children (named, for example, Mary and Sally), the experimenter handed over stickers one at a time, giving a running tally: "One sticker for Mary, one sticker for Sally. Two stickers for Mary, two stickers for Sally. Three stickers for Mary. Four stickers for Mary." So Sally would end up with two and Mary would end up with four. Then the experimenter paused for seven seconds, doing nothing and avoiding eye contact, as the children's spontaneous responses were captured on video. The children were then asked whether the distribution was fair.

Children in Sally's position usually said that it was not fair, they looked unhappy, and they often asked for more. If asked, children in Mary's position were likely to agree that this was unfair, but they didn't respond to this unfairness in the same way—they weren't bothered by it. The nicest thing that an advantaged child was seen to do was hand over a sticker after a disadvantaged child complained—but fewer than one in ten did this. And remember that these children weren't dealing with anonymous strangers; they were sitting next to their classmates, often their friends.

Children are sensitive to inequality, then, but it seems to upset them only when they themselves are the ones getting less. In this regard, they are similar to monkeys, chimpanzees, and dogs, all of whom show signs of being bothered by getting a smaller reward than someone else. For instance, researchers have done studies with pairs of dogs, in which each dog does a trick. One dog is then rewarded with a nice treat, while the other gets a lesser treat. The researchers find that the dog offered a lesser treat will sometimes act, well, pissed, and refuse to eat it.

Children can also be spiteful in their preferences. The psychologists Peter Blake and Katherine McAuliffe paired up four- to eight-year-olds who had never met, placing them in front of a special apparatus that was set up to distribute two trays of candy. One of the children had access to a lever that gave her the choice either to tilt the trays toward herself and the other child (so that each child got whatever amount of candy was on the nearest tray) or to dump both trays (so that nobody got any candy).

When there was an equal amount of candy in each tray, the children almost never dumped. They also almost never dumped when the distribution favored themselves—say, four candies on their tray, and one candy on the other child's tray—though some of the eight-year-olds did reject this choice. But when this distribution was reversed to favor the other child, children at every age group frequently chose to dump both trays. They would rather get nothing than have another child, a stranger, get more than they did.

Further evidence of children's spiteful natures comes from a series of experiments I've just completed in collaboration with Karen Wynn and Yale graduate student Mark Sheskin. We offered children between five and ten years of age a series of choices about how to divide tokens (which could later be exchanged for toys) with another child whom they would never meet. For instance, they would choose between a distribution where each child got one token and a distribution where each child got two tokens. Reasonably enough, when we offered them this choice, they tended to choose the latter option—they got more, and so did the other person.

But we also found that social comparison matters. Consider an option where the chooser and the other child each get one token versus an option where the chooser gets two tokens and the other child gets three. You might think that the latter is the better choice because both children get more; it's greedier *and* it's more generous. But choosing a 2/3 split over a 1/1 split means that the chooser will get relatively less than the other child. This was unpleasant to the children we tested, and they often chose 1/1, giving up an extra token so that they wouldn't end up with a relative disadvantage.

Or take an option where each gets two tokens versus an option where the chooser gets one and the other child gets nothing. The 2/2 option is better for all involved in absolute terms, but the advantage of the 1/0 option is that the chooser gets relatively more than the other child. The older children preferred 2/2, but the five- and six-year-olds preferred the 1/0 option; they would rather have a relative advantage, even at a cost to themselves. Such responses are reminiscent of a medieval Jewish folktale about an envious man who was approached by an angel, and told that he could have anything he wanted—but his neighbor would get double. He thought for a moment, then asked to have one of his eyes plucked out.

FAIRNESS is more than deciding the best way to distribute the positive. We also have to determine how to allocate the negative. This brings us to punishment and revenge, the darker side of morality.

If we were always kind to one another, the issue of punishment would never arise. But, as the anthropologist Robert Ardrey once remarked, "We are born of risen apes, not fallen angels." Some of us are tempted to cheat and kill and succumb to selfish impulses, and for the rest of us to survive in the presence of these individuals, we need to make this bad behavior costly. Indeed, some scholars, such as the philosopher Jesse Prinz, view outrage as more important to morality than empathy and compassion, those sweeter sentiments we discussed in the last chapter.

Let us start with revenge—the personal form of punishment, directed against those who have wronged us personally or who have harmed our family or friends. Revenge has certain distinctive features. Adam Smith describes our feelings toward a man who has murdered someone we love: "Resentment would prompt us to desire, not only that he should be punished, but that he should be punished by our means, and upon account of that particular injury which he had done to us. Resentment cannot be fully gratified, unless the offender is not only made to grieve in his turn, but to grieve for that particular wrong which we have suffered from him."

Inigo Montoya, the character in *The Princess Bride* who seeks to avenge his father's death, echoes this sentiment. Montoya tells the man in black his plan: he will approach the murderer and say, "Hello. My name is Inigo Montoya. You killed my father. Prepare to die!" The killer must know precisely why he is being punished and by whom. Then, and only then, can Montoya kill him. (And when he does, it is deeply satisfying.)

These requirements make sense once we appreciate the link between revenge and status. As the philosopher Pamela Hieronymi says, "A past wrong against you, standing in your history without apology, atonement, retribution, punishment, restitution, condemnation, or anything else that might recognize it as a *wrong,* makes a claim. It says, in effect, that you can be treated in this way, and that such treatment is acceptable." This is one purpose of apologies—to repair the victim's status. If you knock me over and say nothing, you are taking away my dignity. A simple "I'm sorry" can do wonders, because you are showing respect for me as a person; you are acknowledging to me, and possibly others, that it is unacceptable to harm me without cause. If you say nothing, you are sending a quite different message. Without an apology, I might be tempted to recover my status through retaliation. If you knock me over and then I knock you over in response, I've shown you that I am a man to be reckoned with, which will make you less likely to harm me in the future. But this works only if you know who knocked you over and why. (If you think that someone else did it, or that I did it by mistake, then I have failed.)

In our modern Western societies, first-person revenge plays a less prominent role than it does in the so-called cultures of honor—the Bedouin, criminal subcultures such as the Mafia, and the cowboy culture of the American West, for example. Individuals living in such cultures cannot rely on external authority to mete out justice, so it's up to each individual to defend himself and those he cares about. A reputation for violence matters in these societies; this is what deters others from attacking or abusing you. Consistent with this theory, psychologists find that individuals in such societies tend to be disapproving of acts of disrespect and forgiving of acts of retribution.

The psychologist Steven Pinker argues that one reason for the drop in violence over history is the decline of such cultures. We've managed, in many parts of the world, to check our appetite for personal retribution. First-party revenge has been largely replaced with third-party punishment, enforced by the government. When my car window was smashed and my belongings were stolen a few months ago, I felt a flash of anger, but really, the problem was best addressed through a police report and a helpful insurance company. If Inigo Montoya were around now, he wouldn't need to storm the castle to bring his father's murderer to justice; the police would do it for him, and fewer people would have to die.

Still, some appetite for revenge exists within most of us. There are all sorts of interactions that the law doesn't help out with—if only nasty gossip or snarky e-mails—so we benefit from some inclination toward payback, some impulse to make those who disrespect us suffer to the appropriate degree. And while we might lack the stomach for enacting our own violent vengeance, we get pleasure from experiencing it in the imagination. The theme of payback shows up over and over in fiction, from classic works such as *Hamlet* and *The Iliad,* to schlocky films like *An Eye for an Eye* and *Death Wish,* to television series like the aptly named *Revenge.*

PUNISHMENT of third parties who haven't personally wronged us is not the same thing as revenge and doesn't have as simple an explanation. Certainly we do have an appetite for third-party punishment. One example is the recent emergence in China of *renrou sousuo yinqing,* or "human flesh search engines"—a phenomenon in which people use the Internet to crowd-source the identity of wrongdoers: adulterers, unpatriotic citizens, amateur pornographic actors, and so on. These self-appointed avengers try to motivate physical and social attacks against these individuals and often succeed in getting them to leave town or lose their jobs. Or remember the cases we discussed earlier, such as the public reaction against Mary Bale after she put a cat into a garbage bin, or against David Cash Jr., who watched the murder of a child and did nothing—both were stalked and threatened by morally outraged strangers.

One can explore this punitive impulse through another game thought up by behavioral economists—the Public Goods Game, which explores the extent to which people will sacrifice for a greater good. There are several variants of this game, but here's an example: There are four players, each unknown to the others (typically they are playing on separate computer terminals), each starting with $20. The game is played as a series of rounds, and at the start of each round the players put money in the middle. This money is doubled and distributed evenly back to the players. Then each player gets a report about how much money he or she now has and what each of the other players did.

Imagine playing such a game. Here are some ways it can turn out.

1. **Nobody puts any money into the middle:** Everyone keeps his or her $20.
2. **Everyone puts in all of his or her money:** The $80 in the pot is multiplied by 2, and then split four ways, so that everyone gets back $40.
3. **You hold back, the other three put in their money:** Your three co-players put in $20 each. Now there is $60 in the pot. It doubles: $120.

Now it's split four ways, and everyone, including you, gets back $30. Since you didn't contribute, you now have $50.

4. **You put in, the others hold back:** Your $20 is doubled to $40, and split four ways, so that everyone gets back $10. The others didn't pay anything, so each of them has his or her original $20 plus $10, for a total of $30. You are left just with $10.

The best overall solution is for everyone to put in money. If each individual contributes, everyone will double his or her money on each round. But at the same time, any individual would make more by not putting in anything. For instance, if everyone else puts in money, an individual is better off opting out—$50 versus $40. And if nobody else puts in money, an individual is still better off opting out—$20 versus $10.

This calculus matches up nicely with situations in everyday life in which engaging in an unpleasant or time-consuming activity leads to an improvement for everyone, but selfish individuals can sit back and reap the benefits without paying the costs. For example, I want a world where people pay taxes—I benefit from roads, the fire department, the police, and so on—but the world I would most prefer from a selfish standpoint is the one where everyone pays taxes but me. The same goes for recycling, voting, organizing our local block party, serving in the military—or my roommate situation in graduate school, where we faced the following options for cleaning the house:

1. **Nobody does anything:** The apartment is filthy, but nobody has to work. We are all mildly unhappy.
2. **Everyone cleans:** The apartment is clean, and we all do a little bit of work. This is the best overall situation.
3. **I do nothing; everyone else cleans:** This is the best solution for me. I have a clean apartment and do no work.
4. **I clean; the others do nothing:** I have a clean apartment but do far more work than everyone else, and I'm miserable.

In public goods games played in the laboratory, people tend to start off playing nice, but inevitably some participants succumb to temptation and opt out to make extra money. Others observe this, and then they too defect. As more people defect, one feels increasingly like a patsy for staying in. And so, while there might remain some stalwart contributors, the situation gradually goes to hell. This is what happened in my roommate situation: it descended into a Hobbesian battle of all against all, and we lived, unhappily, in squalor.

This looks grim. But in the course of history humans were somehow able to overcome the temptations of defection and free-riding—otherwise, practices such as warfare, big-game hunting, and shared child care could never have come into existence.

And this brings us back to punishment. If the government stopped punishing tax cheats, more people would cheat on their taxes; if evading the draft weren't illegal, more people would evade the draft. The threat of fines and imprisonment helps deter free riders. Now, appealing to state-sponsored sanctions is little help from an evolutionary perspective, since we formed cooperative groups long before there were governments and police. But it hints at a solution to the problem of free riders, which is that *individuals* are motivated to punish one another and that punishment, and fear of punishment, motivate better behavior.

Ernst Fehr and the economist Simon Gächter explored this idea using a modified public goods game. As in the usual game, participants got to see what everyone else did (again, just as a series of numbers; they didn't actually know who any of the other players were). But now a participant could spend his or her money to take away money from another person. In particular, a person who noticed that someone hadn't contributed in the last round could then pay his or her own money to lower the sum that the offender ended up with in the current round—a form of third-party punishment.

This punishment, crucially, was *altruistic:* a participant who chose to punish knew that he was giving up something to promote a good outcome (perhaps better behavior by the free rider in the future, or perhaps the simple enforcement of justice). The money taken from the punishee disappeared; it didn't go to any participant, and the punisher didn't continue to play with the punishee, and so if this did improve the punishee's behavior, it wouldn't help the punisher personally.

Even so, 80 percent of participants punished at least once. And this punishment, which tended to be directed at those who contributed less than average, solved the problem of defection. Soon enough, just about everyone was contributing. Such punishment makes cooperation possible.

BUT is an appetite for altruistic punishment really an evolved instinct? One problem with this proposal is that it's vexingly hard to explain how such behavior could evolve through natural selection. Even if our society works better when free riders are brought into line through punishment, still, someone has to do the punishing, and if it is costly, as it is in the lab games, then we have the free-rider problem all over again. What's keeping an individual from hanging back when he or she sees wrongdoing and benefiting from the altruistic punishment of others—in other words, being a free rider when it comes to punishing free riders? Now, we might be motivated to punish those who shirk from punishing free riders—but then are we also motivated to punish those who shirk from punishing those who shirk from punishing free riders?

Perhaps altruistic punishment could have evolved through some sort of group selection (groups that contain these punishers do better than groups that don't), or perhaps punishers thrive because other individuals like them and prefer to interact with them. But an alternative is that there is no evolved propensity for altruistic punishment in the first place.

In support of this idea, in a recent review of the literature from sociology and anthropology, the philosopher Francesco Guala finds that altruistic punishment is rare—or even nonexistent—in the small-scale societies of the real world. Now, as we saw earlier, there are plenty of direct and indirect ways to make wrongdoers, including free riders, suffer. But such real-world punishment tends to be done in ways that are not costly to the punisher, either because they don't involve confrontation (for example, gossip), or because the group as a whole does it, so that no single individual takes a hit.

Furthermore, although humans everywhere do punish free riders, it turns out that people from different societies react to this punishment in different ways. When free riders from countries such as Switzerland, the United States, and Australia are punished, they shape up and get nicer. But in certain other societies, such as Greece and Saudi Arabia, people who have been punished for free riding don't feel ashamed; they get mad and try to get even. They go looking for those who most likely did the punishment and punish them back, something dubbed "antisocial punishment." This response, as you would expect, makes things worse, and the situation collapses into chaos. (Not surprisingly, antisocial punishment tends to occur in countries with, as the authors of the cross-cultural study put it, "weak norms of civic cooperation.") This suggests that third-party punishment could not have evolved as a solution to the problem of free riding.

In my view, the psychology of third-party punishment is little more than the psychology of revenge writ large. That is, we have evolved a tendency to retaliate against those who harm us and who harm the people we love because by doing so we deter such behavior in the future. When we extend these sentiments to cases that we are not directly involved in, it is through the exercise of empathy. We imagine ourselves in the victim's shoes and respond as if we ourselves were being harmed. Third-party punishment, then, reduces to revenge plus empathy.

This is similar to Adam Smith's view: "When we see one man oppressed or injured by another, the sympathy which we feel with the distress of the sufferer seems to serve only to animate our fellow-feeling with his resentment against the offender. We are rejoiced to see him attack his adversary in his turn, and are eager and ready to assist him." But I think Smith is slightly off base when he says that the perceived resentment of the victim is a necessary spur to punishment. After all, I think that someone who tortures kittens should be punished, but this isn't because I believe that the kittens themselves would want vengeance. The relevant question isn't "What does the victim want?" It is "What would *I* want, if it were me or someone I cared about in the position of the victim?"

Consistent with the idea that our appetite for third-party punishment is parasitic on empathy, it varies according to our relationship with the victim and the person harming the victim. We are drawn to punish those who harm individuals that naturally inspire empathy, such as kittens; those whom we care about; and those who are part of our group, tribe, or coalition. We are less motivated to punish when our empathetic connection is with the aggressor. Few Americans, upon hearing that Navy SEALs killed Osama bin Laden, felt a desire that these men be punished.

Even young children have some appreciation of the logic of third-party punishment, as demonstrated by the psychologists David Pietraszewski and Tamsin German. In their study, researchers told four-year-olds about a child who had pushed another child and taken her toy, then asked who would be mad at the aggressor. The children understood that the victim was likely to be mad, but they also appreciated that a friend of the victim was more likely to be mad than a classmate.

This explanation for third-party punishment—that it stems from our desire for revenge—also explains some of the odder features of our punitive sentiments. Most notably, people are surprisingly indifferent to the actual consequences of punishment. One study explored people's judgments about how to penalize a hypothetical company for harms caused by faulty vaccines and birth control pills. Some people were told that a higher fine would make companies try harder to make safer products—a punishment that would improve future welfare. Others were told that a higher fine would likely cause the company to stop making the product, and since there weren't other good alternatives on the market, the punishment would make the world worse. Most people didn't care about the negative consequences of the second scenario; they wanted the company fined in both cases. In other words, people are more concerned that punishment should injure the punisher than that it should make the world a better place. The psychology of revenge is at work here: in Smith's words, "He must be made to repent and be sorry for this very action."

This insensitivity to consequences is typical for desires, which are usually blind to the forces that explain their existence. Sexual desire exists because it leads to baby making, but the psychology of sexual desire is unmoored from any interest in babies. Hunger exists because eating keeps us alive, but this isn't why we usually want to eat. Similarly, we want to punish, but we don't think about the purpose of punishment, a point nicely made by, yes, Adam Smith: "All men, even the most stupid and unthinking, abhor fraud, perfidy, and injustice, and delight to see them punished. But few men have reflected upon the necessity of justice to the existence of society, how obvious soever that necessity may appear to be."

Most toddlers do not live in a culture of honor. There is usually a Leviathan that will resolve conflicts and punish wrongdoers—such as a parent, babysitter, or teacher. Things do change in middle childhood, when children often find themselves in societies where tattling is discouraged and one is expected to fight one's own battles. Many middle schools and high schools are much like the Wild West. But two-year-olds are permitted to cry or run away or find an adult when someone smacks them; they aren't required to retaliate.

This doesn't mean that children are innocent of retributive desires. They are hardly pacifists, after all. Young children are highly aggressive; indeed, if you measure the rate of physical violence through the life span, it peaks at about age two. Families survive the Terrible Twos because toddlers aren't strong enough to kill with their hands and aren't capable of using lethal weapons. A two-year-old with the physical capacities of an adult would be terrifying.

Children's moralizing impulses are sometimes reflected in violence but are also expressed in a more subtle way. Children tattle. When they see wrongdoing, they are apt to complain about it to an authority figure, and they don't need to be prompted to do so. In one study, two- and three-year-olds were taught a new game to play with a puppet; when the puppet started to break the rules, the children would spontaneously complain to adults. In studies of siblings between the ages of two and six, investigators found that most of what the children said to their parents about their brothers or sisters counted as tattling. And their reports tended to be accurate. They were ratting their sibs out, but they were not making things up.

It's not just siblings who enjoy telling on each other. The psychologists Gordon Ingram and Jesse Bering explored tattling by children in an inner-city school in Belfast and concluded, "The great majority of children's talk about their peers' behavior took the form of descriptions of norm violations." They noted that it was rare for children to talk to their teachers about something good that someone else had done. As in the sibling study, most of the children's reports about their peers were true. The children who lied were not the tattlers but the tattlees, who would often deny being responsible for their acts. Children also don't tattle about insignificant things: one study found that three-year-olds will tattle when someone destroys an artwork that someone else made, but not when the individual destroys an artwork that nobody cares about.

Part of the satisfaction of tattling surely comes from showing oneself to adults as a good moral agent, a responsible being who is sensitive to right and wrong. But I would bet that children would tattle even if they could do so only anonymously. Like the strangers who participate in the human flesh search engines, they would do it just to have justice done. The love of tattling reveals an appetite for payback, a pleasure in seeing wrongdoers (particularly those who harmed the child, or a friend of the child) being punished. Tattling is a way of off-loading the potential costs of revenge.

It is hard to tell whether babies also have an appetite for justice. Here is the experiment that I wish we could do to find out: Show a baby a good character and a bad character, using our standard methods (such as having one character help someone up a hill and another block that individual's path). Then, one at a time, put the good character and the bad character alone on a stage, facing the baby. Next to the baby's hand is a large red button, and the baby is gently shown how to press on it. When the button is touched, the character will act as though it's been given an electric shock—it will scream and writhe in pain. How will babies respond to this? Will they snatch their hand back when the good guy screams? Will they continue to press it for the bad guy? What if it is a difficult button to press—will babies push down on it, their little faces red with exertion, so as to enact just punishment?

I doubt that we will ever do this study. My colleagues, more fastidious than I am, have ethical concerns.

But we have done other studies that offer clues to babies' punitive motivations. In one study with Kiley Hamlin, Karen Wynn, and Neha Mahajan, we did a variant of the good guy/bad guy experiments described in the first chapter. In one scenario, one puppet struggled to open a box, one puppet helped to lift the lid, and another slammed the lid shut. In the other scenario, a puppet rolled a ball to one puppet who rolled it right back, and to another who took the ball and ran away. Instead of asking whether infants preferred to interact with the good or the bad puppet, we asked twenty-one-month-olds either to choose which of the two to reward by giving it a treat or to choose which of the two to punish by taking away a treat. As predicted, we found that when asked to give a treat, they chose the good character; and when asked to take away a treat, they chose the bad one.

One problem with this study, though, is that it was set up so that children were basically forced to choose a puppet to reward and a puppet to punish. We don't know, then, whether toddlers have an urge to reward and an urge to punish, let alone whether they feel that rewarding and punishing are the right things to do. Also, given the physical demands of rewarding and punishing, we had to use toddlers instead of infants in this study, and they may well have learned some of the rewarding and punishing behavior from watching other people.

To explore how babies think about reward and punishment at an earlier age, we decided to look at what five- and eight-month-olds thought of other individuals who rewarded and punished. Would they prefer someone who rewarded a good guy to someone who punished a good guy? Would they prefer someone who punished a bad guy over someone who rewarded a bad guy? For each contrast, by adult lights at least, one individual is acting justly and the other is not.

We tested the babies by first showing them the scenarios with the box—one puppet would help open the box; the other would slam it shut. Then we used either the good guy or the bad guy as the main character of an entirely new scene. This time the puppet rolled the ball to two new individuals in turn: one who rolled it back (nice) and the other who ran away with it (mean). We wanted to see which of these two new characters the babies preferred—the one who was nice to the good guy or the one who was mean to the good guy; the one who was nice to the bad guy or the one who was mean to the bad guy.

When the two characters were interacting with the good guy (the one who had helped open the box), babies preferred to reach for the character who was nice to it as opposed to the one who was mean to it—probably because babies tend to prefer nice puppets overall. Indeed, the five-month-olds also preferred to reach for the character who was nice to the bad guy. Either these younger babies weren't keeping track of the whole sequence of events, or they just preferred nice puppets, regardless of whom they were interacting with.

But the eight-month-olds were more sophisticated: they preferred the puppet who was mean to the bad guy over the one who was nice to it. So at some point after five months, babies begin to prefer punishers—when the punishment is just.

WE HAVE talked so far about certain capacities for judgment and feeling. While perhaps not present in the first few months of life, these capacities are natural in the sense that they are a legacy of our evolutionary history, not cultural inventions.

I have described these capacities throughout as *moral.* This is because they share significant properties with what adults view as moral—they are triggered by acts that affect others' well-being; they relate to notions such as fairness; they connect to feelings such as empathy and anger; and they are associated with reward and punishment. Also, once toddlers learn enough language to talk about their judgments, they use terms that, for adults, are explicitly moral, such as *nice, mean, fair,* and *unfair.* What first shows up in looking time and preferential reaching in a baby appears later as the topic of moral discourse in a toddler.

Still, the moral life of babies is profoundly limited relative to our own. This was appreciated by the psychologist Lawrence Kohlberg, who, about fifty years ago, came up with an influential theory of moral development. He claimed that young children think about morality first in terms of simpler notions such as self-interest (what's good is what brings me pleasure) and then in terms of parental authority (what's good is what my parents say is good). They become more sophisticated as they mature, until, ultimately, morality is understood in terms of abstract rules and principles, similar to the systems developed by moral philosophers. The end point is a consistent and broad theory of right and wrong.

Few contemporary psychologists would endorse Kohlberg's account. The research we've discussed shows that he underestimated the moral sophistication of children. He also overestimated the moral sophistication of adults. Few adults are Kantians or utilitarians or virtue ethicists; we don't normally think about morality as philosophers do. Rather, we possess what the psychologist David Pizarro has dubbed a "hodgepodge morality"—"a fairly loose collection of intuitions, rules of thumb, and emotional responses."

But Kohlberg is right that adult morality is influenced by rational deliberation. This is what separates humans from chimpanzees and separates adults from babies. These other creatures just have sentiments; we have sentiments plus reason. This wouldn't be so important if our evolved sentiments were perfectly attuned to right and wrong. If our hearts were pure, we wouldn't need our heads. Unfortunately, our evolved system can be bigoted and parochial and sometimes savagely irrational, and this is what we'll turn to next.

4

OTHERS

S ome people are the world to us, and others hardly matter at all. As Emily Dickinson wrote, "The soul selects
its own society / Then shuts the door." We'll see that it's
part of our nature to make such distinctions; even babies
do it.

But we can also rebel against our parochial biases. Consider the famous story of the Good Samaritan, which begins
with a lawyer asking Christ what he should do to inherit
eternal life. Christ asks him what is written in the law, and
the lawyer responds by saying that we should love God and
we should love "thy neighbor as thyself." Christ says that
this is correct, and then the lawyer follows up, asking: "And
who is my neighbor?" Christ responds with this parable:

A certain man went down from Jerusalem to Jericho,
and fell among thieves, which stripped him of his rai-
ment, and wounded him, and departed, leaving him

half dead. And by chance there came down a certain
priest that way: and when he saw him, he passed by
on the other side. And likewise a Levite, when he was
at the place, came and looked on him, and passed by
on the other side. But a certain Samaritan, as he jour-
neyed, came where he was: and when he saw him, he
had compassion on him, And went to him, and bound
up his wounds, pouring in oil and wine, and set him
on his own beast, and brought him to an inn, and took
care of him.

Christ asks the lawyer which of these three men was the
neighbor of the victim, and the lawyer responds, "He that
shewed mercy on him." And Christ then says: "Go, and do
thou likewise."

The moral of the story isn't hard to figure out. The
Samaritans were despised by the Jews, which might be why
the lawyer didn't just answer, "the Samaritan"—he couldn't
bear to say the name. Plainly, then, what we have here is
an injunction to ignore traditional ethnic boundaries. As
the philosopher and legal scholar Jeremy Waldron puts it,
"Never mind ethnicity, community, or traditional categories of neighbor-ness"—the point of the story is that the
mere presence of the stranger makes him a neighbor and
thus worthy of love.

This is a radical position. For much of human history,
and for many societies now, our moral obligations extend
only to neighbors whom we already know. The geographer
and author Jared Diamond notes that in the small-scale

societies of Papua New Guinea, "to venture out of one's territory to meet [other] humans, even if they lived only a few miles away, was equivalent to suicide." The anthropologist Margaret Mead was famously romantic about the lifestyles of small-scale societies and viewed them as morally superior in many regards to modern societies—but she was blunt about their feelings toward strangers: "Most primitive tribes feel that if you run across one of these subhumans from a rival group in the forest, the most appropriate thing to do is bludgeon him to death."

Perhaps some of this is bluster. Regardless of one's sentiments, attempting to kill someone is a risky act. You might fail and get killed yourself, or you might succeed and then have to contend with vengeance from his kin and tribe. But even if outright violence is an extreme reaction, the natural reaction when meeting a stranger is not compassion. Strangers inspire fear and disgust and hatred.

In this regard, we are like other primates. In *The Chimpanzees of Gombe,* Jane Goodall describes what happens when a gang of male chimpanzees comes across a smaller group from another tribe. If there is a baby in the group, they may kill and eat it. If there is a female, they will try to mate with her. If there is a male, they will often mob him, rip flesh from his body, bite off his toes and testicles, and leave him for dead.

And yet things have changed. I often fly into strange cities, but I hardly expect that strangers will jump on me in the airport and try to bite off my toes and testicles. Indeed, even cultures in which traveling and travelers are rare often have elaborate codes for hospitality and the proper treatment of visitors. Any adequate theory of moral psychology has to explain both our antipathy toward strangers and how we sometimes manage to overcome it.

BABIES make distinctions between familiar and strange people almost immediately. Newborn babies prefer to look at their mother's face rather than at a stranger's face; they prefer their mother's smell; and they prefer her voice. This last discovery came about through the use of an inspired experimental method. Researchers placed babies in bassinets with headphones on their ears and a pacifier in their mouths and calculated the average rate at which each baby sucked on its pacifier by measuring the time between the end of one period of sucking and the beginning of the next. Then the babies heard either their mother or a strange woman reading Dr. Seuss's *And to Think That I Saw It on Mulberry Street*. Babies could use their sucking behavior to control which voice they heard—for half the babies, they would hear their mother if the gaps between sucks was shorter than their average; for half, if it was longer. Babies younger than three days of age were able to figure this out, and they used the timing of their sucking to listen to what they wanted—which turned out to be the sound of their mother's voice.

Since babies can't know ahead of time what their mom looks like or smells like or sounds like, these preferences must be due to learning: babies see and smell and hear this woman who has been caring for them, and this is whom they come to prefer.

Not only do babies like familiar people, they also like familiar kinds of people. We can explore this using looking-time methods. Earlier, I talked about how babies, like adults, look longer at what is surprising. Babies also share with adults a tendency to look longer at what they like, and we can use this to explore their preferences. It turns out that babies who are raised by a woman look longer at women; those raised by a man look longer at men. Caucasian babies prefer to look at Caucasian faces, as opposed to African or Chinese faces; Ethiopian babies prefer to look at Ethiopian faces rather than Caucasian faces; Chinese babies prefer to look at Chinese faces rather than Caucasian or African faces.

If you saw these biases in adults, you might assume that they reflected a preference for others of their own race. But this isn't likely true for babies. They don't often look into mirrors, and they wouldn't understand what they were seeing if they did. Instead, babies are developing a preference based on the people they see around them. Consistent with this, babies raised in ethnically diverse environments— such as Ethiopian babies living in Israel—show no preference on the basis of race.

These findings support a simple theory of the developmental origin of racism: Babies have an adaptive bias to prefer the familiar, so they quickly develop a preference for those who look like those around them and a wariness toward those who don't. Since babies are usually raised by those who resemble them, white babies will tend to prefer white people; black babies black people; and so on. Racist views get elaborated in the course of development; children learn facts about specific groups; they pick up scientific or religious or folk explanations about why and how human groups are different; and they come to absorb cultural lessons about whom to fear, whom to respect, whom to envy, and so on. But the seeds of racism are there from the very start, in a simple preference for the familiar.

I used to believe this, but I don't anymore. I think there is convincing evidence for a better theory of the origin of racial bias, one supported by research with both adults and young children.

LET's look at adults first. Laboratory studies find that adults automatically encode three pieces of information when we meet a new person: age, sex, and race. This fits our everyday experience. After meeting someone, you might quickly forget all sorts of details, but you are likely to remember whether you were talking to a toddler or an adult, a man or a woman, and someone of the same or a different race.

In an influential article, the psychologists Robert Kurzban, John Tooby, and Leda Cosmides point out that there is something strange about this triad. The focus on sex and age makes sense—our ancestors would have needed to appreciate the difference between a man and a woman, or a three-year-old and a twenty-seven-year-old, in order to conduct any kind of social interaction, from procreation to child care to warfare. But race is the odd man out. The physical cues that correspond to what we now see as races are determined by where people's ancestors came from, and since our ancestors traveled mostly by foot, the typical person would never have met anyone belonging to what we would now call "a different race."

Kurzban and his colleagues conclude that attention to race per se could not have evolved through natural selection. Instead, they argue that race matters only insofar as it piggybacks on *coalition*. Like many other primates, humans live in groups that come into conflict, sometimes violently. It would be useful, then, to be predisposed to understand such coalitions, to break the world into Us versus Them. Race becomes important because in some societies people learn that skin color and certain body features indicate which of many conflicting groups an individual belongs to. This is in much the same way that we might learn that different sports teams have different-colored uniforms; there is nothing inherently interesting about the color of the uniforms—they matter because of what they signal. Racial bigotry develops, then, in much the same way as a child growing up in Boston will come to associate a Red Sox uniform with Us and a Yankees uniform with Them.

Now, there may be other reasons why race is salient. For one thing, our hominid ancestors may have regularly encountered other hominid species. If so, we may well have evolved cognitive mechanisms to reason about these species, and may then have applied this mode of reasoning to other human groups within our own species. This would explain our tendency to *biologize* race, sometimes thinking, incorrectly, of distinct human groups as if they were distinct species, rather than coalitions. Or our interest in race could get a boost as a by-product of a general perceptual bias to favor the familiar—what is sometimes described as the "mere exposure" effect. This phenomenon applies to all manner of things: for instance, we like arbitrary squiggles more if we've seen them before. We already know that babies prefer to look at familiar people and familiar kinds of people; perhaps this is the origin of a same-race preference that persists throughout development.

Finally, a focus on race could be a by-product of an evolved interest in who is and isn't family. Kin has always mattered; it makes perfect Darwinian sense to favor someone who looks like you, because that individual is likely to share more of your genes. Instead of being a proxy for coalition, then, race could be proxy for kinship.

But while these other factors might play a role, there is compelling support for the race-as-cue-to-coalition theory. To test their hypothesis, Kurzban and colleagues used a method known as the memory-confusion paradigm. Researchers give people a series of pictures of people's faces, each with a sentence attributed to that person. Later, researchers ask participants to recall who said what. Given enough picture/sentence pairs, participants inevitably make mistakes, and those mistakes reveal what characteristics we naturally encode as meaningful. If one hears something from a young Asian woman and later forgets the source, it is more likely to later be attributed to a young Asian woman (or another young person, or woman, or Asian) than to an elderly Hispanic man. Moviegoers are more likely to get Laurence Fishburne confused with Samuel Jackson than with Lindsay Lohan.

Kurzban and his colleagues' memory-confusion study used pictures and statements by black and white people but they added a clever twist: sorting the people into two groups (with equal numbers of white and black people in each group) and dressing them in distinctly colored basketball jerseys. They found that participants still made mistakes based on race, misattributing statements like "I need to do some stretching" or "I just want to get out and play," but now when people got it wrong, they were most likely to do so based on jersey color, not skin color. To put this in real-world terms, a sports fan—at least when watching sports—is thinking more about team membership than about the skin color of the individual players.

This way of making sense of race fits well with the work of the psychologists Felicia Pratto and Jim Sidanius, who argue that societies form hierarchies based on three factors: age, sex, and a third, variable category that is sometimes race but may also be religion, ethnicity, clan, or any other social factor.

THE coalition theory also fits well with some recent studies of young children. If coalition is what matters most, one wouldn't expect children to focus on skin color or any other physical feature. Rather, they should pay attention to something that is uniquely human—language. Because speech changes much quicker than physical features—if groups separate for any period of time, they will begin to talk differently—language is a superior indicator of coalition and group membership.

This connection between language and coalition is explicit in the Old Testament. While the word *shibboleth* can now be used more broadly to mean a custom or belief that distinguishes a class or group of people, it originated as a specifically linguistic test of whether an individual was one of Us or one of Them. As the story goes, the Gileadite tribe captured the fords of the Jordan leading to Ephraim, where their recently defeated rivals had lived. To ensure that no Ephraimite refugees made it past their checkpoint, the Gileadites made everyone who sought to pass say the word *shibboleth*. Ephraimites didn't have a "sh" sound in their dialect, so if the refugee said *sibboleth,* the Gileadites knew to kill him. The Americans used a similar trick in the Pacific theater during World War II. Sentries at American checkpoints would shout at unfamiliar approaching soldiers, telling them to repeat the word *Lollapalooza.* Many Japanese people have difficulties pronouncing the "L" sound, so if they shouted back a distorted version of the word, the sentry would open fire.

Young babies can recognize the language that they have been exposed to, and they prefer it to other languages even if it is spoken by a stranger. Experiments that use methodologies in which babies suck on a pacifier to indicate their preferences find that Russian babies prefer to hear Russian, French babies prefer French, American babies prefer English, and so on. This effect shows up mere minutes after birth, suggesting that babies were becoming familiar with those muffled sounds that they heard in the womb.

The psychologist Katherine Kinzler and her colleagues have looked at the consequences of linguistic preference for how babies come to navigate their social worlds. In one experiment, they tested ten-month-olds in Boston and Paris. The babies listened to both an English speaker and a French speaker, and then each speaker held out a toy. The Bostonians tended to reach for the one offered by the English speaker; the Parisians went for the one offered by the French speaker. Other studies found that twelve-month-olds would rather take food from a stranger who speaks their language than from one who speaks a different language; two-year-olds prefer to give a gift to a speaker of their language; and five-year-olds prefer a child who speaks their own language as a friend.

Such choices make sense. It is easier, after all, to be friends with someone who speaks the same language, and, other things being equal, someone who speaks the same language is more likely to share one's preferences for toys and food. What's more interesting, though, is that we see the same effect with *accents*. Babies prefer to look at a speaker without an accent, even if the speaker with an accent is perfectly comprehensible. When choosing friends, five-year-olds are more likely to choose children who speak American English as opposed to French-accented English, and when learning about the function of a new object, four- and five-year-olds trust a native speaker more than an accented speaker. This suggests that children's preferences are driven by some degree of cultural identification, conveyed via language, just as predicted by the coalitional theory.

As YOU can imagine, there is plenty of research into the development of racial bias in children. The first experimental procedure was developed in the 1930s. An adult showed children pairs of dolls—a white doll and a black or brown doll—and asked questions like "Who would you like to play with?," "Which looks bad?," and "Which has the nice color?" In the 1970s, an expanded version was developed. Researchers showed children a picture of a white boy and a black boy and tested them with questions like "Here are two boys. One of them is a kind boy. Once he saw a kitten fall into a lake and he picked up the kitten to save it from drowning. Which is the kind boy?"

It is perhaps not so surprising that white children were drawn to the white child for the good things and the black child for the bad things. But what was shocking to many was that the first studies, done by the psychologists Kenneth and Mamie Clark, found that black children also tended to favor the white child. This study, which was cited in the *Brown v. Board of Education* decision that ended school segregation in the United States, might well be the most important developmental psychology finding in American history.

These studies have their critics. The psychologist Frances Aboud points out that there is something absurd about the demands being put on participants. Children are forced to choose, and there is only one dimension of difference—race.

The only options are to favor one's own group (which would be racist) or favor the other group (which would be racist in a different sense, as well as perverse). Children have no opportunity to opt out and say race doesn't matter.

But better-designed experimental methods confirm that racial biases are established by the age of six. Consider the research of the psychologists Heidi McGlothlin and Melanie Killen, who presented white children between the ages of six and nine with images of ambiguous situations, such as a picture of a child in a playground sitting in front of a swing with an expression of pain, with another child standing next to her. Sometimes the standing child was black and the sitting child was white; sometimes the races were reversed. Other scenes involved acts that could be interpreted as cheating and stealing. Children were asked to describe the scenes and to answer questions about them. In these studies, unlike the earlier ones, they were not forced to take race into account. But they did: white children were more likely to describe these ambiguous situations as corresponding to bad acts when the white child could be seen as the victim and the black child could be seen as the perpetrator. Importantly, though, this held only for children in all-white schools. White children in racially heterogeneous schools weren't influenced by the race of the characters.

Other studies find that children often favor peers of the same race and think that they are better people—but again this holds mostly in racially homogeneous schools. When the studies are run in heterogeneous schools, children don't care about race. Such results provide some support for what social psychologists call the "contact hypothesis"—the notion that, under the right circumstances, social contact diminishes prejudice. Apparently, the mixed-race schools provide the right circumstances.

What about younger children? Studies with three-year-olds find that when they get to choose whom to accept an object from or engage in an activity with, gender matters— boys tend to choose the male, girls the female—and age matters, with children tending to choose a child over an adult. And as we've just discussed, language matters as well: children tend to choose individuals who speak the same language and don't have a foreign accent. But race doesn't matter for the three-year-olds: white children don't choose whites over blacks, for example. Only later do racial biases start to creep in, and only for children raised in certain environments. We might have natural biases to favor some groups over others, but apparently we are not natural-born racists.

And even for the older children who do take race into account, it's not as important as language. For instance, when white five-year-olds were asked to choose between a white child and a black child as a friend, they tended to prefer the white child. But when asked to choose between a white child with an accent and a black child without one, they chose the black child.

NEITHER race nor language is necessary to sort people into coalitions. There is a large body of research showing that it takes very little to make a coalition that really matters: to establish group loyalty, to pit people against one another.

The most famous studies here were developed independently by two European social psychologists. Muzafer Sherif was born in 1906 in Turkey and was as a young man nearly murdered by the Greek army; he later spent time in prison in the 1940s for his opposition to the Nazis. Henri Tajfel, born in 1919 in Poland, was a Jew who fought with the French against the Nazis and spent five years as a prisoner of war. To put it mildly, then, both men had personal experience with coalitions.

Sherif and Tajfel were both interested in what it takes to form an Us that clashes with a Them. Now, one possible way of exploring this would have been to look at real-world conflicts, but these reflect long and complex histories—an Israeli might hold many legitimate grievances against a Palestinian and vice versa—and Sherif and Tajfel wanted to determine the *minimum* that it takes to divide people. Instead of examining conflicts with long historical records, then, they each conducted experiments designed to create social divisions where none had previously existed.

In 1954, Sherif invited twenty-two fifth graders—white middle-class boys from what he described as "established families"—to attend a summer camp at Robbers Cave State Park in Oklahoma. The boys were split into two groups, each housed in a separate cabin; neither group knew of the other's existence. During the first week of the camp, each group explored the area, played games, and had an all-around good time. And each group named itself: "the Rattlers" and "the Eagles."

Then the experimenters set up first contact. Sherif, who posed as the camp janitor to observe the interactions, noted that one of the boys, upon hearing but not seeing the other group, called them "the nigger campers." The researchers arranged tournaments between the groups, and relations slowly went from cautious animosity to something quite a bit worse. These small societies began to emphasize their distinct customs: the Rattlers would cuss; the Eagles would take pride in their clean language. They made flags. They objected to eating together in the mess hall. They continued to use racial epithets, though everyone was white—it seems as if these terms were used as all-purpose expressions for "others." In written tests, the boys from each group said that members of their own tribe were stronger and faster than their foes.

After the Rattlers won a few competitions, the Eagles stole their flag, set it on fire, and put up its charred remains. The Rattlers retaliated and destroyed their rivals' cabin while the Eagles were at dinner. The Eagles won a tournament and the Rattlers stole their prized trophy—knives that had been given to them by the psychologists.

Sherif then moved to the next phase of the experiment, which was figuring out how to bring the groups together—in other words, seeking world peace in a test tube. Many attempts, such as shared meals and shared movies, failed, but the researchers finally succeeded by introducing a problem that threatened both groups' existence:

a mysteriously cut water pipe. The factions were brought together by a common cause, perhaps a common enemy.

The Robbers Cave experiment demonstrated that you could create warring communities in a couple of weeks. Still, the situation did encourage individuals to identify with their group: not only did the psychologists facilitate competition between the groups, but each boy spent a week with his own group before he even knew about the other group, and it does seem reasonable for a boy to trust his friends more than strangers. Could coalitions emerge without all of this social support?

This was Tajfel's question. He designed a simple experiment in which he asked adults to rank a series of abstract paintings. He then randomly told half of them that they had shown a preference for the works of Paul Klee and told the other half that they preferred the works of Wassily Kandinsky. This was enough to make people feel a sense of group membership. When later asked to distribute money to other Klee lovers and other Kandinsky lovers, participants would give more to the group that they belonged to—even if they themselves didn't profit from doing so. These findings have been replicated many times; some studies find that you can divide people using the Platonic ideal of randomness—the toss of a coin.

Such "minimal-group" studies have been done with children as well. The psychologist Rebecca Bigler and her colleagues did a series of experiments in which children in summer programs were divided up arbitrarily—some got blue T-shirts and others got red T-shirts. They found that if the children's teachers mentioned these distinctions and used them to divide children into competing teams, robust in-group preferences emerged—the children preferred children of their own color (of shirt, that is) and allocated more resources to their group. Other researchers found that explicit cues from a teacher weren't even necessary; they could create group preferences just by giving the children different-color T-shirts or categorizing them based on the toss of a coin. Children in these experiments gave more money to their own group, predicted that their own group would behave better, and were more likely to remember bad acts that were done by an out-group member.

Now, people won't seize on just *any* distinction. If someone is sitting at one side of a crowded table, she can divide the group into those who are sitting on her side versus those who are sitting on the other side, or those who are on her right versus those on her left—but neither of these divisions would be the basis for psychologically natural groups. That would be *too* minimal. Rather, children and adults glom on to differences that matter to the other people around them. We are social creatures, so distinctions that are as arbitrary as heads versus tails, red shirts versus blue shirts, and Klee lovers versus Kandinsky lovers can matter to us, but only when we see that others take them seriously. It's not quite right, then, to say that we form groups solely on the basis of something as arbitrary as a coin toss. It's not the toss per se but the fact that the toss is done in a social situation where the outcome clearly matters to other people.

As another illustration of the social nature of categories,

recall that even babies are capable of distinguishing people according to the color of their skin. But children display no early-emerging bias to choose friends on the basis of skin color: preschoolers don't care about race, and neither do older children in certain mixed schools. If skin color is socially relevant—if black kids sit at one table and white kids at another—children will pick up on this. If not, they won't. We start off prepared to make distinctions, but it's our environments that tell us precisely how to do so.

MANY of the generalizations that we make about social groups have some basis in reality. The science writer David Berreby begins his book *Us and Them* with the observation that on the streets of his neighborhood in New York he sees people, almost always women, pushing children in strollers; when he sees a white adult with a nonwhite child, he assumes that the adult is the parent, but when he sees a nonwhite adult with a white child, he assumes that the adult is a nanny.

Berreby asks rhetorically if there's something wrong with him for thinking this. The answer might be yes if he thought that this pattern had no exceptions—if the idea of a nonwhite adult being the parent of a white child was *impossible*. But Berreby knows full well that it is a generalization, not an absolute rule. As a different example, one might notice that there are a lot of Jewish university professors. Jews make up between 1 and 2 percent of the total American population and 4 percent of the population in New Haven, Connecticut, the city where I live and teach.

I haven't seen any statistics, but I can assure you the proportion of my colleagues who are Jewish is a lot higher than 4 percent.

The origins of these generalizations are better understood through history and sociology than through psychology, neuroscience, or evolutionary biology. It would be absurd to explain the gross disparities between whites and blacks in America, for instance, without reference to the legacy of slavery and Jim Crow.

Keep in mind also that, in the world, just as in the lab, distinctions that start off as arbitrary can become real if enough people believe that they are. This is why social differences are so slow to eradicate: they are self-perpetuating. Berreby describes attending primary school in California, where half the students were white and half were black. For administrative purposes, teachers sorted the children into groups by astrological sign, and the categories took on social significance—as he puts it, "We Tauruses soon came to feel that we belonged together," and soon the Tauruses tended to act similarly, which convinced some of the teachers of the truth of astrology. Or consider the belief held by some Asians that children born in the Year of the Dragon are superior. A study of Asian immigrants to the United States shows that children born in 1976, which was a Dragon year, actually do turn out to be better educated than children born in other years. This isn't because the year itself really makes a difference, of course; it is because people believe that it does. The research finds that Asian mothers of Dragon babies are themselves better educated, richer, and slightly older than other Asian mothers—and hence better able to adjust their birthing strategies to have Dragon children.

While the origin of group differences takes us outside the sciences of the mind, the question of how we learn about these differences is bread-and-butter psychology, and the answer is simple: humans (and other creatures) are natural statisticians. The only way to cope with the present is by making generalizations based upon the past. We learn from experience that chairs can be sat upon, that dogs bark, and that apples can be eaten. Of course, there are exceptions— fragile chairs, mute dogs, and poisonous apples—and it's worth it to be on guard for such outliers. But life would be impossible if we weren't constantly going with the odds; otherwise, we wouldn't know what to do with a new chair, dog, or apple.

We do statistics on people as well. As the social psychologist Gordon Allport put it in his classic book, *On the Nature of Prejudice,* we "must think with the aid of categories. . . . We cannot possibly avoid this process." If I'm walking down the street and need to ask for directions, I won't ask a toddler, because my stereotype about toddlers is that they aren't good at giving directions, and I won't ask someone who is screaming into the air, because such a person fits my stereotype of someone who is insane, and insane people tend to be neither reliable nor helpful. If I hear about a killer or rapist on the loose, I might resolve to keep my eyes open for him—yes, *him,* because while it might be a woman, my intuitions are guided by the statistics. And, indeed, various studies have found that when people are asked about athletic achievement, criminality, income, and so on, their stereotypes of racial and ethnic groups tend to be accurate.

So what's not to like? Well, one concern is moral. Even if stereotypes are accurate, it may sometimes be wrong to utilize them. The issues here are subtle: we are not morally bothered by *some* generalizations about people. We are comfortable with laws and policies that discriminate on the basis of age, for instance. This is because we are forced to do so (we can't let everybody drive); because the stereotypes are so clearly rooted in facts (four-year-olds are really too young to drive); and because such policies apply to a slice of everyone's life span, not to a subset of the population, so they seem fairer. Sooner or later, everyone will get his or her chance. As another example, life insurance companies are allowed to make generalizations based on whether a person smokes and how much he or she weighs.

But the use of stereotypes based on gender, race, or ethnicity is more fraught. This is in part because it can cause suffering—even if the stereotypes are accurate, the costs that are borne by those discriminated against may outweigh the increased efficiency of the people doing the discriminating—and in part because it can violate certain notions of fairness. A T-shirt printed by the satirical magazine *The Onion* says, "Stereotypes Are a Real Time-Saver"— but there are instances where it's just wrong to treat an individual on the basis of the group he or she belongs to; it's better to take the extra time.

A further problem is that stereotypes are influenced by

coalitional bias, not just empirical data. We are powerful statistical learners for chairs, dogs, and apples, but when it comes to people, our biases can distort our conclusions. At the moment the groups are formed, no real difference exists between the Klee lovers and the Kandinsky lovers, or the red-shirt children and the blue-shirt children, but the participants will come to think that real differences exist and will believe that their own groups are objectively superior. We see this outside the lab as well. After World War II started, Americans switched their attitudes about the Chinese and the Japanese. The Japanese, who had been regarded as progressive and artistic, became sly and treacherous; the Chinese went from sly and treacherous to reserved and courteous. Similarly, the Russians were brave and hardworking when they were fighting Hitler with the Americans in 1942 and cruel and conceited in 1948 as the Cold War dawned.

Indeed, just thinking of someone as a member of an out-group influences our feelings toward him or her. We have seen that babies and children prefer to interact with people who speak with a familiar accent; similarly, adults tend to rate individuals with certain non-native accents as less competent, intelligent, educated, and attractive. Other studies find that we are prone to think of members of highly unfamiliar out-groups as lacking emotions that are seen as uniquely human, such as envy and regret. We see them as savages, or, at best, as children.

THE typical participants in a psychology experiment are university or college students from North America or

Europe, and these may well be the least racist people in the world. Even when tested in the most anonymous of contexts, they tend to be diligently nonracist. In fact, race is taboo for this population. It meets two criteria for being taboo: it's the stuff of obscenity (racial terms are prime epithets), and it's the stuff of comedy (there are comedians who make their living with material of the form "White people do *this* and black people do *that*"). In both of these regards, race falls into the same category as human waste and sexual intercourse, two topics we will address in the next chapter.

Children don't start off seeing race as taboo. In one study, inspired by a once-popular game called "Guess Who?," researchers showed an array of forty pictures of individual people, arranged in four rows of ten, to a group of mostly white children between the ages of eight and eleven. The experimenters then pointed to one of the pictures and told the children to narrow the array down to that picture by asking the fewest possible yes/no questions (such as "Is your person a woman?"). When all the pictures showed white people, ten- and eleven-year-olds did better than the eight- and nine-year-olds, which isn't surprising. But when some of the pictures showed white people and others showed black people, the older children did worse, because they avoided asking questions such as "Is your person white?" They had reached the point in development at which there is a psychic cost to even mentioning race. Indeed, social psychologists find that many of their overtly nonprejudiced white research subjects experience a pressing anxiety about appearing racist when interacting with blacks.

It is one of the more interesting discoveries of psychology, then, that even the least racist people in the world have unconscious racial biases. A black face, flashed on a computer screen too fast to consciously perceive, tends to trigger thoughts of aggression among white subjects; they are more likely to complete a word fragment like "HA_E" as "HATE." Black male faces also tend to lead to greater responses in an area of the brain called the amygdala, which is associated with fear, anger, and threat, among other things. In the Implicit Association Test, or IAT, most subjects are quicker to associate white faces with positive words like *joy* and black faces with negative words like *horrible* than to do it the other way around.

These studies get a lot of play in the popular media, where they are sometimes portrayed as a means to flush out hidden racists. The worst example I ever saw was during an episode of the television show *Lie to Me,* where a crack team of psychologists and investigators uses a muddled version of the IAT to determine which of a group of firemen has committed a hate crime. They find that one firefighter is slower than the rest to associate positive words like *principled* with black faces such as Barack Obama's, and this settles it. "I'm not a racist," he later protests. His interrogator snaps back: "You don't think you are." This is the sort of media depiction that makes social psychologists wince. Even if the firefighters were tested on the actual IAT, it wouldn't help ferret out the racist. These methods were developed to gather aggregate data about people's unconscious biases. They are not racist-detectors.

At the other extreme, some critics have argued that such findings tell us little about stereotyping and prejudice in the real world. Who cares about subtle measures such as reaction time, skin conductance, or the activation of the amygdala? But in fact, these measures correlate with considerations that really matter, such as how awkward someone is when interacting with someone from another race. Furthermore, the same implicit biases show up when people make real-world decisions such as whether to hire someone for a job or whether to assist someone who is crying out for help.

This research illustrates how we can be at war with ourselves. Part of a person might believe that race should play no role in hiring decisions (or even that racial minorities should get an advantage), while another part guides the person against choosing a black person. This tension can reflect a moral struggle; one's explicit view about what's right clashes with one's gut feelings.

MY BET is that a hundred years from now, we are likely to still reason in terms of human groups; we will keep some of our biases and hold to some of our prejudices.

This is in part because group differences really do exist. For example, Americans often stereotype students from some Asian countries as being academically more successful than average, and indeed, Asian applicants to universities have higher-than-average SAT scores. Now, one can make it taboo to discuss this, or taboo for anyone other than Asians to discuss it, but, absent brainwashing or mass hypnosis, you can't rewire people's brains to make their knowledge go away.

And some such generalizations are likely to persist. The groups we view as races and ethnicities share similarities for some of the same reasons that the groups we view as families do. Just as members of an immediate family share genes that make them more likely to have certain distinctive traits, so do members of larger human groups that are collections of families. Most of all, people who live together— families or collections of families—will come to share certain properties over time: they will come to eat distinctive foods, engage in certain activities, speak in distinctive ways, and hold certain values. Cultural differentiation happens quickly, as we see in cases where nations get split, as in East and West Germany, and North and South Korea.

Another reason why our biases are here to stay has to do with our coalitional natures. We favor our own groups. This is evident in the minimal-group experiments, and it's obvious in the real world, where we are pulled by bonds of country, neighborhood, and kinship. The tightest bonds here are kin. There have been all sorts of attempts to dissolve the special ties of family, to replace it with other groups, such as the state or the church. All have failed. Indeed, race and ethnicity share something with kinship: when classifying people as falling into one category or another, even the most liberal and determinedly antiracist people understand that this as a question about who your biological relatives are. As the psychologist Francisco Gil-White points out, when someone says that they are half Irish, one quarter Italian, and one quarter Mexican, this isn't a statement about their attitudes or affiliations; it's a statement about the ethnicities of their ancestors.

On the bright side, our tendency to sort ourselves and others into groups affords us real pleasures. People don't *want* their cultures and languages to be extinguished; we get joy from belonging to a specific community. And while many of us disapprove of those who think worse of other groups, it's not usually seen as wrong to be proud of, and concerned about, your own group. When I was a child growing up in Quebec, the Jews in my community were actively involved with helping Jews in Russia—strangers in an impossibly distant country who mattered because they were our people. Citizens of France are outraged if a foreign government unfairly imprisons a French citizen; Italians take pride in the accomplishments of other Italians they'll never meet. As I was writing this chapter, I received an invitation from a colleague to go to a political event in support of someone who, if elected, "would be the first Chinese American senator to serve in the continental United States." Are you surprised to hear that the person who sent the invitation is herself Chinese American?

Even those who are fiercely opposed to religion and nationalism will seek out the joys of community in other ways, through their immediate family, or their circle of friends, or their professional community. Now, seeing oneself as part of the community of psychology professors, to take a random example, might differ from seeing oneself as a Catholic, or a Greek, or an American. But one still experiences the same feelings of warmth, pride, and belonging. Berreby goes so far as to call our focus on human groups "one of the natural founts of human imagination and creative pleasure."

One might object that the benefits of our parochial nature can never outweigh its costs. For every in-group there is an out-group, and that's where the trouble lies. We would have no Holocaust without the Jews and Germans; no Rwandan massacre without the Tutsis and Hutus. Still, it's not clear whether there is any alternative to dividing humanity into groups. Nobody knows whether a truly universalist ethic is humanly possible, whether we can be truly indifferent to ties of culture, country, or blood and still be good and decent people. The philosopher Kwame Anthony Appiah notes that even engagement with distant strangers "is always going to be engagement with particular strangers; and the warmth that comes from shared identity will often be available." American Christians will send money to fellow Christians in the Sudan; writers will campaign for the freedom of writers around the world; women in Sweden will work for women's rights in South Asia, and so on. Appiah cites Cicero on this point: "Society and human fellowship will be best served if we confer the most kindness on those with whom we are most closely associated."

Also, we can use our intelligence to override our coalitional biases when we feel that they have started to run amok. We create treaties and international organizations aimed at protecting universal human rights. We employ procedures such as blind reviewing and blind auditions that are designed to prevent judges from being biased, consciously or unconsciously, by a candidate's race—or anything other than what is under evaluation. We establish quota systems and diversity requirements to ensure sufficient representation by a minority group, taking the decision out of the hands of individuals who have their own preferences and agendas.

My point isn't that the solutions listed above are the right ones. Indeed, they can't all be right, since they conflict with one another. (Race-blind admission processes for a university ignore race; quotas and diversity requirements explicitly take race into account.) Rather, the point here is that we can engineer certain situations, with the help of custom and law, to eradicate bias where we think that bias is wrong. This is how moral progress happens more generally. We don't typically become better merely through good intentions and force of will, just as we don't usually lose weight or give up smoking just by wanting to and trying really hard. But we are smart critters, and we can use our intelligence to manage our information and constrain our options, allowing our better selves to overcome those gut feelings and appetites that we believe we would be better off without.

This is how we cope with our natural propensity to favor our own group over others. But it turns out that there are even uglier aspects of our natures that we need to overcome.

5

BODIES

D isgust is a powerful force for evil. If you want to exterminate or marginalize a group, this is the emotion to elicit. The chemist and writer Primo Levi tells how the Nazis denied Jewish prisoners access to toilets, and the effect that this had: "The SS escort did not hide their amusement at the sight of men and women squatting wherever they could, on the platforms and in the middle of the tracks, and the German passengers openly expressed their disgust: people like this deserve their fate, look at how they behave. These are not Menschen, human beings, but animals, it's as clear as day."

Now, one needn't *actually* make others disgusting to trigger such a response; the more usual method is to use the power of the imagination. You can tell stories about how filthy certain people are and how bad they smell. Voltaire said of the Jews: "These people were so negligent of cleanliness and the decencies of life that their legislators were obliged to make a law to compel them even to wash their hands." You can use metaphor, as when the Nazis described "the Jew" as "a being disgustingly soft and porous, receptive of fluid and sticky, womanlike in its oozy sliminess, a foul parasite inside the clean body of the German male self." Often the hated group is compared to disgusting creatures such as rats and cockroaches. This is the rhetoric used in all genocidal movements, against the Armenians, the Tutsi, and so on.

The groups that elicit disgust don't have to be ethnicities or races. George Orwell is eloquent about the role of disgust in class divisions.

> Here you come to the real secret of class distinctions in the West. . . . It is summed up in four frightful words which people nowadays are chary of uttering, but which were bandied about quite freely in my childhood. The words were: The lower classes smell.
>
> That was what we were taught—the lower classes smell. And here, obviously, you are at an impassable barrier. For no feeling of like or dislike is quite so fundamental as a physical feeling. Race-hatred, religious hatred, differences of education, of temperament, of intellect, even differences of moral code, can be got over; but physical repulsion cannot. You can have an affection for a murderer or a sodomite, but you cannot have an affection for a man whose breath stinks—habitually stinks, I mean. However well you may wish him, however much you may admire his mind and character,

if his breath stinks he is horrible and in your heart of hearts you will hate him.

Earlier in the book we explored the role that empathy plays in motivating moral behavior. Empathy makes one more likely to care: it boosts compassion and altruism. Disgust has the opposite effect: it makes us indifferent to the suffering of others and has the power to incite cruelty and dehumanization.

IT IS easy to conjure up the feeling of disgust. Imagine opening a food container, sniffing deeply, and discovering that it is hamburger gone bad. Most people would get a certain feeling that includes a flash of nausea. This feeling is accompanied by a special facial expression (a "yuck" face— nose scrunched, mouth shut, tongue pushed forward) and a distinctive motivation: get that away from me. You don't want to smell it, you don't want to touch it, and you certainly don't want to eat it.

Certain objects, substances, and experiences reliably elicit this reaction. Paul Rozin, the preeminent researcher on the topic of disgust, has developed a scale to measure people's "disgust sensitivity." Here are some items that Rozin and his colleagues ask subjects to evaluate. Just how disgusting do you find these experiences?

- You see a bowel movement left unflushed in a public toilet.
- Your friend's pet cat died, and you have to pick up the dead body with your hands.

- You see a man with his intestines exposed after an accident.
- While you are walking through a tunnel under a railroad track, you smell urine.

Your mileage may vary. When I read these aloud in classes and presentations, some people wonder what the fuss is about; others gag. One student in a large Introduction to Psychology class ran out of the lecture hall when I showed these sentences on a PowerPoint slide. Rozin and colleagues have found that people's disgust sensitivity ratings predict how willing they are to actually engage in disgusting activities, such as picking up a cockroach or touching the head of a freshly killed pig.

Through experimental research and cross-cultural observation, we know that people everywhere are repelled by blood, gore, vomit, feces, urine, and rotten flesh—these evoke what Rozin dubs "core disgust." Unfortunately for us, these substances are also the stuff of life. As the title of a well-known children's book says, "Everybody Poops." All manner of substances squirt, drip, and ooze from our bodies and from the bodies of those we love. These vary in how repulsive they are. Feces, urine, and pus are bad indeed, but people willingly ingest one another's semen and saliva; sweat is not as bad as snot; and, at least in vampire fiction, the drinking of blood can be erotic, not gross. Intriguingly, one body product is hardly disgusting at all—tears. Rozin suggests that tears are immune from disgust because we think of them as uniquely human, but I find William Ian Miller's explanation more plausible: tears lack the physical properties of disgusting substances because of "their clarity, their liquidity, their non-adhering nature, their lack of odor, and their clean taste."

Some people have to deal with these substances for a living, including those who work with the wounded, the diseased, and the dead; others purposely engage in disgusting activities to show how tough they are, or how spiritual, or they do it to entertain others, as on the television show *Fear Factor*. All other things being equal, though, we generally strive to avoid the items on Rozin's core disgust list.

But we don't start off this way; babies are innocent of disgust. As Freud put it in *Civilization and Its Discontents*, "The excreta arouse no disgust in children. They seem valuable to them as being a part of their own body which has come away from it." If left unattended, young children will touch and even eat all manner of disgusting things. In one of the coolest studies in developmental psychology, Rozin and his colleagues did an experiment in which they offered children under two something that was described as dog feces ("realistically crafted from peanut butter and odorous cheese"). Most of them ate it. Most also ate a whole small dried fish, and about a third ate a grasshopper.

Then, sometime in early childhood, a switch is thrown, and children become like adults, disgusted by much of the world. Psychologists have often wondered what motivates this change, and many follow Freudian theory and blame the trauma of toilet training. When my own children were young, I read one of Penelope Leach's excellent books on parenting, which advised:

> *Don't try to make the child share your adult disgust at feces. He just discovered that they come out of him. He sees them as an interesting product belonging to him. If you rush to empty the potty; change him with fastidious fingertips and wrinkled nose; and are angry when he examines or smears the contents of his potty, you will hurt his feelings. You don't have to pretend to share his pleasurable interest—discovering that adults don't play with feces is part of growing up—but don't try to make him feel they are dirty and disgusting. If he knows his feces are disgusting to you, he will feel that you think he is disgusting too.*

While Leach might be correct that a parent's overt disgust is disrespectful to the child, everything else in this passage is mistaken. It's not that the child discovers that "adults don't play with feces," as if this were some arbitrary cultural practice, akin to "adults don't wear footed pajamas." Rather, children come to find feces gross. And this insight isn't dependent on observing an adult's reaction. After all, a lot of people read Leach's book and took her advice, and yet here we are, more than twenty years after its publication, and people are still disgusted at poo.

The toileting theory falls short in other ways. Other societies have very different practices when it comes to urination and defecation (and some don't even have toilets)—yet disgust is universal. Blood and vomit and rotten meat are disgusting but have nothing to do with toilet training. And even if it were true that children find their body products gross only because adults find them gross, this would only push the question back: Why do *adults* respond that way?

A more plausible theory is that core disgust serves an adaptive purpose. According to this theory, disgust isn't learned but rather emerges naturally once babies have reached a certain point in development. There is some sense to this timing; if disgust kicked in too early, babies would be disgusted all the time at their wastes and wouldn't be able to do anything about it. Natural selection wouldn't be that needlessly cruel.

If disgust is an adaptation, what is it an adaptation for? The most popular explanation is that disgust evolved to ward us away from eating bad foods. Indeed, the English word itself derives from the Latin, meaning "bad taste."

This theory has much to support it. First, as Darwin observed, the distinctive facial expression of disgust corresponds to the acts of trying not to smell something, blocking access to the mouth, and using the tongue to expel anything already within. It's no accident that we don't open our mouths wide when disgusted. Indeed, the "yuck face" is the same expression one gets when actually retching, and this may be its origin. Second, the feeling of nausea associated with disgust serves to discourage eating. Third, our disgust reactions can be triggered by thoughts of eating the wrong foods. As Darwin put it, with perhaps a bit of Victorian exaggeration: "It is remarkable how readily and instantly retching or actual vomiting is induced in some persons by the mere idea of having partaken of any unusual food, as of an animal which is not commonly eaten." Fourth, even controlling for an overall increase in the rate of nausea, pregnant women are exceptionally disgust-sensitive during the same period that the fetus is most sensitive to poison. Fifth, the anterior insular cortex, which is implicated in smell and taste, becomes active when people are shown disgusting pictures.

Disgust cannot be entirely hardwired, of course, because people vary considerably in what disgusts them. The idea of eating rat, beetle, or dog makes me gag, but people raised in some societies find these foods perfectly yummy. Some learning must take place, then—a conclusion that is consistent with the bad foods theory of disgust. Humans face what Rozin has dubbed the "omnivore's dilemma"—we eat a huge range of foods, but some of them can kill us—so we need to learn what we can and cannot eat in a local environment. In the course of this learning, food, and particularly meat, is guilty until proven innocent. Nobody ever told me that it is gross to eat fried rat; I find it gross because, during the critical period of childhood, people around me never ate it.

Some have argued that the food-based theory is incomplete and that disgust has evolved to warn us away from pathogens and parasites more generally. The anthropologist Valerie Curtis and her colleagues surveyed more than forty thousand people from 165 countries over the Internet to find out what images disgusted them. They found that pictures indicating potential disease were rated as particularly gross: a skin lesion depicting pus and inflammation, for instance, was viewed as more disgusting than a picture of a clean burn. People were also somewhat disgusted by someone made up to look feverish and spotty-faced. This theory also captures why the smell of an unwashed stranger can be so repulsive—being unclean is a sign of disease.

CHARLES Darwin, always an astute observer of human nature, tells the story of his own disgust. In Tierra del Fuego, he writes, "a native touched with his finger some cold preserved meat which I was eating at our bivouac, and plainly showed disgust at its softness; whilst I felt utter disgust at my food being touched by a naked savage, though his hands did not appear dirty."

People can be disgusting. If it's true that disgust evolved in part to prevent disease, then the disgustingness of people follows naturally—we are disease vectors. But we are disgusting in a more basic way. We are fleshy things and we are associated with all of the substances that elicit core disgust. *"Inter faeces et uriam mascimur,"* in the words of Saint Augustine—We are born between urine and feces.

Disgust may be morally neutral when elicited by a dead rat or a puddle of vomit, but disgust at our fellow human beings is more troubling. Now, disgust is not identical to repulsion or hatred. You can hate someone who doesn't disgust you at all in a visceral sense—though there is often the temptation to use the rhetoric of disgust toward those we despise: "He makes me sick!" And you can feel disgust without hatred, repulsion, or any sort of negative feeling at all. Changing your child's diaper or cleaning up her vomit might be revolting, but it doesn't make you hate your child. Still, disgust ups the odds. To be grossed out by someone is, other things being equal, to be repelled by him.

Disgust is the opposite of empathy. Just as empathy leads to compassion in many (but not all) circumstances, disgust usually (but not always) leads to repulsion. Empathy triggers an appreciation of another's personhood; disgust leads you to construe the other as diminished and revolting, lacking humanity.

Experimental research shows that feelings of disgust make us judge others more harshly. In the first experiment along these lines, the psychologists Thalia Wheatley and Jonathan Haidt hypnotized participants to feel a flash of disgust whenever they saw an arbitrary word. When the participants later read stories of a mild moral transgression, those who saw the word rated the behavior as more immoral than those who didn't. In other experiments, participants were asked to make judgments at a messy, disgusting desk; or in a room that had been blasted with a fart spray; or after being shown a scene from the movie *Trainspotting* in which a character puts his hand into a feces-filled toilet; or after being asked to write about a disgusting experience. All of these situations made the participants more morally disapproving about the acts of other people. Even eating a bitter food, which evokes a sensation akin to physical disgust, makes people harsher toward moral transgressions. And consistent with these experimental findings, individuals with high disgust sensitivity have harsher attitudes toward certain other people, such as immigrants and foreigners.

The consensus from the world and from the lab is clear: disgust makes us meaner.

SEXUAL practices are part of Rozin's disgust scale. Respondents are asked to rate how disgusting it is for an adult woman to have sex with her father or for a thirty-year-old man to seek sexual relationships with eighty-year-old women. Many people do see such acts as disgusting. And they see them as immoral as well.

Our moral response to certain sexual activities is really puzzling from an evolutionary point of view. Most of the moral judgments I have been discussing throughout this book can be understood as evolved adaptations. The warmth we feel toward those who are kind and honest and the outrage we feel toward cheaters and free riders can be seen as adaptive solutions to the challenges of individuals living with one another in a small society. Our reactions to unfairness emerge from our evolved obsession with status; our reactions to assault and murder follow from the importance of surviving and having one's kin survive. We think it is worse to intentionally kill someone than to knowingly allow the person to die (even when rescuing them would be trivially easy), because no society can survive if individuals could kill one another at will, but it's less critical that we be obliged to save one another.

Other aspects of our moral thought are not themselves

adaptations, but they are natural extensions of adaptations. Our brains did not evolve to disapprove of modern crimes like arson and drunk driving, but these behaviors are seen as morally wrong because they fall into the general categories of intentional and negligent harm. I doubt that the logic of gift giving is encoded in our genes; rather, our intuitions about what's appropriate to give, and our feelings of gratitude or disappointment, can be explained (at least in part) in terms of evolved concerns about status, respect, and reciprocity.

But sexual morality is different. Yes, it's easy enough to see how any creature that reproduces through sex would evolve a desire to engage in sexual intercourse along with a desire to avoid certain sex acts that either don't lead to reproduction (such as sex with nonhuman animals) or don't lead to the right sort of reproduction (such as sex with parents, siblings, or one's adult sons or daughters). The mystery for moral psychologists isn't why we would engage in certain types of sex while avoiding other types; it's why we should be so concerned with the sex that other people are having.

For example, sexual intercourse between two people of the same sex is forbidden in much of the world and is sometimes punishable by death. In the United States, it was only in 2003 that the Supreme Court, in *Lawrence v. Texas,* deemed sodomy laws unconstitutional; up until then, thirteen states had laws against same-sex sexual relationships. Many prominent social and religious figures continue to decry homosexual relationships as immoral, and homosexuals are victims of bullying, harassment, and even murder.

In a recent poll (May 2012), 42 percent of adults said that "gay or lesbian relations" are morally wrong.

It used to be worse, of course. Take Thomas Jefferson, whose wise words on our moral natures are quoted at the start of this book. In 1777, Jefferson proposed the following law for Virginia: "Whosoever shall be guilty of Rape, Polygamy, or Sodomy with man or woman shall be punished, if a man, by castration, if a woman, by cutting thro' the cartilage of her nose a hole of one half inch diameter at the least." As brutal as this now seems, Jefferson was merciful by the standards of the era. His proposal was rejected because it wasn't harsh enough; the legislature wanted, and ended up with, the death penalty for these acts.

What's particularly noteworthy here is Jefferson's conflation of rape—always a crime for obvious reasons—with consensual sexual acts such as sodomy. Our disapproval of such acts is perverse from an evolutionary perspective. After all, there is no genetic downside to homosexual activity. There's no risk of malformed offspring, and there might be an overall benefit in establishing and strengthening social bonds through sexual contact.

Now, *exclusive* homosexuality does have negative reproductive consequences for the individual. But, still, given the fierce nature of mate competition, it makes no sense for men to be bothered by other males who are exclusively homosexual. A good Darwinian would predict the opposite. Men who have sex with one another (or who devote themselves to any other harmless nonreproductive activity instead of trying to impregnate women) are pulling themselves out of the mating market, giving every other male a relative advantage. Male homosexuals should inspire gratitude, not disapproval. Women should be the only ones bothered by male homosexuals, just as men should be the only ones bothered by female homosexuals.

So much the worse for evolutionary explanations, then. Perhaps our moral disapproval has cultural roots. But finding a cultural function of this restriction is no easier. It's sometimes said that societies condemn homosexuality because encouraging reproductive sex helps to keep the population large. But women, not men, are the limiting factor in the production of children, so this would only explain disapproval of female homosexuality. Indeed, given the emphasis through human history on controlling the sex lives of women, one would have predicted that lesbians would be the sole focus of moral censure, not gay men.

Incest is another sexual behavior that is condemned in just about every culture. People often have explicit explanations for this restriction. When the anthropologist Margaret Mead questioned a member of an Arapesh tribe about what he would think of a person who married his sister, he explained that marrying outside the family was necessary to build alliances: "What, you would like to marry your sister? What is the matter with you anyway? Don't you want a brother-in-law? Don't you realize that if you marry another man's sister and another man marries your sister, you will have at least two brothers-in-law, while if you marry your own sister you will have none? With whom will you hunt, with whom will you garden, whom will you visit?" In our society, one might raise concerns about consent, psychological harm, or the possibility of deformed children.

But while there might be perfectly sensible reasons for opposing incest, our instinctive repugnance at the thought of this act comes from a deeper place. As the psychologist Steven Pinker points out, parents of teenage children have all sorts of concerns, but they don't usually worry that their kids will sneak off to have intercourse with one another. Teenagers do not refrain from sibling incest because they're concerned that they will have a shortage of in-laws to hunt and garden with or because they are worried about deformed children. Sibling incest is rare simply because most siblings don't want to have sex with one another; the very idea is disgusting.

There is an evolutionary logic to this disgust response. It's clearly a bad idea to have children with your close relatives, because of the likelihood that the child will inherit two copies of an allele that would be harmless on its own but deleterious in a pair. When people do have sex with kin, it is often by mistake, as when siblings, separated early in life, meet and get married and only learn later that they are blood relatives. Co-residence during childhood is one of the cues that seem to trigger the mental system that steers us away from incest. People respond to this cue even when they are not actually related by blood, which explains why a stepfather who enters the family when the daughter is past a certain age, as opposed to being around when she was a baby, is more likely to later be sexually attracted to her. He is also more likely to kill her. (I should add the obvious

here, which is that most stepparents, even those who enter
the family late, never assault their children, sexually or otherwise. Most of us are moral beings, and there is a large
chasm between desire and action.)

But none of this explains why incest committed by *other
people* bothers us so. Consider a well-known hypothetical,
carefully constructed by Jonathan Haidt to avoid the consequences that are usually connected to incest, such as concerns about coercion or deformed children:

> *Julie and Mark are brother and sister. They are travel-
> ing together in France on summer vacation from col-
> lege. One night they are staying alone in a cabin near
> the beach. They decide that it would be interesting and
> fun if they tried making love. At the very least, it would
> be a new experience for each of them. Julie was already
> taking birth control pills, but Mark uses a condom too,
> just to be safe. They both enjoy making love, but they
> decide never to do it again. They keep that night as
> a special secret, which makes them feel even closer to
> each other. What do you think about that? Was it ok
> for them to make love?*

Most people say that Julie and Mark did something
wrong. Interestingly, when asked to articulate the basis
for this judgment, most cannot, a phenomenon that Haidt
describes as "moral dumbfounding." It just feels wrong.

If you distrust these sorts of artificial examples, here's a real one. In 2010, a political science professor from Columbia University (who studies game theory, of all things) was charged with "third-degree incest" for having consensual sex with his twenty-four-year-old adult daughter. The legal charges were accompanied by sensationalistic coverage in newspapers and blogs, and there were demands that he be fired from his position. Clearly, many people thought his actions were immoral.

Laws against incest, even those that apply to consenting adults, can certainly be defended on consequentialist grounds. Knowing that one's young son or daughter will be an acceptable sexual partner in the future might distort the relationship between a parent and a child. More generally, sexual relationships might be incompatible with the special ties that hold between certain blood relatives, even as adults, so society might be better off if such relationships are not permitted. But these concerns were probably not the source of many people's disapproval of the professor. Rather, his activity grossed them out—it was seen, in the words of the *New York Daily News,* as "a sick sexual relationship." There might be good reasons to ban consensual incest, but we wouldn't be so quick to come up with these reasons if we weren't already disgusted by the idea in the first place.

I DON'T think it is a coincidence that the sex acts that we disapprove of are the very same ones that we think of as disgusting. Rather, disgust is part of the solution to the problem of sexual morality.

Disgust is our natural default toward certain sex acts, and, as we have seen, disgust triggers repulsion and rejection. The psychologist Nilanjana Dasgupta and her colleagues found that viewing disgusting images led to more negative implicit attitudes toward homosexuality, while a study that I did with the psychologists Yoel Inbar and David Pizarro found that exposing people to a bad smell—a fart spray—made them report less warmth toward gay men.

This predicts that an individual's disgust sensitivity should be related to his or her attitudes about sexual behavior. To explore this idea, Yoel Inbar, David Pizarro, and I measured the disgust sensitivity of a broad sample of American adults (leaving out any questions about sexual disgust) and found that greater sensitivity was associated with more conservative attitudes on a range of political issues—and the association was particularly strong for sex-related issues such as abortion and gay marriage. The effect held even when we factored out gender, age, and religious affiliation. In a second set of studies, adding Yale philosopher Joshua Knobe to our team, we tested students at the University of California, Irvine, and Cornell University. This population is highly socially liberal and, when explicitly asked, tends to be unbiased toward homosexuals. Still, the students' disgust sensitivity scores correlated with their implicit attitudes about homosexuals: the more disgust-sensitive they were, the more negative their attitudes.

But why is sexual activity disgusting in the first place? Rozin and his colleagues have suggested that while disgust evolved to defend the physical body, it has transformed over

the course of human history to a more abstract defense of
the soul. We are now disgusted by anything that threatens
our self-image as pure, elevated beings and reminds us that
we are animals. So people who ignore the sexual boundaries prescribed by our cultures are seen as disgusting and
beastly: "Insofar as humans behave like animals, the distinction between human and animals is blurred, and we see
ourselves as lowered, debased, and (perhaps most critically)
mortal."

Similarly, the philosopher Martha Nussbaum argues
that while "primary disgust" (elicited by feces, blood, and
the like) evolved to steer us away from contaminants, disgust toward people is motivated by a desire to denigrate
members of other social groups; it is "a stratagem adopted
to cordon off the dominant group more securely from its
own feared animality." The reasoning goes something like
this: "If those quasi humans stand between me and the
world of disgusting animality, then I am that much further
from being mortal/decaying/smelly/oozy myself."

I find these proposals unlikely. They are far too abstract
and intellectual. A seven-year-old who is grossed out at the
thought of cooties, or who gasps in revulsion upon hearing
what her parents have been up to in the bedroom, is not
upset because she has been reminded that she is an animal,
or because she worries about death. In fact, abstract concerns about animality and mortality aren't tied to revulsion in the first place. If reminders of our animal nature
disgusted us, then evolutionary trees and diagrams of the
double-helix structure of DNA should make us retch, as

they are stark reminders of our biological natures. Similarly, death may scare or sadden people, but it doesn't gross us out. Dead bodies are certainly disgusting, but nobody gags at the sight of mortality tables.

Sex is disgusting for a much simpler reason. It involves bodies, and bodies can be disgusting. The problem with the exchange of bodily fluids isn't that it reminds us that we are corporeal beings; it is that such fluids trigger our core disgust response. Other drives shut down or inhibit this response—including love and lust. But disgust is the natural default.

STILL, Rozin and Nussbaum are on to something when they say that our intuitions about morality are influenced by concerns about purity. Physical cleansing is part of the rituals of many religions, as in baptism by Christians and Sikhs, and *wudu* (the washing of certain parts of the body prior to worship) in Islam. This hints at a relationship between physical cleanliness and spiritual cleanliness. We see this connection as well in language. *Clean* and *dirty,* for instance, can refer to properties of physical objects but also to reputations and policies. We can describe offensive language as "filth," intentions as "pure," and so on.

And then there is the Macbeth effect. The psychologists Chen-Bo Zhong and Katie Liljenquist did a series of studies in which they asked some of their participants to think about their prior bad deeds. These individuals, reminded of their moral impurity, ranked cleaning products (like soap and toothpaste) as more desirable and were more likely to choose an antiseptic wipe over a pencil as a gift. In a follow-up study, the psychologists Spike Lee and Norbert Schwarz asked people to role-play a scene where they conveyed a malicious lie by either voice mail or e-mail. Then the participants evaluated consumer products. Those who did the evil act over voice mail (with their mouths) preferred mouthwash; those who did it over e-mail (using their hands) preferred hand sanitizer. And this cleaning actually did help to alleviate guilt and shame. When Shakespeare had Lady Macbeth scrub her hands after the stabbing of King Duncan, he knew what he was doing.

In another study, Zhong and his colleagues found that reminders of cleanliness make subjects more disapproving toward acts like watching pornography. This makes sense considering the connection with physical cleanliness—just as someone who is very physically clean might be concerned about getting physically dirty again, someone who has become morally pure might be motivated to avoid moral contamination.

Even a subtle reminder of purity can have an effect. The psychologists Erik Helzer and David Pizarro approached students in a public hallway and asked them a series of questions about, among other things, their political orientation. Students who were approached while they were standing next to a hand-sanitizer dispenser tended to state that they were more conservative than students who weren't standing close to the dispenser. In a second experiment, students were brought into the laboratory. Some of them were reminded of purity—there was a sign saying "Experimenters: Help keep the lab clean by using hand wipes!"—and they were asked to wipe their hands before using the keyboard. In comparison to those who didn't get purity reminders, these subjects rated themselves as more politically conservative and were more disapproving of actions that could be seen as sexually impure, such as "While house-sitting for his grandmother, a man and his girlfriend have sex on his grandmother's bed" and "A woman enjoys masturbating while cuddling with her favorite teddy bear."

An increased focus on purity, then, influences the moral assessment of others' actions, particularly in the domain of sex. Now, in these experiments, purity was influenced by subtle situational factors, such as seeing a Purell dispenser or cleaning one's hands with an antiseptic wipe. In the real world, social movements often rely on reminders of purity that are anything but subtle. The term *ethnic cleansing* is a new one, but the idea is very old—one can justify the expulsion of a group on the grounds that they taint the purity of a nation.

In fact, most people alive are committed to systems of belief and practice that put great emphasis on keeping one's body and soul pure. I am speaking, of course, of the major religions, such as Christianity, Islam, Hinduism, and Judaism. These emphasize what anthropologist Richard Shweder and his colleagues describe as an ethics of divinity, which revolves around concepts such as "sacred order, natural order, tradition, sanctity, sin, and pollution." It is little wonder that these religions are so deeply invested in the morality of sexual behavior.

IF I am correct, then, the moral outrage directed toward those who engage in incest, homosexuality, bestiality, and so on is not a biological adaptation. Individuals who disapprove of these activities do not reproduce more than those who are indifferent, and societies with many such disapproving individuals are not more successful than those without them. Instead, this aspect of moral psychology is a biological accident. It just so happens that evolved systems that keep us away from parasites and poisons respond in a certain negative way to sexual activity. Over the course of history, this aversive reaction has been reinforced, directed, and sanctified by various cultural practices, including religion and law.

Does our response to sexual behavior even count as morality? Under some theories, it doesn't. The psychologist Elliot Turiel defines morality as "prescriptive judgments of justice, rights, and welfare pertaining to how people ought to relate to each other"; Jonathan Haidt defines it in terms of "interlocking sets of values, virtues, norms, practices, identities, institutions, technologies, and evolved psychological mechanisms that work together to suppress or regulate self-interest and make cooperative societies possible." The issues that I have discussed in earlier chapters—including compassion, fairness, and punishment—mesh well with these definitions.

But sexual morality is not about "justice, rights, and welfare," and it's not necessarily about "how people relate

to each other." After all, sexual morality can often extend
to a person by him- or herself, or to a person and something else that's not a person but rather animal, vegetable,
or mineral. Nor is it obvious that our sexual morality serves
to "make cooperative societies possible." It didn't evolve for
that purpose (or for any purpose), and there is little reason to believe that it serves any such role in the here and
now. Imagine that some virus were to spread tomorrow that
had a very specific effect—it destroyed part of the anterior
insula, so that people no longer felt the emotion of disgust.
Our other moral capacities would remain fully intact, so we
would still recognize the wrongness of sexual crimes such
as rape and pedophilia, as these are wrong on more general
grounds. But the instinctive "Yuck" reaction that drives
many people's responses to the consensual sexual activities
of others would disappear. Is it really so obvious that if this
were to happen, society would fall apart? Hardly.

So by certain definitions, what I've been calling sexual
morality isn't morality at all. But all this shows is that the
definitions are incomplete. Our response to sexual violations may be a biological accident, but it feels no different
from other moral responses that have evolved as adaptations. Sexual morality is connected to guilt, shame, and
anger. It fuels a desire for punishment. And it is codified
in law and custom, just like other sorts of moral restrictions. For example, the book of Leviticus in the Hebrew
Bible states that sex between men is punishable by death;
this rule appears right next to the punishment for cursing
your parents (death), the punishment for blasphemy (death

by stoning), and the punishment for a priest's daughter if she becomes a prostitute (death by burning). All of this is preceded by a poetic plea for kindness to the handicapped ("Thou shalt not curse the deaf, nor put a stumbling-block before the blind"). Some contemporary legal systems do put forbidden sexual acts such as homosexuality into their own special category, but still, they are thought of as crimes in precisely the same way as murder and assault.

And many people believe that they should be crimes and that disgust is a reliable moral guide. In a famous article, the physician and bioethicist Leon Kass made the case for what he calls "the wisdom of repugnance":

> *Revulsion is not an argument; and some of yesterday's repugnances are today calmly accepted—though, one must add, not always for the better. In crucial cases, however, repugnance is the emotional expression of deep wisdom, beyond reason's power fully to articulate it. Can anyone really give an argument fully adequate to the horror which is father-daughter incest (even with consent), or having sex with animals, or mutilating a corpse, or eating human flesh, or even just (just!) raping or murdering another human being? Would anybody's failure to give full rational justification for his or her revulsion at these practices make that revulsion ethically suspect? Not at all.*

My own view is different. I think that the intuitions associated with disgust are at best unnecessary (after all, there are other reasons to argue against rape or murder) and at worst harmful in that they motivate irrational policies and license savage behavior.

For one thing, even if we knew nothing about psychology or evolution, a brief look at the history of disgust illustrates its unreliability as a moral cue. The revulsion that Nazis felt toward the Jews, or that most Americans felt toward interracial marriage, is precisely the same sort of revulsion that many of us currently feel toward certain groups and activities. Since it is clear that disgust got it wrong in the past, why should we trust it now?

But the real argument against disgust isn't merely that it sometimes leads us astray. Nothing is perfect. It is easy to think of cases where reasonable deliberation led people to conclusions that we now recognize as morally abhorrent, or where an empathetic response turned out to be the immoral one. But when reason goes wrong, it is because the premises were faulty, or there was a mistake in logic. When empathy goes wrong, it is because it was unfairly or arbitrarily applied, or because it led to the violation of other considerations, such as fairness. Disgust is different. Relying on disgust is like relying on a coin toss. When a coin toss gives the wrong answer, it's not because you are throwing it the wrong way. It gives the wrong answer for the same reason that it sometimes gives the right answer—by accident.

Repugnance is different in this regard from the other moral capacities we have been discussing. The rest of morality has emerged through processes, such as biological evolution and cultural innovation, which are sensitive to the problems faced by self-interested individuals who have to get along with other self-interested individuals. Evolution brought our species partway toward a solution, giving rise to sentiments such as compassion for those who suffer, anger at cheaters and free riders, and gratitude to those who are kind. These are inspired solutions, evolved over millennia, to the problems that faced us as humans living in small groups. As individuals who now live in a much different world, we can build from this, stepping away from our own specific circumstances and developing and endorsing moral principles of broad applicability. Such principles reflect values that, as rational and reflective beings, we are willing to sign on to. *This* deserves to be called wisdom.

6

FAMILY MATTERS

A young woman meets a much younger man and takes
him into her home. He suffers from serious limitations. He cannot walk or talk or even sit up; he cannot be
left alone and must be fed and bathed. He often screams
and cries at night, and she spends the first years with him in
a sleep-deprived fog. Still, this is the most important relationship of her life. She would die for him. She dedicates
many years to nursing him as he gradually becomes able to
walk, to toilet himself, and to speak. After they have been
together for a bit over a decade, he becomes interested in
other women and begins to date, and eventually he leaves
her home and marries someone else. The woman continues
to love and support him, helping to raise the children that
he has with his new wife.

If this younger man were a grown stranger, the woman's
actions would be seen as saintly or insane. But this descrip-
tion summarizes a typical relationship between mother and

son. In some regards, knowing that the woman is his mother makes her sacrifice all the more impressive, because now we can add additional considerations—if he's not adopted, she kept him inside her body for nine months, suffering pain, nausea, and exhaustion. Then she gave birth, an act that is terribly painful and physically risky. She might then have fed him from her own body for months or years afterward.

The point of this story, told by Alison Gopnik in *The Philosophical Baby,* is that family is special. Knowing that they are mother and son changes how we think of the woman's actions. If she were indifferent toward her child, unwilling to make these sacrifices, treating him just as she would a stranger, many people would judge her to be immoral, repellently so. We feel the same, though perhaps to a lesser degree, when the parent is a father instead of a mother.

Our best theories of adult moral psychology have little to say about these sorts of judgments. Most research in the field, including my own, focuses on how people make sense of, judge, and respond to the actions of unrelated strangers. We have little to say about how people think about interactions between parent and child, brother and sister, and other closely related individuals. It is typical that the index of the *Moral Psychology Handbook,* a collection of essays by the top scholars in the field, has no entries for "mother," "son," or "family."

I think this is a mistake. To understand our moral natures, we need to appreciate the special status of certain close relationships. This requires liberating ourselves from certain philosophical assumptions and taking seriously what we can learn from both the study of evolution and the study of babies.

THE relationship between moral psychology and moral philosophy is intimate. Moral philosophers such as Immanuel Kant, David Hume, and, of course, Adam Smith could be seen as the founders of contemporary moral psychology. Many of the contemporary leading figures in the field— the researchers whose work I have been discussing in this book—have had some philosophical training. And, as we shall see, the theories and methods and even the experimental stimuli of moral psychology often come directly from moral philosophy.

It is not moral philosophy in general, however, that influences how we do our work, but rather a particular strand of moral philosophy—one that focuses primarily on the question of which actions are morally obligatory, which are optional, and which are forbidden. Philosophers in this area are split into two main camps: *consequentialists* (who judge actions on the basis of their outcomes, such as whether they increase the sum of human happiness) and *deontologists* (who propose that certain broader principles should be respected, even if they lead to worse consequences).

Consequentialists might argue that torturing a person, even an innocent person, would be the right thing to do if it led to overall better consequences—if it caused more overall pleasure than pain, or saved more lives than it ended, or led to a greater proportion of individuals achieving their goals than not. (I'm being vague here, because consequentialists don't always agree about which sorts of consequences matter.) In contrast, some deontologists will insist that torture is always wrong because it violates certain absolute principles, such as a restriction against violating a person's intrinsic dignity. For such a deontologist, torturing someone would be wrong even if it saved a million innocent people.

Moral philosophers often proceed by thinking up complex and unnatural moral dilemmas and using their intuitions about these problems to refine their theories. This is similar to what some psychologists do, but the difference is that the psychologists are interested in people's beliefs about what's right and wrong, while the philosophers are interested in what's *really* right and wrong. Moral intuitions are sometimes contradictory: we might think X is morally good and Y is morally bad, even though X and Y are identical scenarios described in different ways. A psychologist can stop there, accepting this inconsistency as an interesting fact about the human mind. A philosopher cannot.

At the same time, though, an adequate moral philosophy can't depart too far from our commonsense intuitions. One wouldn't take seriously a moral theory that said that torturing babies for fun was a good thing to do. Such a conclusion would be so unrelated to what we naturally think of as right and wrong that it wouldn't be a moral theory at all. The working moral philosopher resolves this tension by engaging in what John Rawls described as "reflective equilibrium"—going back and forth between general principles and specific cases, ultimately coming to a point where a theory captures certain intuitions but rejects others. As a result, moral theories do end up making counterintuitive claims. There are deontologists such as Kant, who tell us that lying is always wrong (Always wrong? Even if the Nazis are at the door, asking if there are Jews in the attic? Yes!) and utilitarians such as Bentham, who say that it's perfectly fine to torture and kill a baby if this action increases the sum total of the world's happiness by even a smidgen (A baby? An innocent little baby? Yes!).

Some of the most influential examples in modern philosophy concern runaway trains. The philosopher Peter Unger offers a scenario in which Bob is the proud owner of a rare, beautiful, and expensive car, a Bugatti. And then something terrible happens.

One day when Bob is out for a drive, he parks his Bugatti near the end of a railway siding and goes for a walk up the track. As he does so, he sees that a runaway train, with no one aboard, is running down the railway track. Looking farther down the track, he sees the small figure of a child very likely to be killed by the runaway train. He can't stop the train and the child is too far away to warn of the danger, but he can throw a switch that will divert the train down the siding where his Bugatti is parked. Then nobody will be killed—but the train will destroy his Bugatti. Thinking of his joy in owning the car and the financial security it represents, Bob decides not to throw the switch. The child is killed. For many years to come, Bob enjoys owning his Bugatti and the financial security it represents.

As we've discussed earlier, Peter Singer offers a variant on this example: Bob is walking by a lake and sees a child drowning in shallow water. Bob could easily wade in and pull the child out, but this will ruin his shoes, which are quite expensive. So Bob walks on, letting the child drown.

These scenarios are constructed so that it's clear that Bob did something wrong through his failure to act. But now consider other failures to act. The world contains many dying children, and Bob can save some of them by giving to charity. He can save a life for far less than the price of a Bugatti or even of a pair of Italian loafers. Unger and Singer argue that Bob's choice not to sacrifice his car or his fancy shoes in order to save the child is really no different from Bob choosing to buy the car and the fancy shoes in the first place instead of going to www.oxfam.org and using the money to save children's lives. So while it's tempting to think that when Bob finds himself in these situations he is an unlucky man, forced to choose whether to sacrifice something of great value or let another person die, it turns out that anybody who is living a comfortable life is continually faced with this very dilemma.

Now, you could point to all sorts of differences here. One is that when Bob fails to throw the switch or wade into the water, he is condemning a specific child to death; when Bob fails to send money to charity, the effects are less discrete. Another is that, in these examples, Bob is the only one who can help; when it comes to charity, Bob is one of many. But Singer and Unger argue that such differences are morally irrelevant. We have different intuitions about X and Y, but

X and Y are, in relevant regards, identical. If they are right, this should worry us as moral beings. If failing to give to charity is equivalent to watching a child drown, we need to seriously rethink how we live our lives.

THERE is another runaway train case—more precisely, a runaway trolley case—that has been hugely influential in moral psychology. In one scenario (the "switch" scenario), a trolley is running out of control down a track. In its path are five people who have been tied to the track. You could throw a switch, which would lead the trolley down a different track. Unfortunately, there is a single person tied to that track and this would kill him. Should you throw the switch or do nothing?

In the second scenario (the "bridge" scenario), a trolley is running out of control down a track. In its path are five people who have been tied to the track. You are standing on a bridge above the track, next to a large stranger. The only way to stop the trolley is to shove the man off the bridge and into the trolley's path, killing him but saving the five. (It won't help to jump yourself; you're too small to stop the trolley.) Should you push the man or do nothing?

The outcome is identical in both situations—both throwing the switch and pushing the man would save five people and kill one. But most people intuitively feel that these cases are different: it is right to throw the switch and wrong to push the man. Apparently, then, we are not natural consequentialists; there is more to the morality of an act than its outcome.

Some philosophers believe that the difference between pushing the man and throwing the switch is captured by a principle known as the Doctrine of Double Effect, or DDE. The DDE, which is often attributed to the Catholic philosopher and theologian Thomas Aquinas, posits a critical moral difference between killing or harming someone as an unintended consequence of causing a greater good to occur (which can be morally permissible) and intentionally causing a death or harm in order to bring about a greater good (which is not permissible).

For example, according to the DDE, it might be permissible to bomb an enemy military base with the knowledge that the bombs will cause the death of some innocents who work at the base. This could be done with the goal of destroying the base, ending the war quickly, and saving millions of lives. The innocents are "collateral damage," like the man in the switch case. But if the bombing were done with the goal of killing the innocent people and thereby intimidating the population into surrendering (again, ending the war quickly, saving millions of lives), this would not be morally permissible under the DDE, because the innocents would be dying to bring about a greater good, like the man in the bridge case. Even though the ultimate goal in the two cases is the same (to win the war), and even though the same number of people die, still, according to the DDE, the second act is worse than the first. In the second case, the deaths of innocents is a means to an end, while in the first case, it is a regrettable by-product.

Psychologists first got into the domain of trolley problems

with the work of the psychologist Lewis Petrinovich and his colleagues in the 1990s. They gave university students different scenarios, including "lifeboat problems"—there are six people on a lifeboat that can hold only five: Would you throw one into the water to drown, and, if so, how do you decide which one?—and trolley problems, using the "switch" version. Subjects were asked whether they would throw the switch if the individual on the sidetrack were a member of the American Nazi Party. What if he were the world's best violist? What if he were a gorilla?

Then, in his doctoral research, the philosopher and legal scholar John Mikhail did a series of studies comparing intuitions about different "switch" and "bridge" scenarios. Soon afterward, in 2001, the neuroscientist Joshua Greene and his colleagues published a paper in *Science* that used brain-imaging techniques to explore how people reason about trolley and trolleylike situations. Greene's paper was the tipping point, inspiring a wave of trolley-problem research by psychologists, neuroscientists, and anthropologists. By now, Web-based surveys have assessed the intuitions of hundreds of thousands of people from different countries and cultures, and variants of trolley problems have been presented to people living in hunter-gatherer societies, to psychopaths, and to patients suffering from various sorts of brain damage. It turns out that all neurologically normal people, not just trained philosophers, draw a moral distinction between the switch case and the bridge case. Even three-year-olds presented with a modified version of the trolley scenarios (using Lego people) will tend to say that throwing the switch is the right thing to do, while pushing the man isn't.

Some scholars see these findings as an indication that humans possess a universal moral faculty analogous to the universal grammar outlined by the linguist Noam Chomsky—one that is partially innate and universal and that includes subtle and abstract principles. There do seem to be some interesting parallels here. Just as much as our linguistic knowledge is unconscious (every English speaker knows that something is wrong with the sentence "John seems sleeping," but only experts can articulate the principle underlying this gut feeling), many of our moral intuitions are due to factors that lie outside our conscious awareness.

But, as Izzat Jarudi and I have argued, language and morality differ quite sharply in some regards. Most of all, linguistic knowledge is distinct from emotion. You might be disgusted or outraged by what somebody says, but the principles that make sense of sentences are entirely cold-blooded. Your eyes do not well with tears as you unconsciously determine the structural geometry of a verb phrase. By contrast, moral judgments are linked to emotions such as compassion and shame and outrage.

The importance of emotion is evident in the bridge version of the trolley scenario. Greene and his colleagues find that people are more willing to use the man as an instrument to stop the runaway train if, instead of shoving him, they can throw a switch that opens a trapdoor that makes him fall onto the track. This shouldn't make a difference from the standpoint of the DDE—in both cases, killing the man is a means to an end—but it makes a psychological difference. Greene argues that this is because the thought of touching the man, of laying your hands on him and *shoving*, gives rise to a powerful emotional response, much more than the thought of just throwing a switch, and this is why most people see this act as morally wrong.

Trolley intuitions can be manipulated in other ways that don't fit any philosophical theory. One clever study looked at effects of cues as to the race of the characters. Is it right to choose to sacrifice an individual named Tyrone Payton to save a hundred members of the New York Philharmonic? Is it right to choose to sacrifice Chip Ellsworth III to save a hundred members of the Harlem Jazz Orchestra? Conservatives were even-handed, but liberals were not; they were more likely to kill a white person to save a hundred black people than vice versa—even though, when asked, they explicitly claimed that race shouldn't be a factor. In another study, people were given trolley problems after seeing a humorous clip from *Saturday Night Live*. This made them more likely to endorse pushing the large man in front of the train.

There are many scholars who are uncomfortable with how bizarre and contrived trolley problems can be. The philosopher Kwame Anthony Appiah observes that the dense trolley literature "makes the Talmud look like Cliff Notes." But there is little doubt that they have proven to be powerful tools for exploring the structure of our intuitions.

As Greene puts it, trolley problems might be the fruit flies of the moral mind.

PHILOSOPHICAL examples and psychological experiments rarely involve intuitions about family members. But it turns out that moral philosophers do use trolley and trolleylike problems to address moral problems that pertain to intimate relationships. Indeed, when philosopher Philippa Foot introduced the trolley problem in 1967, it was intended to explore the morality of *abortion,* looking at cases in which the death of the fetus results from actions taken to save the life of the mother. The general idea here is that we can think more clearly about these controversial and emotionally fraught cases if we translate them into simplified dilemmas involving strangers.

The scenario with Bob's Bugatti might also tell us something about family. It is used to make the case that we should care more about the fates of distant strangers. Now, even for a consequentialist like Peter Singer, some selfish preference makes sense, since the most efficient system is often one in which everyone takes care of himself and those close to him first. Adam Smith makes this point well: "Every man is, no doubt, by nature, first and principally recommended to his own care; and as he is fitter to take care of himself than of any other person, it is fit and right that it should be so." Just as the instruction for using oxygen masks in airplane emergencies (you first, then your children) is the best system for ensuring that everyone survives, a system where we give ourselves and our own families priority might be the best way to maximize happiness for all.

But Singer's point is that there are limits—the resources we give to ourselves and those we love are far too great. It is a moral mistake, he argues, to lavish our children with luxuries in order to make them just a bit happier when the same resources could be used to save the lives of strangers. The Bugatti trolley example is intended as a stark illustration of why this is the case.

This is one way to do moral philosophy. One develops general and abstract principles—perhaps very simple ones, as in consequentialism—by thinking about examples with strangers, and then one extends these principles to family and friends. A philosopher might also argue that it is the interactions between strangers that are the interesting ones. We need, after all, to know how to deal with the billions of individuals who share the world with us. Indeed, if it's true that our natural moral sensibilities are nonexistent or blunted when it comes to faraway people, this is precisely where philosophy might need to step in. Intimate relationships can take care of themselves.

But this is the wrong way to do moral psychology. From the standpoint of looking at human nature and human interactions, it makes no sense to start with strangers and view family and friends as a special case. That goes against everything we know about how morality evolved in the species and develops in the individual.

Imagine that we could start again, without taking moral

philosophy as a foundation. If we build our moral psychology from evolutionary biology and developmental psychology instead of philosophy, things begin to look very different.

Evolution first. The natural history of morality began with small groups of people in families and tribes, not a world in which we regularly interact with thousands of strangers. Think of summer camp in the middle of nowhere, not midtown Manhattan. Our social instincts, therefore, evolved to help us deal with people we see frequently, not to guide our interactions with anonymous strangers. Because we engaged in continued and repeated interactions with other members of our group, those individuals who helped others, were gratified by the help of others, and were motivated to punish or shun those who behaved badly would have out-reproduced those without these sentiments, and this explains why our minds now work as they do. The logic of natural selection further dictates that our altruistic and moralizing impulses should be discriminating—there is a strong reproductive benefit to being biased to favor friends and family over strangers, and one would expect this to be incorporated as part of an innate moral sense.

Now, there is no consensus as to the precise evolutionary origins of our moral instincts and moral understanding. Some claim that our moral sense follows directly from the benefits of cooperative behavior, especially among related individuals. Others argue for a two-stage account in which initial moral instincts are established, and then a dedicated system for the acquisition of moral norms emerges as society gets larger. There are also debates over whether group selection—natural selection at the level of communities—plays a role in the origin of morality. There is particular controversy, as we've seen, over the evolutionary origins of our impulse to punish cheaters, free riders, and other bad apples. Did our punitive nature evolve because groups that include members who punish do better than those that don't (a group selection account), or did it evolve because punishers are attractive to others and therefore are more likely to survive and reproduce (an individual selection account)? Or is punishment of third parties an accidental spillover of a more narrow proclivity toward revenge (a view that I proposed in chapter 3)? All of these are open questions, presumably to be resolved through the tools of evolutionary modeling, cultural and physical anthropology, and experimental research with humans and other animals.

But not everything is up for grabs. All evolutionary accounts of the origins of morality emphasize the importance of community, friendship, and especially kinship. This was appreciated in Darwin's own speculation about the origin of our moral capacities: "Any animal whatever, endowed with well-marked social instincts, *the parental and filial instincts being here included,* would inevitably acquire a moral sense or conscience, as soon as its intellectual powers had become as well, or nearly as well developed, as in man."

Consider now development. Humans are the mama's boys of the biosphere. We have the longest childhoods of any creature—an extended period of serious vulnerability—which leads to special bonds between parents and children.

This might help us understand why our social and moral lives are so intricate compared to those of other creatures.

In particular, some scholars see this early period as critical; they see altruism as emerging from the care we give to our helpless offspring. This theory is supported by an unusual piece of evidence: the multiple roles of the hormone *oxytocin*, which is released during labor to facilitate contractions and during stimulation of the nipples to facilitate the flow of milk. But while oxytocin has evolved for its role in maternal care, it has broader effects. When oxytocin is in your system, you feel calm and mellow and friendly; in economics games, people dosed with the hormone become more trusting and more generous. And those individuals who have alleles that make them more receptive to oxytocin tend to be more empathetic and less susceptible to stress. Accordingly, oxytocin has been called "the love hormone," "the cuddle chemical," "the milk of human kindness," and the "moral molecule."

There is a lot more to morality, of course, than warm feelings. Oxytocin can't explain why we send money to distant strangers or get outraged at those who harm others. Indeed, the response that oxytocin generates is itself morally complex: it makes us nicer to those close to us but might increase our parochial biases; one study found that snorting oxytocin makes you more positive toward your own group but also more willing to derogate members of other groups.

Still, it is a neat finding that the same molecule involved in childbirth and breastfeeding is implicated in sex and kindness. This supports the idea that some of our moral sentiments have their origin in the relationship between mother and child.

NOT everyone who studies moral psychology focuses on abstract philosophical cases. The anthropologist Richard Shweder developed one of the most influential alternatives to the standard view, proposing a trinity of moral foundations. There is an ethics of *autonomy*, which focuses on individual rights and freedoms. This is the dominant moral foundation for most Westerners, and certainly most Western philosophers; it's the sort of morality that makes you think up trolley problems. But there is also an ethics of *community*, which focuses on notions including respect, duty, hierarchy, and patriotism, and an ethics of *divinity*, which focuses on pollution and purity, sanctity and sacred order.

This theory has been extended and developed by the psychologist Jonathan Haidt, who argues that we possess a sextuplet of distinct moral foundations—care/harm, fairness/cheating, loyalty/betrayal, authority/subversion, sanctity/degradation, and liberty/oppression. These are evolved universals, but they admit of variation, like dials on an equalizer, and can be set in unique ways. For instance, Haidt argues that political liberals emphasize care/harm and fairness/cheating but deemphasize the other foundations, while political conservatives care about all of them equally. This is why, for example, conservatives care more than liberals do about respect for the national flag (as this is associated with loyalty), children's obedience toward parents (authority), and chastity (sanctity).

I'm sympathetic to these approaches, but they don't go far enough, in my view, in acknowledging the special status of family and friends. My own cartography of our moral lives is different. It takes as a starting point the sorts of individuals that our moral judgments and sentiments apply to.

First, there are *kin*. We care for close blood relatives and feel outraged at those who might harm them. Kindness to kin is the original form of morality and emerges directly through natural selection; since relatives share genes, it means that kindness to kin is, in a very real way, kindness to oneself. While other species have bonds of kinship, humans take this further—we moralize these bonds. We not only have strong ties between parent and child, for instance, but also feel that others *should* have such bonds; we disapprove of parents who are indifferent to their children's fate. Some moral principles also apply specially to kin, such as certain prohibitions on sexual relationships, discussed in the previous chapter.

A second category includes those individuals who are part of our community or tribe. Call this the *in-group*. As with kin, the moral notions here relate to harm and helping, care and obligation. Our sentiments toward in-group members have evolved as adaptations to group living, existing because of the mutual benefit that arises when individuals within a group cooperate with one another.

Some of these sentiments extend to the protection of the group as a whole, such as respect for those who uphold the values of the community and hatred of heretics and apostates. Loyalty is a virtue; betrayal is a sin—and a very serious one. It was treachery, and not lust or anger, that earned sinners a place in Dante's ninth, deepest, circle of hell.

Loyalty toward the in-group can clash with loyalty toward kin. Dante himself viewed the betrayal of one's kin as less severe than betrayal of one's friends or political party. Cain, who killed his brother Abel, is punished less than Antenor, who opened the gates of Troy to Greek invaders. The worst sinner of all, for Dante, was the betrayer of Christ, Judas Iscariot.

Here Dante was following scripture. Religious texts, not surprisingly, insist that the religious in-group is more important than kin. In the Gospels, Christ is explicit that he is there to replace the family, not support it: "I came not to send peace, but a sword. For I am come to set a man at variance against his father, and the daughter against her mother. . . . And a man's foes shall be they of his own household. He that loveth father or mother more than me is not worthy of me: and he that loveth son or daughter more than me is not worthy of me." One sees the same preference in the Hebrew Bible, which states: "If thy brother, the son of thy mother, or thy son, or thy daughter, or the wife of thy bosom, or thy friend, which *is* as thine own soul, entice thee secretly, saying, 'Let us go and serve other gods' . . . thou shalt surely kill him," and then explains why: "because he hath sought to thrust thee away from the LORD thy God."

The third category is that of *strangers*—those individuals whom we do not interact with regularly and who are not thought of as part of our group. While the force that drives the evolution of morality toward kin is genetic overlap, and the force that drives morality toward the in-group is the logic of mutual benefit, the force that drives morality toward strangers is . . . nothing. We are capable of judging the actions of strangers as good and bad, but we have no natural altruism toward them, no innate desire to be kind to them.

As an analogy, consider the psychology of number. Humans and other creatures are prewired with some understanding of mathematics. But, as the psychologist Karen Wynn has argued, our initial foundations are incomplete: in particular, there is no dedicated brain system for reasoning about zero. It was a relatively recent discovery that zero is a number, and children find this idea difficult to grasp. Coming to see strangers as falling into the moral domain is as much a human accomplishment as coming to appreciate that zero is a number.

Now, the suffering of a stranger might well trigger empathy. To witness someone in distress—a child attacked by a pack of dogs, say, screaming in agony—is unpleasant, even if you have never seen the person before. Even babies find it painful to witness another in pain, as do creatures such as monkeys and rats. But as we saw earlier, empathy is not compassion. It doesn't necessarily lead to the desire to help. Adults who live in small-scale societies respond to strangers with hatred and disgust, and toddlers get highly anxious when they encounter strangers; they experience fear, not fondness. And while we do see all sorts of spontaneous kindness by babies and young children—soothing, sharing, helping, and the like—these are directed toward family and friends.

Of course, many adults transcend our initial indifference toward strangers, just we now appreciate that zero is a number. But this is because of how we were raised and the societies in which we live; we did not start off that way.

THE categories of kin, in-group, and stranger are porous. Much moral persuasion aims to shift people from one category to another. Those who are intent on fomenting genocide will try to persuade others that those individuals who might have previously been thought of as part of their in-group (the Jewish Germans in Germany of the 1940s, say, or the Tutsi in Rwanda of the 1990s) are actually strangers. Those who wish to motivate kindness toward distant people will work toward a shift in the opposite direction, using pictures and stories and personal details so that these individuals will feel less like strangers and more like members of our in-group, and numerous studies have found that we really are more likely to help others when we see their faces and hear their names.

The metaphor of kinship is powerful as well: if one wants to strengthen the bonds of a group, one way to do so is describe it as a family or brotherhood or sisterhood. Many societies have a system of "fictive kin," where genetically unrelated individuals are talked about, and presumably thought of, as blood relatives. Where I was raised in Montreal, my neighbors and other friends of my parents were described as aunts and uncles, and it took me an embarrassingly long time to figure out who was my real kin.

Fictive kinship doesn't have to be imposed from above. The writer Rachel Aviv reports on the lives of homeless gay teenagers living on the streets of New York and observes that they form elaborate fictive families. Roles such as mother and father are determined not by age but by knowledge and by the ability and willingness to serve as a mentor. These relationships become extended and complex. Aviv describes how one homeless boy, Ryan, became a father, and when the children he mentored went on to mentor others, he became a grandfather: "'The beauty of the gay family is that you can walk into Union Square and you have an in—you're not alone,' he said. 'I can go up to a stranger and ask who his gay mother is. And it's like, Oh my God, I'm your uncle!' He added, 'A lot of us lost our biological families, so the gay family fills the void.'"

Philosophers often miss the importance of these bonds. William Godwin, a committed utilitarian (and the father of Mary Shelley, author of *Frankenstein*), once asked his readers to imagine that we could rescue only one person from a fire—an illustrious archbishop whose work brings pleasure and insight to thousands, or the archbishop's valet, who happens to be our father. Godwin concluded that the right answer is to leave Dad behind. But for many of us, this solution doesn't strike us as moral; it seems appalling. As Adam Smith observed, "The man who should feel no more for the death or distress of his own father, or son, than for those of any other man's father or son, would appear neither a good son nor a good father. Such unnatural indifference, far from exciting our applause, would incur our highest disapprobation."

I WANT to end by returning to the trolley problem. Most people say that you should throw the switch to save five people at the expense of one. One standard interpretation of this response is that we are moral consequentialists along the lines of Bentham and Mill. In the absence of emotional distractions, our judgments about right and wrong are based on how the world will be affected if one acts or doesn't act. Since five deaths are worse than one death, the choice is clear.

But there is an alternative interpretation. Perhaps our intuition in the switch case isn't driven by moral considerations at all. After all, the individuals in this case are anonymous and abstract; they are strangers. As Richard Shweder argues, then, we might treat the dilemma as little more than a math problem: Which is less, one or five? The majority who answer that the right act is to switch the trolley are reasoning in the same way that they would if asked whether to destroy one object or five objects. Actually, this experiment has been done: if you establish a trolley scenario with teacups at the ends of the tracks instead of people, participants also tend to throw the switch and destroy one teacup rather than five.

This proposal differs from the view that people are being moral consequentialists, and it does so in a way that's testable, as there are differences between moral and nonmoral judgments. For example, I don't like raisins. But this is a preference, not a moral attitude, so I don't care whether other people like raisins and don't think raisin eaters should be punished. I wouldn't feel guilty if I ate a raisin, and I don't admire others who abstain. My raisin shunning has none of the signatures of a moral judgment. I also don't like baby killing. This is a moral attitude, though, so all of these implications *do* follow. I believe other people shouldn't kill babies and that baby-killers should be punished. I would feel guilty if I killed a baby myself and would admire someone who stopped another person from killing a baby.

I think that our intuition about the switch case is more like raisin eating than baby killing. People might agree that it's the "right thing" to throw the switch, but this is an abstract intellectual decision, not a moral one, and hence there is little disapproval of those who fail to throw the switch and little desire to punish them, and so on. After all, we don't blame people who choose to allow strangers to die in the real world by not giving enough to charity, so it would be strange if we blamed them for allowing strangers to die in the trolley problem by choosing not to kill someone.

Also, it's not clear that we always do make a moral distinction between the death of five strangers and the death of one stranger. Yes, people care about number when forced to choose between five and one. But without this sort of explicit contrast, the numbers hardly matter. One study asked one group of subjects to donate money to develop a drug that would save the life of a single sick child and asked another group to donate money to develop a drug that would save the lives of eight sick children. The two groups offered the same amount.

This insensitivity holds for higher numbers as well. Imagine you were to read about the severe drought crisis in West Africa. Would it make a difference to you if you read that 80,000 people might die . . . or 400,000 . . . or 1.6 million? If you believed that 1.6 million people were at risk would you be twenty times more concerned than if you believed that there were 80,000? Twice as concerned? Most likely, the number would have no effect at all.

From this perspective, the typical response in the switch case reflects indifference, not morality. This helps us understand a set of otherwise mysterious findings. Individuals with damage to the ventromedial prefrontal cortex often develop a blunting of emotions, similar to psychopaths, and they tend to advocate the pushing of the man in the bridge case more often than normal people. That is, they treat the bridge case just like the switch case. College students with borderline psychopathic traits do the same. These findings are often cited—with a bit of glee at tweaking the consequentialists—as evidence that the bad guys and the brain-damaged are striving for the greatest good for the greatest number, just like Bentham and Mill!

The alternative, though, is that these individuals are not reasoning morally at all. Lacking normal empathetic responses, they think of the bridge case in the same way that normal individuals look at the switch case, as yet another math problem. Since one is less than five, they say: Push.

Most of the rest of us don't think it's right to push in

the bridge case, though. The person is still a stranger, but a stranger in the flesh, and it no longer seems justified to kill the one to save five. I agree with Joshua Greene that this situation elicits a strong emotional response; pushing someone to his death feels unpleasant—it feels *wrong*—in a way that throwing a switch doesn't. But the question remains as to why this is so. Why does it bother us to harm someone up close and personal?

One possibility is that we've evolved a specific aversion to assaulting another individual without some sort of provocation. Putting aside morality, such an act, even directed toward a stranger, is extraordinarily dangerous. You might fail and get killed yourself. Or you might succeed, in which case you have to contend with your victim's family and friends, who will be out for your blood. So such an aversion makes adaptive sense. Alternatively, this emotional response might emerge as a result of how we are raised as children; it might be shaped by the punishments and disapproval of the adults around us when we try to inflict harm on those around us.

In any case, it's not merely that we are reluctant to kill strangers; as we'll see in the next chapter, we are often nice to strangers, particularly those whom we can visualize as distinct individuals. If you tell subjects that a little girl needs a drug to live, and show a picture of her and tell the subjects her name, *now* they give more to create that drug—actually, they give quite a bit more than they would give to save the lives of eight children whose names and faces they don't know. If I were walking through the woods near my house and saw a child drowning in the lake, I would quickly wade in to save her, even if it ruined my shoes. And I'm sure I would throw a switch to divert a runaway train from killing a child, even if it meant the destruction of my precious car (not a Bugatti, in my case, but a 2005 Toyota RAV4).

But we shouldn't be too smug about our moral powers. I read every day about the suffering of strangers in faraway lands, and I know I can improve their lives, but I rarely make the effort. When I'm in a big city, I often find myself in the position of the Good Samaritan in the tale from the Gospels, passing someone slumped on the side of a road, probably sick, hungry, plainly in need of assistance. If the person were my *kin*—my sister, my father, my cousin—I would rush over to help; if he or she were in my *in-group*—my neighbor, a colleague from my university, someone I play poker with—I would also help. But it's always a stranger, so I usually turn away and keep walking. Most likely, you do the same.

7

How to Be Good

I t would be naive to deny that many seemingly altruistic acts are done out of self-interest. A lot of charity goes not to the most needy or most worthy but to projects that the givers themselves benefit from, as when wealthy parents give millions to elite universities in the hopes of getting their children accepted. Also, as the sociologist Thorstein Veblen observed, charitable giving is the perfect way to advertise one's wealth and status. It's also a good way to attract sexual and romantic partners; it hardly hurts to be seen as generous and caring.

Still, people do help others in ways that don't benefit themselves, and some of this is perfectly anonymous. The Yale psychologist Stanley Milgram is best known for his studies on obedience in which he brought people into his laboratory and found that many of them would follow instructions to administer a deadly electric shock to a stranger. But Milgram was also interested in kindness, and in 1965, he did an experiment in which he scattered stamped, addressed letters all over New Haven, dropping them onto sidewalks and placing them in telephone booths and other public places. Most letters arrived at their destinations, which means that the good people of New Haven had picked them up and put them into mailboxes—simple acts of kindness that could never be reciprocated. This kindness is selective: Milgram found that the letters tended to be delivered if they had a name on the front—"Walter Carnap"—but not if they were addressed to "Friends of the Nazi Party."

Our goodness is evident in other ways as well. Most societies no longer punish people by mutilating them—Thomas Jefferson's proposal that a woman should be punished for polygamy by "cutting thro' the cartilage of her nose a hole of one half inch diameter at the least" would not be adopted now. Attitudes about the family have changed—in many countries it is no longer lawful for men to rape their wives or for parents to beat their children. Some people are so concerned about the fate of nonhuman animals that they deprive themselves of delicious foods such as veal scaloppine and comfortable clothing such as fur coats. Many believe in rights such as freedom of speech and freedom of religion and believe that it is wrong to keep others as slaves or to discriminate on the basis of race.

Some see our goodness as evidence for divine intervention. The biologist Francis Collins has proposed that this sort of enlightened morality cannot be explained by biological evolution and has concluded that a benevolent God must have inserted a moral code into us. The social commentator Dinesh D'Souza concludes that "high altruism"—goodness toward nonrelatives, bearing no conceivable genetic or material reward—is, in the words of C. S. Lewis, best explained by "the voice of God within our souls." And in 1869, the co-discoverer of natural selection, Alfred Russel Wallace, observed that humanity has transcended evolution in many regards, including in our "higher moral faculties," and he concluded that there must be some superior intelligence shaping the development of our species.

Now, one can take these claims as metaphorical, as poetic expressions of awe at our wondrous capacities. But Collins, D'Souza, and Wallace all mean it literally—they are claiming that God *actually did something to us,* presumably in the few million years since we split off from other primates. Since our beliefs and choices emerge from the workings of our physical brains, this means that, at some point in our evolution, God literally restructured the human brain. It follows, then, that careful neuroscientists should be able to find the brain areas that God modified and observe how his divine handiwork differs from the more prosaic products of biological evolution. If Collins and others are right, then, our advanced morality could lead us to the greatest discovery in the history of science—decisive proof of the existence of God.

But they are not right. The mere existence of altruistic motivations that serve no reproductive purpose—even those that motivate choices that are bad for us and bad for our genes, as when we risk our lives to save strangers—is fully consistent with biological evolution. After all, natural selection is not clairvoyant; it responds to current contingencies, not to anticipated future environments, so maladaptive behavior in the here and now is fully consistent with evolutionary theory. This is easy enough to see in other domains. Lust presumably evolved to motivate people to engage in reproductively relevant sexual behaviors, yet many men get aroused by pornography and go on to spill their seed in a manner that does nothing to increase their chances of producing children and grandchildren. Is this wasteful activity an evolutionary mystery, and thereby proof of divine intervention? Of course not. Similarly, certain altruistic tendencies that have evolved through natural selection might be triggered now by situations that have no biological payoff.

Collins, D'Souza, and Wallace are right when they claim that certain puzzling aspects of our morality are not accidents: they manifest a design and a purpose that need to be accounted for. But, as I have argued throughout this book, it is mistaken to assume that these higher moral faculties are part of human nature. Insights such as the wrongness of slavery could hardly be innate if they weren't appreciated by people hundreds of years ago, and even certain aspects of morality that are assumed by many to be part of our innate endowment, such as kindness toward strangers, actually turn out to be lacking in babies and young children.

These critics are like men marveling at eyeglasses and arguing that since natural selection couldn't have created such intricate wonders they must be the handiwork of God.

They are forgetting the third option. *We* made them. Similarly, our enhanced morality is the product of human interaction and human ingenuity. We create the environments that can transform an only partially moral baby into a very moral adult.

CONSIDER first the power of custom. My emphasis throughout the book has been on moral sentiments and moral judgments, but neither of these is necessary for good behavior.

Think about tipping. This act is purely altruistic in the sense that it helps others at a cost to oneself, without any tangible benefit. But it typically lacks a moral motivation. Few people, as they are about to leave behind a few dollars or add a bit to their credit card, actively take the perspective of the person who just served them, flinching at his imagined outrage at being stiffed or warming in the empathetic appreciation of her pleasure at getting an 18 percent tip. Few of us think about the moral logic of tipping, mulling over how little servers get paid and concluding that we really should hand over something extra. Few of us experience any other-directed motivation at all. We just calculate the tip and leave it, with nothing in our heads but the math.

Now, it is possible that this thoughtless action is the result of prior contemplation: perhaps each of us at one time thought about the logic and morality of tipping and decided it was the right thing to do, and over time this kindness turned into reflex. This is how we succeed at complicated activities like tying our shoes—we start by consciously attending to our actions, and soon awareness fades; we proceed on autopilot. Perhaps this is true of morality more generally. As Aristotle noted, one of the traits of virtuous individuals is that they aspire to turn thoughtful good behavior into mindless habit, to grow into the sorts of people who do the right thing without ever thinking about it.

Still, much of the behavior that we see as good is picked up as part of one's culture, as custom, and never ruminated upon. It is like learning to speak. When a two-year-old learns that dogs are called "dogs," she will not usually ask why dogs have this particular name or why things have names at all. These are good questions, and they may occupy her when she gets older, but young children have to learn many tens of thousands of words, and the way to do this is by simply copying what others do, not working out the logic behind it. Indeed, much of what we learn is unconscious. As a result of my upbringing, for instance, I prefer to keep a certain physical distance from other people. But I notice this only when I'm with people who have been raised differently, just as I am conscious of what we call things in English only when hearing a speaker of another language use different words.

Or recall Herodotus's story about how Darius brought together the Greeks who would burn the bodies of their dead fathers with the Indians who would eat the bodies of their dead fathers. Each group was horrified at the acts of the other, because they believed that their own custom was the only appropriate way to treat the dead. They believed this, not because they had each previously engaged in a process of choosing between the alternative ways of treating the dead, but because they had never thought of the alternatives in the first place. Herodotus ends this story by writing, "One can see by this what custom can do," and he goes on to call custom "king of all."

We are most influenced by the behaviors that we see repeatedly, but even brief experience can have an effect. Researchers have studied how children between the ages of about six and eleven behave after observing the charitable acts of strangers. In a typical experiment, children played a bowling game and got some sort of reward afterward, such as tokens they could trade in for prizes. Before playing, children watched someone else play, either an adult or another child, and then saw that person donate some proportion of his or her reward into a charity jar for the poor. The more that this first person donated, researchers found, the more the child donated. The experience of watching the other person was more powerful than explicit exhortations to give to charity—in fact, some studies found that preaching had a *negative* effect.

As any parent would tell you, though, children pick up bad behaviors along with the good. If the model puts nothing in a jar, children often put in nothing as well—even though they would otherwise have given a little. Interestingly, some studies find that children are more influenced by bad behavior than by good. In a recent set of experiments by the psychologist Peter Blake and his colleagues, three- to six-year-olds watched as their parent gave away resources to another adult. Children saw Mom or Dad either being quite selfish (giving one out of ten stamps) or very generous (giving nine out of ten stamps). Later, when dividing up their own resources with another child, children imitated the parent's example more strongly when the parent gave very little than when their parent gave a lot. It's as if they were looking for an excuse to be selfish and the bad behavior of their parent provided it.

One can learn to be good without much moral motivation, then, just by mimicking the goodness of others. But this just pushes the question back: Why are the *others* so nice? Where do these customs come from? In the United States two hundred years ago, it was the custom of whites to keep black slaves. Indeed, many people considered slavery to be a moral institution, a conclusion derived in part from biblical justification and in part from the genuine belief that this arrangement was best for all members of the society, including the slaves. A white child raised in such a society would be prone to absorb such views, just as she would learn how to talk and how to tip and how close to stand to strangers.

ONE way to think about our changing moral attitudes is in terms of "the moral circle." This metaphor was developed by William Lecky, a nineteenth-century historian, and was popularized by Peter Singer in his 1981 book, *The Expanding Circle*. The moral circle encompasses those individuals whose fates we are concerned with, who matter to us.

Lecky believed that the circle starts small and expands over history: "Men come into the world with their benevolent affections very inferior in power to their selfish ones, and the function of morals is to invert this order. . . . At one time the benevolent affections embrace merely the family, soon *the circle expanding* includes first a class, then a nation, then a coalition of nations, then *all humanity,* and finally, its influence is felt in the dealings of man with the animal world." In *The Descent of Man,* Darwin approvingly cites Lecky and goes on to observe that, over the course of our species' development, our sympathies "became more tender and widely diffused, so as to extend to the men of all races, to the imbecile, the maimed, and other useless members of society, and finally to the lower animals."

Darwin's remark about "other useless members of society" reminds us, first, of the many changes in how we talk about certain groups since 1871—nobody today would so casually describe mentally or physically impaired individuals as "useless." Second, and more importantly, his phrase reminds us that the engine that drives the expansion of the moral circle cannot be sheer self-interest. Expanding the moral circle doesn't necessarily confer any material gains upon us; we don't profit by caring more for "the imbecile" and "the maimed."

One force that can expand the circle is personal contact—when people are of equal status, working toward a common goal, interactions between individuals often reduce prejudice. Military units and sports teams are two frequently cited examples, but various studies from the 1950s have confirmed the power of personal contact in a range of other circumstances: white housewives living in desegregated public housing, white police officers who were assigned black partners, and so on. Parents are being reasonable, then, when they try to extinguish racism in their children by putting them in racially diverse schools—since, under the right conditions of contact, the children will expand their moral circles to include members of other races.

Another important factor in expanding the circle is exposure to stories. The philosopher Martha Nussbaum explains how stories teach children to empathize and identify with people whose perspectives and identities may be very different from their own: "We see personlike shapes all around us: but how do we relate to them? . . . What storytelling in childhood teaches us to do is to ask questions about the life behind the mask, the inner world concealed by the shape. It gets us into the habit of conjecturing that this shape, so similar to our own, is a house for emotions and wishes and projects that are also in some ways similar to our own; but it also gets us into the habit of understanding that that inner world is differently shaped by different social circumstances."

Now, stories are not necessary for relating to the minds of others. As we discussed earlier, even one-year-olds think of the "personlike" shapes around them as having emotions and wishes and projects that are distinct from their own. But Nussbaum is talking about *habit*, not ability, and it is worth taking seriously her claim that exposure to stories makes us more prone to think about the minds of other people. Also, there are some "personlike shapes" whom we wouldn't naturally tend to consider. I had never given much thought to the plight of prisoners in solitary confinement, but after reading a moving journalistic discussion, I now feel differently.

Stories can elicit compassion on a case-by-case basis, but they can also lead us to question our moral principles and our habits of behavior. As the psychologist Steven Pinker puts it, "Exposure to worlds that can be seen only through the eyes of a foreigner, an explorer, or a historian can turn an unquestioned norm ('That's the way it's done') into an explicit observation ('That's what our tribe happens to do now')." This is the point that Herodotus was making when he told the story of the Greeks and the Indians. Travel broadens, and literature is a form of travel.

Now, some object that this explanation ignores the moral complexity of literature. The literary critic Helen Vendler writes that "treating fictions as moral pep-pills or moral emetics is repugnant to anyone who realizes the complex psychological and moral motives of a work of art." The legal scholar Richard Posner points out that many of the great stories express terrible values—rape, pillage, murder, human and animal sacrifice, concubinage, and slavery in the *Iliad;* anti-Semitism, racism, and sexism in the works of Shakespeare and Dickens; and so on. Posner concludes, "The world of literature is a moral anarchy."

He notes as well that there is little evidence that frequent readers are any nicer than everybody else. The Nazis were famously literate; Joseph Goebbels was said to love Greek tragedy. Some psychologists would disagree here, citing recent findings that people who read more fiction have somewhat higher social skills than people who prefer nonfiction. But even if this is true, it doesn't follow that they are nicer people. Also, it's unclear what to make of this sort of correlation; perhaps it's not that reading makes one more social but instead that social people enjoy fiction more. Women read more fiction than men, and this may be because women are, in certain regards, more social than men. And along these lines, Jennifer Barnes, a former graduate student in my lab, found that adults who suffer from mild forms of autism, and hence who are socially impaired, are less interested in fiction than a more normal population. So while it's clear that one's social and empathetic capacities influence one's interest in fiction, we can't be confident that the effect goes in the other direction.

Still, the right fiction at the right time can have an effect. There is significant historical evidence that literature, movies, television shows, and the like really have influenced the trajectory of human history, which supports Nussbaum's rebuttal to Posner—the Nazis might have read a lot, but they didn't read the right sort of books. Harriet Beecher Stowe's 1852 book, *Uncle Tom's Cabin,* the bestselling novel of the nineteenth century, helped whites to imagine slavery from the perspective of slaves and played a significant role in changing Americans' attitudes toward the institution. Dickens's *Oliver Twist* prompted changes in how children were treated in nineteenth-century Britain; the work of Aleksandr Solzhenitsyn introduced people to the horrors of the Soviet gulag; movies such as *Schindler's List* and *Hotel Rwanda* expanded our awareness of the plights of people (sometimes in the past, sometimes in other countries) whom we might never encounter in real life.

For a more recent example, consider how radically the treatment of racial and sexual minorities in the United States has changed over the last few decades. Much of the credit here should go to television; we often relate to characters on our favorite shows as if they were our friends, and millions of Americans regularly interacted with pleasant and amusing and nonthreatening blacks and gays on programs like *The Cosby Show* and *Will and Grace*. This can be powerful stuff; it might well be that the greatest force underlying moral change in the last thirty years of the United States was the situation comedy.

I admit that this is just a hunch, but it's backed up by evidence from other countries, where the introduction of television has had an observable effect on moral beliefs. Robert Jensen and Emily Oster find that when rural Indian villages start to get cable television, more women attend school, people find spousal abuse less acceptable, and there is a decrease in the preference for sons over daughters. Jensen and Oster suggest that these changes result from exposure to soap operas, which tend to present more cosmopolitan values. Similar findings have emerged from studies in Brazil and Tanzania.

There is no law of nature, though, stating that the messages conveyed through stories have to be morally good ones. For every story that expands the moral circle, motivating the audience to take the perspective of a distant other, one can find another that shrinks it, describing how people outside the in-group are evil or disgusting. For every *Uncle Tom's Cabin* and *Schindler's List* there is a *Birth of a Nation* and a *Protocols of the Elders of Zion*. Any theory of moral change has to explain why the expansive stories have more purchase than the cruel ones and why we are motivated to create such good stories in the first place.

No DISCUSSION of morality would be complete without discussing religion, as many see this as a major force for moral progress.

Actually, many people, especially in America, take this further—they think you cannot be good without believing in God. Many Americans say that they would not vote for an otherwise qualified atheist to be president—in fact, atheists come off worse in this regard than Mormons, Jews, and homosexuals. When people are asked about who shares their vision of American society, atheists are at the bottom. They are seen as self-interested and immoral, as both potential criminals and snooty elitists.

Some suggest that even if individuals can be good without God, still, they owe some of that goodness to having grown up in a society founded on religious ideals. The philosopher and legal scholar Jeremy Waldron argues that many of the key moral insights that lead us to care about others have their origin in the teachings of the great monotheistic faiths: "Challenging the limited altruism of comfortable community has been one of the great achievements of the Western religions. . . . What I have in mind are the prescriptions of the Torah, the uncompromising preaching of the Prophets and the poetry of the Psalmist aimed specifically to discomfit those whose prosperity is founded on grinding the faces of the poor, on neglecting the stranger, and on driving away the outcast. I have in mind too the teaching and example of Jesus Christ in associating with those who were marginal and despised, and in making one's willingness to feed the hungry, clothe the naked, take in the stranger, and visit those who are in prison a condition of one's recognition of Him."

If Waldron is right, then religion explains, at least in part, the expansion of the moral circle. Other scholars, though, hold the opposite view, agreeing with Christopher Hitchens that religion is "violent, irrational, intolerant, allied to racism and tribalism and bigotry, invested in ignorance and hostile to free inquiry, contemptuous of women and coercive toward children."

Now, any fair-minded observer would have to agree that many moral projects that we now see as positive, such as the establishment of major international charities and the American civil rights movement, have been grounded in religious faith and supported by religious leaders. But it should be equally obvious that some of the most horrific atrocities in history have been motivated by religious faith. Supporters of religion can go through the Bible and the Koran and cite the enlightened parts; religion's critics can easily rattle off long passages that we now see as morally grotesque, such as divine approval of genocide, slavery, and mass rape. Indeed, some passages reflect a moral code that is almost comically cruel, as in the story of how "little children" teased the prophet Elisha about his baldness ("Go up, thou bald head") and so Elisha cursed them, and then two she-bears came out of the woods and "tare forty and two children of them."

There has to be an answer to the question of whether religion has been a net gain or a net loss for our species, but nobody knows what the answer is, and I'm not sure anyone ever will. The problem is that religion is *everywhere*. Right now (and for as far back as we know), most people are religious: most of us believe in one or more Gods; most believe in some sort of afterlife; most engage in some sort of religious practice. This makes it difficult to separate the influence of religion from every other aspect of being human and makes it particularly hard to assess claims about nonreligious societies and individuals. Certainly there are atheists who are moral, but perhaps their morality benefits from the religiosity of those societies in which they live. Certainly there are decent countries with a large proportion of atheists, such as Denmark, but such countries are just a few generations from being devout, so perhaps they have inherited their virtues from their religious past. Asking how humanity would fare without religion is like asking what things would be like if we had three sexes instead of two, or if humans could fly.

We might have better luck with a more modest question: Are the religious individuals in a society more moral than the secular ones? Many researchers have looked into this, and the main finding is that there are few interesting findings. There are subtle effects here and there: some studies

find, for instance, that the religious are slightly more prej-
udiced, but this effect is weak when one factors out other
considerations, such as age and political attitudes, and exists
only when religious belief is measured in certain ways.

The only large effect is that religious Americans give
more to charity (including nonreligious charities) than
atheists do. This holds even when one controls for demo-
graphics (religious Americans are more likely than average
to be older, female, southern, and African American).

To explore why this relationship exists, the political scientists Robert Putnam and David Campbell asked people
about life after death, the importance of God to morality, and various other facets of religious belief. It turns out
that *none* of their answers to such questions were related to
behaviors having to do with volunteering and charitable
giving. Rather, participation in the religious community
was everything. As Putnam and Campbell put it, "Once we
know how observant a person is in terms of church attendance, nothing that we can discover about the content of
her religious faith adds anything to our understanding
or prediction of her good neighborliness. . . . In fact, the
statistics suggest that even an atheist who happened to
become involved in the social life of the congregation (perhaps through a spouse) is much more likely to volunteer
in a soup kitchen than the most fervent believer who prays
alone. It is religious belongingness that matters for neighborliness, not religious believing."

This importance of community, and the irrelevance
of belief, extends as well to the nastier effects of religion.

The psychologist Jeremy Ginges and his colleagues found a strong relationship between religiosity and support for suicide bombing among Palestinian Muslims, and, again, the key factor was religious community, not religious belief: mosque attendance predicted support for suicide attacks; frequency of prayer did not. Among Indonesian Muslims, Mexican Catholics, British Protestants, Russian Orthodox in Russia, Israeli Jews, and Indian Hindus, frequency of religious attendance (but again, not frequency of prayer) predicts responses to questions such as "I blame people of other religions for much of the trouble in this world."

It might seem perverse to conclude that religious beliefs are toothless when it comes to morality. Take suicide bombing. Even if one's attitude is best predicted by religious attendance and not religious belief, it does seem reasonable to conclude, as Richard Dawkins does, that someone who believes that God wants them to kill infidels is going to be a lot more enthusiastic about killing infidels than someone who doesn't believe in God in the first place. More generally, religions make explicit moral claims, about abortion, homosexuality, duties to the poor, masturbation, and just about everything else. Surely *this* would have an effect on the psychologies of their followers?

Maybe, but an alternative is that religious belief does not cause moral belief—it reflects it. This is a view defended by the journalist and scholar Robert Wright in *The Evolution of God*. Wright is particularly interested in the expansion and contraction of what we have been describing here as the moral circle, and he tracks how monotheistic religions have changed their attitudes toward those outside the group. For Wright, these shifts correspond to more general cultural changes. When the moral circle contracts, perhaps because of war or some other external threat, people "tend to find a scriptural basis for intolerance or belligerence." When it expands, "they're more likely to find the tolerant and understanding side of their scriptures." Believing that scripture itself causes these changes is like concluding that newspaper headlines cause plane crashes.

This doesn't necessarily mean that religious belief is irrelevant to morality. It might serve as an *accelerant*—part of a self-reinforcing system. Individuals or societies who are inclined to hate some group of people—homosexuals, say—will seek support from religious texts and the words of religious figures; once they find it, this can reinforce and justify and intensify their hatred. Those who are inclined toward compassion or justice can find support for this as well, and hence religion can ground causes that even the staunchly secular will deem morally positive.

WE HAVE considered some of the forces that drive moral change, but we've ignored so far the complexity of many moral decisions. This is particularly the case with regard to the moral circle, where we have followed scholars like Lecky and Darwin in assuming that the bigger the circle, the better. This is a plausible enough position to start from; one might say that the main problem with humanity up to now is that our circle of concern has tended to be so cruelly small.

But it's not hard to see that a bigger moral circle isn't always a better one. Should we expand our circle to fetuses, treating them as morally equivalent to children? What about embryos? Zygotes? Some would say yes all the way down, and indeed, many believe that society's refusal to protect these individuals from destruction is a moral wrong on a par with the Holocaust. What about nonhuman animals? In Paris in the 1500s, lowering a cat onto a fire was considered an acceptable form of public entertainment; as one historian put it: "The spectators, including kings and queens, shrieked with laughter as the animals, howling with pain, were singed, roasted, and finally carbonized." We don't do this anymore; should the next step be to stop hunting animals, eating them, and using them for medical research? Some would say yes to all of this too, but then what about the proper treatment and protection of skin cells? Personal computers? Viruses? Not everything has moral weight, and a too-big moral circle makes life worse for those individuals who plainly do have rights and moral worth. If a zygote is treated the same as a child, this may harm pregnant women; if we choose not to experiment on nonhuman animals, this may hinder the treatment of disease in people. These are the sorts of dilemmas that we have to deal with.

The recognition of these problems suggests a missing ingredient in our story so far. This is reason. When thinking about morality, we make inferences, ferret out inconsistencies, and explore analogies. We can assess clashing claims by seeing how well they capture our intuitions about situations that are both real and imaginary. In doing all of this, we are exercising the same capacity that we use to develop scientific theories and deal with practical problems, like setting up a business or planning where to go on vacation. This capacity might be more developed in some people, but we all possess it. It has driven moral progress over history: just as we've used reason to make scientific discoveries, such as the existence of dinosaurs, electrons, and germs, we've also used it to make moral discoveries, such as the wrongness of slavery.

I am aware that this position will seem outlandish to some. It is certainly unfashionable. The current trend in psychology and neuroscience is to downplay rational deliberation in favor of gut feelings and unconscious motivations. The political and cultural commentator David Brooks provides an articulate defense of this trend in his bestselling book *The Social Animal.* He argues that what matters is not cold-blooded rationality but what lies beneath: "emotions, intuitions, biases, longings, genetic predispositions, character traits, and social norms." Psychology and neuroscience, Brooks tells us, "[remind] us of the relative importance of emotion over pure reason, social connections over individual choice, character over IQ."

The fall of reason is particularly dramatic in the study of moral psychology. This is in large part due to the work of the psychologist Jonathan Haidt, who in a classic 2001 paper argued that "moral reasoning does not cause moral judgment; rather, moral reasoning is usually a post hoc construction, generated after a judgment has been reached"; he claimed that moral intuitions drive moral reasoning "just as surely as a dog wags its tail."

While nobody is insisting that reason is entirely impotent—Brooks is clear that we can sometimes use our intelligence to override our gut, and Haidt concedes that some experts (such as professional philosophers) do sometimes engage in moral deliberation—the upshot here is that reason is a bit player on the moral stage. This conclusion connects contemporary psychology with an important faction within moral philosophy, one whose rallying cry comes from David Hume: "Reason is, and ought only to be the slave of the passions, and can never pretend to any other office than to serve and obey them."

I will concede that there is something true about Hume's claim. As we discussed earlier, without some initial spark of caring, we wouldn't be moral beings in the first place. Furthermore, some of our moral judgments (like those we explored in chapter 5, having to do with disgust and purity) are plainly not the result of reason, and, as Haidt has observed, our explanations for such judgments are often nothing more than post hoc justifications. More generally, many factors influence our judgments and our actions without our even realizing it: Washing our hands (a reminder of purity) makes us more morally disapproving, and so does the sight of a messy room or the whiff of fart spray. We are more willing to help others if there is the smell of fresh bread in the air or if we have just found a small sum of money.

But none of this shows that reason is irrelevant. After

all, many moral intuitions *can* be justified. People are not tongue-tied when asked why drunk driving is wrong, or why it is a good thing to hold the door open for someone on crutches. We are not at a loss when asked why it is worse to kill someone than to yell at them, or why it would be wrong for an employer to pay the black workers less than the white ones. If challenged on these points—by a child, say—we would justify them by reference to concerns about harm, fairness, and equity.

And such reasoning does make a difference in the real world. This has been chronicled by various scholars, such as Robert Coles, who studied the struggles faced by black and white children in the American South during the civil rights movement, and Carol Gilligan, who interviewed young women deciding whether to get an abortion. Reading their work, we can observe people working to resolve moral problems and can see how this reasoning sometimes drives them toward conclusions that conflict with the views of those around them. Interview studies find that individuals who are vegetarians for moral reasons have little problem articulating the rationale for their decision, sometimes giving arguments based on the infliction of harm ("Once my eyes were opened to the widespread sadism and torture inflicted upon farm animals, I could never eat another creature again") and sometimes drawing upon the language of rights ("In all fairness, the rights of animals to live and enjoy their lives must take precedence over our 'right' to eat whatever we desire"). When the psychologists Karen Hussar and Paul Harris interviewed forty-eight six- to ten-year-olds who became vegetarians in nonvegetarian households, they found that *all* of the children gave moral justifications for their decision.

This sort of deliberation is the stuff of life. Nobody who has ever watched children interact could miss the enthusiasm with which they debate everyday moral dilemmas, arguing about whether a teacher was being cruel when she punished a student or whether it is right to download music without paying for it. And adults, of course, ruminate and worry and argue all the time about the right thing to do—not just when it comes to abortion, capital punishment, and other grand questions of morality and politics, but about more local issues as well: How should we handle our colleague with the drinking problem? What do I do about the relative who is apparently not intending to pay me back the money she owes me? How bad is it if I don't get my book manuscript to my editor on time?

Moral deliberation is ubiquitous, but psychologists typically overlook it. This is in part because everybody loves counterintuitive findings. Discovering that individuals have moral intuitions that they struggle to explain is exciting and can get published in a top journal. Discovering that individuals have moral intuitions that they can easily explain, such as the wrongness of drunk driving, is obvious, uninteresting, and unpublishable. It is fascinating to discover that individuals who are asked to assign a punishment to a criminal are influenced by factors that they are unaware of (like the presence of a flag in the room) or that they would consciously disavow (like the color of the criminal's skin). It is boring to find that individuals' proposed punishments are influenced by rational considerations such as the severity of the crime and the criminal's previous record. Interesting: We are more willing to help someone if there is the smell of fresh bread in the air. Boring: We are more willing to help someone if he or she has been kind to us in the past.

We sometimes forget that this bias in publication exists and take what is reported in scientific journals and the popular press as an accurate reflection of our best science of how the mind works. But this is like watching the nightly news and concluding that rape, robbery, and murder are part of any individual's everyday life—forgetting that the nightly news doesn't report the vast majority of cases where nothing of this sort happens at all.

THE capacity for reason takes time to emerge, so the moral life of a baby is necessarily limited. A baby will possess inclinations and sentiments; he or she might be motivated to soothe another in pain or to feel angry at a cruel act or to favor someone who punishes a wrongdoer. But a lot is absent; most of all, the baby lacks a grasp of impartial moral principles—prohibitions or requirements that apply equally to everyone within a community.

Such principles are at the foundation of systems of law and justice. Peter Singer points out that explicit statements of impartiality show up in every religion and every moral philosophy. They are expressed in the various forms of the Golden Rule, as in Christ's command, "As you would that men should do to you, do ye also to them likewise," or Rabbi Hillel's statement, "What is hateful to you do not do to your neighbor; that is the whole Torah; the rest is commentary thereof." When Confucius was asked for a single word that summed up morality, he responded, "Is not reciprocity such a word? What you do not want done to yourself, do not do to others." Immanuel Kant proposed as the core of morality: "Act only on that maxim through which you can at the same time will that it should become a universal law." Adam Smith appealed to the judgment of an impartial spectator as the test of a moral judgment, and Jeremy Bentham argued that, in the moral realm, "each counts for one and none for more than one." John Rawls suggested that when ruminating about a fair and just society, we should imagine that we are behind a veil of ignorance, not knowing which individual we will end up as, and Henry Sidgwick wrote that "the good of any one individual is of no more importance, from the point of view of the Universe, than the good of any other."

Singer suggests that the logic of impartiality is a discovery that arises over the course of human history from the need to justify one's actions to other rational beings. If your explanation for hitting another person is simply "I wanted to," this is just an expression of selfish desire and carries no weight. What's so special about you that your pleasure should have priority over the other person's pain? But responses such as "He hit me first" or "He stole my food" are actual justifications because they imply that anyone in the same situation (including the person you hit) could have done the same. Singer approvingly quotes Hume here, who notes that someone who is offering a true justification has to "depart from his private and particular situation and must choose a point of view common to him with others." This is what it means to offer a *reason*. As Pinker puts it, commenting on Singer's proposal: "As soon as you try to persuade someone to avoid harming you by appealing to reasons why he shouldn't, you're sucked into a commitment to the avoidance of harm as a general goal."

We've been focusing on the specific case of harm, but the logic holds more generally. Individuals who benefit from working together on projects such as big-game hunting or shared child care need to coordinate their behavior, and some people will occasionally have to sacrifice for the greater good. This can succeed only if there are systems of reward and punishment that apply impartially within the community. The need for impartiality is most clear when it comes to the distribution of goods, such as food. If an individual tries to take everything, shouting, "I want it!" the situation devolves into a fight, and everyone is worse off. But statements such as "I want an even share" or "I want more because I worked harder" can be appreciated by rational beings, because, again, these standards, in principle, apply to all of us.

Under this account, impartiality emerges as a reasoned solution to the problem of coordinating the actions of rational and self-interested beings. But empathy might play a role as well. When you take the perspective of others, it becomes clear that your desires are not special. It's not only that I don't want to be harmed, it's also that *he* doesn't want to be harmed, and *she* doesn't want to be harmed, and so on. This can support the generalization that *nobody* wants to be harmed, which can in turn support a broader prohibition against harm. Empathy and impartiality are often mutually reinforcing: the exercise of empathy makes us realize that we are not special after all, which supports the notion of impartial principles, which motivates us to continue to empathize with other people.

As an example of how empathy and reason work together, consider parental behaviors that psychologist Martin Hoffman calls *inductions*. These occur when a child has harmed or is about to harm someone, and the parent urges the child to take the victim's perspective, saying things like "If you throw snow on their walk they will have to clean it up all over again" or "He feels bad because he was proud of his tower and you knocked it down." Hoffman estimates that children between the ages of two and ten receive about four thousand inductions a year. We can see these as empathetic prods, attempts to get children into the habit of taking the perspective of others. But they also serve as a repeated argument, making the point over and over again to the child: *You are not morally privileged.*

Young children are not just passive recipients of moral arguments. They can also generate such arguments, and we see here a sort of recapitulation of how our ancestors might have been forced to appeal to reason to justify their actions. When the psychologists Melanie Killen and Adam Rutland recorded the interactions of a group of three-and-a-half-year-olds playing alone in a room, with no adults present, they captured this process of moral persuasion perfectly:

> *Ruth:* (holding up two Fisher-Price people) Hey, I want the green person. How about if we trade? Here, you can have this one (gives a blue person to Michael). And I can have the green one. Okay? (reaches for the green person that Michael is holding).
>
> *Michael:* No! We already did trade. I want this one (holds on to the green one). I want it now and you had it already.
>
> *Lily:* Hey, you can both have my spoons, if you want? (shows her spoons to Michael and Ruth).
>
> *Ruth:* No, I want the green person.
>
> *Michael:* I'm not trading any of mine (hovers over his toys).
>
> *Lily:* (sings) I'm not trading any of mine.
>
> *Ruth:* (sings) I'm not trading any of mine.
>
> *Lily:* Well, that's not fair because *I* don't have any people (pouts).
>
> *Michael:* (to Ruth) Give her one of them.
>
> *Ruth:* But you have three and she has none and I have one. So that's not fair.
>
> *Lily:* Yeah, because I have none.
>
> *Ruth:* (to Michael) You know what? If you give me the green and then I'll give her the red one and then we'll all have one.

Michael: Well, if you don't give me the red one then I
   won't invite you to my birthday party.
Lily: But I don't have any people.
Ruth: Okay, I'll give you this one (to Lily) and I'll take
   this one from Michael and then we'll all have one,
   okay?
Michael: (gives orange person to Ruth) Okay, but can
   we trade again tomorrow?
Ruth: (sings) Birthday party! (takes the orange person
   from Michael and gives the red person to Lily).
Lily: (sings) Birthday party!
Michael: (sings) Birthday party!

We know from the research reviewed earlier in this book
that young children are stingy when asked to distribute
resources. They might strongly endorse a principle of equal
division when it comes to other people, but when they
themselves are in a position to hand out resources, they tend
to keep the lion's share. But we see relatively little stinginess
in the interaction between Ruth, Lily, and Michael. They
deal well with one another—in large part because they have
to. Like Singer's hypothetical individuals from our distant
past, they can't get away with "I want to": they are forced to
provide, and live up to, objective justifications.

And their justifications are relatively sophisticated.
There is more singing than in your average philosophy seminar, and Michael does threaten Ruth at one point, but they
are also appealing to impartial principles—not just stating
demands or expressions of preference. Lily and Ruth both

insist (and Michael ultimately agrees) that it's "fair" that each of the children gets at least one toy (as when Lily says, "Well, that's not fair because I don't have any people"). And Michael himself appeals to a principle that dictates that an individual toy gets to be shared over time ("I want it now and you had it already").

It was not inevitable that the dispute ended where it did. Michael might have responded to Lily and Ruth by arguing that there were other reasons why he should keep all of his toys—perhaps he owned them, or perhaps he just enjoyed them so much more than everybody else. He might well have convinced the other children that one of these other considerations overrode the principle of equal division. Reasoning can take us in surprising directions.

Once we have a commitment to impartial principles, this can trump our self-interest. We sacrifice to do what we feel is right. Some examples of this include Oskar Schindler, who risked everything to save Jews from the Holocaust, and Paul Rusesabagina, who sheltered Tutsis during the Rwandan genocide. But my own favorite illustration comes from Rick Blaine in *Casablanca*, played by Humphrey Bogart. The movie ends with Rick explaining to his lover Ilsa Lund why she has to go with her husband and leave him behind, and he grounds his explanation in an eloquent statement of moral impartiality: "Look, I'm no good at being noble, but it doesn't take much to see that the problems of three little people don't amount to a hill of beans in this crazy world."

We should keep this quote in mind when we consider the increasingly popular view that we are slaves of the passions—that our moral judgments and moral actions are the product of neural mechanisms that we have no awareness of and no conscious control over. If this view of our moral natures were true, we would need to buck up and learn to live with it. But it is not true; it is refuted by everyday experience, by history, and by the science of developmental psychology.

It turns out instead that the right theory of our moral lives has two parts. It starts with what we are born with, and this is surprisingly rich: babies are moral animals, equipped by evolution with empathy and compassion, the capacity to judge the actions of others, and even some rudimentary understanding of justice and fairness. But we are more than just babies. A critical part of our morality—so much of what makes us human—emerges over the course of human history and individual development. It is the product of our compassion, our imagination, and our magnificent capacity for reason.

ACKNOWLEDGMENTS

Morality has interested me for as long as I can remember, but the impetus for this book was a lecture series that I gave at Johns Hopkins University in 2007 and 2008. The topic was "The Cognitive Science of Religion," and two of my lectures explored the relationship between morality and religious belief. I thank the Metanexus Institute, the John Templeton Foundation, and the Krieger School of Arts and Sciences for supporting these lectures. I am grateful as well to Steven Gross for coordinating my visits and talking with me about these issues.

After completing these lectures, I put morality aside for a while to complete a book on a quite different topic (pleasure) but then returned to it in 2010, when I wrote an article called "The Moral Life of Babies" for the *New York Times Magazine*. I am grateful to my editors Alex Star and Jaime Ryerson for their interest in this topic and for their extensive editorial guidance. At this point, my agent Katinka Matson convinced me to take the plunge. This is my third book with Katinka. She is wise, honest, and fiercely supportive—I'm lucky to have her on my side.

In 2011, I was asked to give the DeVane Lectures at Yale, on the topic "The Moralities of Everyday Life." These lectures served as a dry run for many of the arguments in this book. I thank the then-president of Yale, Richard Levin, and the then-provost (now president), Peter Salovey, for giving me this opportunity. I am also grateful for their work in ensuring that Yale is such a fine intellectual community. There is no better place in the world to be a teacher and a scholar.

The Yale baby studies described here were funded by grants from the National Science Foundation and the National Institutes of Health. I am very grateful for their support.

As this book took shape, many colleagues and friends answered questions, read passages, gave advice, and just helped me talk through the issues. I thank Catherine Alexander, John Bargh, Rodolfo Cortes Barragan, David Berreby, Peter Blake, Adam Cohen, Val Curtis, John Dovidio, Carol Dweck, Brian Earp, Deborah Fried, John Gibbs, Adam Glick, Kiley Hamlin, Edie Hofstatter, Frank Keil, Melanie Killen, Joshua Knobe, Valerie Kuhlmeier, Robert Kurzban, Marianne LaFrance, Megan Mangum, Gregory Murphy, Shaun Nichols, Kristina Olson, Wendy Phillips, David Pizarro, David Rand, Laurie Santos, Sally Satel, Richard Shweder, Luca Surian, and Karen Wynn. I owe a special debt to Tamar Gendler and Joshua Greene for many conversations about these issues, and for sharp comments on earlier drafts.

I discussed many of these ideas in an undergraduate

seminar on moral psychology, and I'm grateful to the students for discussion and debate. And I went over a first draft of this book with my lab group, composed of undergraduates, graduate students, and postdoctoral fellows. I thank the following for their wise and constructive comments: Konika Banerjee, Jennifer Barnes, Lindsey Drayton, Thalia Goldstein, Lily Guillot, Jonathan Phillips, David Pietraszewski, Alex Shaw, Mark Sheskin, Christina Starmans, and Annie Wertz.

I thank my editor at Crown, Rachel Klayman, for her faith in this project and her wise counsel throughout. Along with her wonderful editorial assistant, Stephanie Chan, she provided extensive and thoughtful comments on earlier drafts, leading me to rethink and restructure many of my arguments. I feel the book is much improved as a result—it's certainly a lot shorter.

I thank my family—close, extended, real kin, and fictive kin, all of them—for their support. And I should include a special shout-out to my teenage sons, Max and Zachary, for their love and companionship, and for countless hours of enjoyable debate. I hope to persuade at least one of them to join the family business.

And this brings me to my biggest thank-you, which is to my wife, Karen Wynn. I am not one of these people who keep family and work separate. Karen directs the Infant Cognition Center at Yale, and all of my own research on baby morality has been as a collaborator on studies led by Karen and her students. The ideas presented in this book have been shaped by my years of discussion with Karen, and I've benefited throughout from her kindness, her brilliance, and her love. She also thought up the title.

NOTES

PREFACE

1 **a writer living in Dallas:** S. Satel, "Desperately Seeking a Kidney," *New York Times Magazine,* December 16, 2007.

1 **others go even further:** L. MacFarquhar, "The Kindest Cut," *New Yorker,* July 27, 2009.

1 **a moral code implanted by God:** Francis Collins, *The Language of God: A Scientist Presents Evidence for Belief* (New York: Free Press, 2006).

3 **"Death to Mary Bale":** L. M. Holson, "The New Court of Shame Is Online," *New York Times,* December 23, 2010.

4 **Thomas Jefferson was right:** or full text of the letter, see "Letter to Peter Carr" (August 10, 1787), www.stephenjaygould.org/ctrl /jefferson_carr.html. For discussion of Jefferson's view on moral psychology, see John Macnamara, *Through the Rearview Mirror: Historical Reflections on Psychology* (Cambridge, MA: MIT Press, 1999).

4 **Adam Smith:** For a thoughtful overview of Smith's ideas about morality, see Michael L. Frazer, *The Enlightenment of Sympathy: Justice and the Moral Sentiments in the Eighteenth Century and Today* (New York: Oxford University Press, 2010).

1. THE MORAL LIFE OF BABIES

7 **The one-year-old decided to take justice into his own hands:** The anecdote is first reported in P. Bloom, "The Moral Life of Babies," *New York Times Magazine,* May 9, 2010.

8 **The Reverend Thomas Martin:** Quoted in Frank Keil, *Developmental Psychology* (New York: Norton, forthcoming).

8 **Even moral philosophers don't agree about what morality really is:** J. Nado, D. Kelly, and S. Stich, "Moral Judgment," in *The Routledge Companion to the Philosophy of Psychology,* ed. John Symons and Paco Calvo (New York: Routledge, 2009), 621–33.

9 **it is a certain type of wrong:** These are among the criteria used by Elliot Turiel and his colleagues to distinguish moral transgressions from what they call "socio-conventional transgressions." See Elliot Turiel, "The Development of Morality," in *Handbook of Child Psychology,* ed. William Damon and R. M. Lerner, vol. 3, ed. N. Eisenberg (New York: Wiley, 2006), 789–857.

10 **John Mikhail has suggested:** John Mikhail, *Elements of Moral Cognition: Rawls' Linguistic Analogy and the Cognitive Science of Moral and Legal Judgment* (New York: Cambridge University Press, 2010).

11 **Jeremy Strohmeyer and David Cash Jr.:** C. Booth, "The Bad Samaritan," *Time,* September 7, 1998.

11 **For other types of moral wrongs, the issue of harm is not as clear-cut:** See, for example, R. Shweder and J. Haidt, "The Future of Moral Psychology: Truth, Intuition, and the Pluralist Way," *Psychological Science* 4 (1993): 360–65; Jonathan Haidt, *The Righteous Mind: Why Good People Are Divided by Politics and Religion* (New York: Pantheon, 2012).

13 **a study of spontaneous helping in toddlers:** F. Warneken and M. Tomasello, "Altruistic Helping in Human Infants and Young Chimpanzees," *Science* 311 (2006): 1301–3.

13 **as Adam Smith put it:** Adam Smith, *The Theory of Moral Sentiments* (1759; repr., Lawrence, KS: Digireads.com, 2011), 30.

14 **Herodotus made this point:** Herodotus, *The Histories,* rev. ed., trans. Aubrey de Selincourt (New York: Penguin, 2003).

14 **My favorite summary of contemporary moral differences:** R. Shweder, "Are Moral Intuitions Self-Evident Truths?," *Crimi-*

nal Justice Ethics 13 (1994): 26. In other writings, though, Shweder is clear that moral universals exist as well; see, for example, R. Shweder, "Relativism and Universalism," in *Companion to Moral Anthropology*, ed. Didier Fassin (New York: Wiley), 85–102.

15 **the tendency of anthropologists to exaggerate how exotic other people are:** M. Bloch, "The Past and the Present in the Present," *Man* 12 (1977): 278–92, quote from 285.

16 **one aspect of morality . . . has long been a no-brainer from an evolutionary point of view:** Richard Dawkins, *The Selfish Gene* (New York: Oxford University Press, 1976).

17 **Adam Smith pointed this out:** Smith, *Theory of Moral Sentiments*, 63.

17 **"subversion from within":** Richard Dawkins, *The God Delusion* (New York: Houghton Mifflin, 2006), 199.

18 **Darwin's theory:** Charles Darwin, *The Descent of Man* (1871; repr., London: Penguin, 2004), 155. See also S. Bowles, "Group Competition, Reproductive Leveling, and the Evolution of Human Altruism," *Science* 314 (2006): 1569–72; E. O. Wilson, *The Social Conquest of Earth* (New York: Liveright, 2012).

18 **An alternative . . . is that the good guys might punish the bad guys:** R. L. Trivers, "The Evolution of Reciprocal Altruism," *Quarterly Review of Biology* 46 (1971): 35–57.

19 **five minutes inside the head of a two-year-old:** Alison Gopnik, *The Philosophical Baby: What Children's Minds Tell Us About Truth, Love, and the Meaning of Life* (New York: Farrar, Straus and Giroux, 2009).

19 **The psychologist Charles Fernyhough describes:** Charles Fernyhough, *A Thousand Days of Wonder: A Scientist's Chronicle of His Daughter's Developing Mind* (New York: Avery, 2009), 5.

20 **The psychologist Alison Gopnik . . . The baby just *is,* trapped in the here and now:** Gopnik, *Philosophical Baby.*

22 **a baby's "naive physics":** See, for example, R. Baillargeon, "Object Permanence in 3½ and 4½ Month Old Infants," *Developmental Psychology* 23 (1987): 655–64; E. Spelke, "Principles of Object Perception," *Cognitive Science* 14 (1990): 29–56. For a review, see E. S. Spelke and K. D. Kinzler, "Core Knowledge," *Developmental Science* 10 (2007): 89–96.

22 **babies can also do rudimentary math:** K. Wynn, "Addition and

Subtraction by Human Infants," *Nature* 358 (1992): 749–50. For a review of extensions and replications, see K. van Marle and K. Wynn, "Quantitative Reasoning," in *Encyclopedia of Cognitive Science,* ed. Lynn Nadel (London: Nature Publishing Group, Macmillan, 2002). For a study of babies' understanding of ratios, see K. McCrink and K. Wynn, "Ratio Abstraction by 6-Month-Old Infants," *Psychological Science* 18 (2007): 740–46.

23 **They like the sound of human voices . . . they like the look of human faces:** For review, see Paul Bloom, *Descartes' Baby: How the Science of Child Development Explains What Makes Us Human* (New York: Basic Books, 2004).

23 **how to freak out a baby:** E. Tronick, H. Als, L. Adamson, S. Wise, and T. B. Brazelton, "The Infant's Response to Entrapment Between Contradictory Messages in Face-to-Face Interaction," *Journal of American Academy of Child Psychiatry* 17 (1978): 1–13.

23 **In one study:** T. Field, N. Vega-Lahar, F. Scafidi, and S. Goldstein, "Effects of Maternal Unavailability on Mother-Infant Interactions," *Infant Behavior and Development* 9 (1986): 473–78; Tronick, Als, Adamson, Wise, and Brazelton, "Infant's Response to Entrapment."

23 **babies know that individuals have goals:** A. Woodward, "Infants Selectively Encode the Goal of an Actor's Reach," *Cognition* 69 (1998): 1–34.

24 **fifteen-month-olds:** K. H. Onishi and R. Baillargeon, "Do 15-Month-Old Infants Understand False Beliefs?," *Science* 308 (2005): 255–58.

25 **previous work by the psychologists David Premack and Ann Premack:** D. Premack and A. J. Premack, "Infants Attribute Value +/– to the Goal-Directed Actions of Self-Propelled Objects," *Journal of Cognitive Neuroscience* 9 (1997): 848–56.

26 **we created animations in which geometrical figures helped or hindered one another:** V. Kuhlmeier, K. Wynn, and P. Bloom, "Attribution of Dispositional States by 9-Month-Olds: The Role of Faces," under review; V. Kuhlmeier, K. Wynn, and P. Bloom, "Attribution of Dispositional States by 12-Month-Old Infants," *Psychological Science* 14 (2003): 402–8; J. K. Hamlin, K. Wynn, and P. Bloom, "Social Evaluation by Preverbal Infants," *Nature* 450 (2007): 557–59. To see examples of what the babies are shown, go

to "Social Evaluation by Preverbal Infants," 2007, www.yale.edu /infantlab/socialevaluation/Helper-Hinderer.html.

27 **Our first set of studies used . . . puppets instead of animations:** Hamlin, Wynn, and Bloom, "Social Evaluation by Preverbal Infants."

28 **We then followed this up with a pair of studies looking at three-month-olds:** J. K. Hamlin, K. Wynn, and P. Bloom, "3-Month-Olds Show a Negativity Bias in Social Evaluation," *Developmental Science* 13 (2010): 923–39.

29 **a "negativity bias":** A. Vaish, T. Grossmann, and A. Woodward, "Not All Emotions Are Created Equal: The Negativity Bias in Social-Emotional Development," *Psychological Bulletin* 134 (2008): 383–403; P. Rozin and E. Royzman, "Negativity Bias, Negativity Dominance, and Contagion," *Personality and Social Psychology Review* 5 (2001): 296–320.

29 **a project led by Mariko Yamaguchi:** M. Yamaguchi, V. Kuhlmeier, K. Wynn, and K. van Marle, "Continuity in Social Cognition from Infancy to Childhood," *Developmental Science* 12 (2009): 746–52.

30 **Kiley and Karen created different sets of morality plays:** J. K. Hamlin and K. Wynn, "Five- and 9-Month-Old Infants Prefer Prosocial to Antisocial Others," *Cognitive Development* 26 (2011): 30–39.

31 **identifying the helper as nice and the hinderer as mean:** J. K. Hamlin, K. Wynn, and P. Bloom, "Social Evaluation by Preverbal Infants," poster presented at the meeting of the Society for Research in Child Development, Boston, 2007.

31 **Adam Smith . . . describes the moral sense:** Smith, *Theory of Moral Sentiments,* 222.

2. EMPATHY AND COMPASSION

33 **some unhappy combination of genes, parenting, and idiosyncratic personal experience:** E. Viding, R. J. R. Blair, T. E. Moffitt, and R. Plomin, "Evidence for Substantial Genetic Risk for Psychopathy in 7-Year-Olds," *Journal of Child Psychology and Psychiatry* 46 (2005): 592–97.

34 **a strategy that parents often use with their children:** Martin L. Hoffman, *Empathy and Moral Development: Implications for Caring and Justice* (New York: Cambridge University Press, 2000).

35 **a thirteen-year-old mugger:** William Damon, *The Social World of the Child* (San Francisco: Jossey-Bass, 1977), 18.

35 **Ted Bundy was puzzled:** Quoted in Paul Bloom, *Descartes' Baby: How the Science of Child Development Explains What Makes Us Human* (New York: Basic Books, 2004).

35 **The serial killer Gary Gilmore summed up the attitude:** Quoted in Bloom, *Descartes' Baby*.

35 **interview with Peter Woodcock:** From Jon Ronson, *The Psychopath Test: A Journey Through the Madness Industry* (New York: Riverhead, 2011), 91.

36 **Some illustrative examples are reported by Charles Darwin:** Charles Darwin, "A Biographical Sketch of an Infant," *Mind* 2 (1877): 285–94.

36 **William responded to the perceived suffering of others:** Darwin, "Biographical Sketch," 289.

36 **William's satisfaction at his own kind actions:** Darwin, "Biographical Sketch," 291.

37 **first hints of guilt and shame:** Darwin, "Biographical Sketch," 292.

37 **"carefully planned deceit":** Darwin, "Biographical Sketch," 292.

37 **"How much money would it take for you to strangle a cat . . . ?":** Michael Sandel, *Justice: What's the Right Thing to Do?* (New York: Farrar, Straus and Giroux, 2009).

38 **psychopathy can be an asset in business and politics:** Paul Babiak and Robert D. Hare, *Snakes in Suits: When Psychopaths Go to Work* (New York: HarperCollins, 2006).

39 **"the look people get right before I stab them":** A. A. Marsh and E. M. Cardinale, "Psychopathy and Fear: Specific Impairments in Judging Behaviors That Frighten Others," *Emotion* 12 (2012): 892–98.

40 **Adam Smith didn't use the word *empathy* . . . but he described it well:** Adam Smith, *The Theory of Moral Sentiments* (1759; repr., Lawrence, KS: Digireads.com, 2011), 13.

40 **"my own throat would feel narrow in sympathy":** John Updike, *Getting the Words Out* (Northridge, CA: Lord John Press, 1988),

17, cited in Elaine Hatfield, John T. Cacioppo, and Richard L. Rapson, *Emotional Contagion* (New York: Cambridge University Press, 1994).

41 **Adam Smith provides another example:** Smith, *Theory of Moral Sentiments,* 13.

41 **mirror neurons:** V. Gallese, L. Fadiga, L. Fogassi, and G. Rizzolatti, "Action Recognition in the Premotor Cortex," *Brain* 119 (1996): 593–609; G. Di Pellegrino, L. Fadiga, L. Fogassi, V. Gallese, and G. Rizzolatti, "Understanding Motor Events: A Neurophysiological Study," *Experimental Brain Research* 91 (1992): 176–80.

41 **comparing it to the discovery of DNA:** V. S. Ramachandran, "Mirror Neurons and Imitation Learning as the Driving Force Behind 'the Great Leap Forward' in Human Evolution," 2009, Edge video, transcript at www.edge.org/3rd_culture/ramachan dran/ramachandran_index.html.

42 **the initial claims about mirror neurons are significantly overblown:** G. Hickok, "Eight Problems for the Mirror Neuron Theory of Action Understanding in Monkeys and Humans," *Journal of Cognitive Neuroscience* 21 (2009): 1229–43; Steven Pinker, *The Better Angels of Our Nature: Why Violence Has Declined* (New York: Viking, 2011); Alison Gopnik, "Cells That Read Minds? What the Myth of Mirror Neurons Gets Wrong About the Human Brain," *Slate,* April 2007, www.slate.com/articles/life/brains/2007/04/cells _that_read_minds.html.

43 **empathy exists to motivate compassion and altruism:** For discussion, see C. Daniel Batson, *Altruism in Humans* (New York: Oxford University Press, 2011). For a review of empathy and sympathy from a developmental perspective, see Hoffman, *Empathy and Moral Development.*

43 **the link between empathy . . . is more nuanced than many people believe:** See also J. Prinz, "Is Empathy Necessary for Morality?," in *Empathy: Philosophical and Psychological Perspectives,* ed. Amy Coplan and Peter Goldie (New York: Oxford University Press, 2010).

44 **Empathy is also influenced by what one thinks of the other person:** T. Singer, B. Seymour, J. P. O'Doherty, K. E. Stephan, R. J. Dolan, and C. D. Frith, "Empathic Neural Responses Are Modulated by the Perceived Fairness of Others," *Nature* 439 (2006): 466–69.

44 **an example from the philosopher Peter Singer of an obviously good act:** P. Singer, "Famine, Affluence, and Morality," *Philosophy and Public Affairs* 1 (1972): 229–43.

44 **the Chinese scholar Mencius:** Quoted in S. Darwall, "Empathy, Sympathy, Care," *Philosophical Studies* 89 (1998): 261–82.

45 **Steven Pinker points out:** Pinker, *Better Angels,* 576.

45 **A real-world case, described by the philosopher Jonathan Glover:** Jonathan Glover, *Humanity: A Moral History of the Twentieth Century* (New Haven: Yale University Press, 2000), 379–80.

46 **Experiments by the psychologist C. Daniel Batson:** C. D. Batson, T. R. Klein, L. Highberger, and L. L. Shaw, "Immorality from Empathy-Induced Altruism: When Compassion and Justice Conflict," *Journal of Personality and Social Psychology* 68 (1995): 1042–54.

47 **Even newborns respond to other people's expressions:** A. N. Meltzoff and M. K. Moore, "Imitations of Facial and Manual Gestures by Human Neonates," *Science* 198 (1977): 75–78.

47 **parents and babies frequently mirror one another's expressions:** C. Trevarthen, "The Concept and Foundations of Infant Intersubjectivity," in *Intersubjective Communication and Emotion in Early Ontogeny,* ed. Stein Bråten (New York: Cambridge University Press, 1998), 15–46.

47 **the sound of crying is unpleasant for babies; it tends to make them cry themselves:** A. Sagi and M. Hoffman, "Empathic Distress in the Newborn," *Developmental Psychology* 12 (1976): 175–76.

48 **Babies cry more at the sound of another baby's cry . . . the cries of a chimpanzee infant:** G. B. Martin and R. D. Clark, "Distress Crying in Infants: Species and Peer Specificity," *Developmental Psychology* 18 (1982): 3–9; M. Dondi, F. Simion, and G. Caltran, "Can Newborns Discriminate Between Their Own Cry and the Cry of Another Newborn Infant?," *Developmental Psychology* 35 (1999): 418–26.

48 **Hungry rhesus monkeys avoid pulling a lever:** S. Wechkin, J. H. Masserman, and W. Terris Jr., "Shock to a Conspecific as an Aversive Stimulus," *Psychonomic Science* 1 (1964): 47–48; J. H. Masserman, S. Wechkin, and W. Terris, "'Altruistic' Behavior in Rhesus Monkeys," *American Journal of Psychiatry* 121 (1964): 584–85.

48 **Rats will press a bar to lower another rat:** G. E. Rice and P. Gainer, "'Altruism' in the Albino Rat," *Journal of Comparative and Physiological Psychology* 55 (1962): 123–25; G. E. J. Rice, "Aiding Behavior vs. Fear in the Albino Rat," *Psychological Record* 14 (1964): 165–70.

48 **one-year-olds will pat and stroke others in distress:** For review, see Hoffman, *Empathy and Moral Development.*

48 **The psychologist Carolyn Zahn-Waxler and her colleagues found:** C. Zahn-Waxler, J. L. Robinson, and R. N. Emde, "The Development of Empathy in Twins," *Developmental Psychology* 28 (1992): 1038–47; C. Zahn-Waxler, M. Radke-Yarrow, E. Wagner, and M. Chapman, "Development of Concern for Others," *Developmental Psychology* 28 (1992): 126–36.

49 **Girls are more likely to soothe than boys:** Zahn-Waxler, Robinson, and Emde, "Development of Empathy in Twins."

49 **research suggesting greater empathy and compassion, on average, in females:** N. Eisenberg and R. Lennon, "Sex Differences in Empathy and Related Capacities," *Psychological Bulletin* 94 (1983): 100–131.

49 **you can see similar behavior in other primates:** Frans de Waal, *The Ape and the Sushi Master: Cultural Reflections of a Primatologist* (New York: Basic Books, 2001).

49 **In one study where rats had the chance to press a bar:** Rice, "Aiding Behavior vs. Fear," 167. For discussion, see S. D. Preston and F. B. M. de Waal, "Empathy: Its Ultimate and Proximate Bases," *Behavioral and Brain Sciences* 25 (2002): 1–71.

49 **Toddlers also sometimes respond egocentrically to others' pain:** Hoffman, *Empathy and Moral Development.*

50 **anecdotes and studies showing spontaneous helping:** For review, see D. F. Hay, "The Roots and Branches of Human Altruism," *British Journal of Psychology* 100 (2009): 473–79.

50 **"'Daddy wants slippers'":** C. W. Valentine, *The Psychology of Early Childhood* (London: Methuen, 1942), 321.

50 **a psychologist wrote about an eighteen-month-old:** Joseph Church, ed., *Three Babies: Biographies of Cognitive Development* (New York: Random House, 1966), 71–72.

50 **And another psychologist . . . described turning her lab into a**

messy home: H. L. Rheingold, "Little Children's Participation in the Work of Adults, a Nascent Prosocial Behavior," *Child Development* 53 (1982): 114–25.

50 **psychologists have found that toddlers help adults:** F. Warneken and M. Tomasello, "Altruistic Helping in Human Infants and Young Chimpanzees," *Science* 311 (2006): 1301–3; F. Warneken and M. Tomasello, "Helping and Cooperation at 14 Months of Age," *Infancy* 11 (2007): 271–94. For review, see Michael Tomasello, *Why We Cooperate* (Cambridge, MA: MIT Press, 2009).

50 **This behavior is impressive:** K. A. Dunfield, V. A. Kuhlmeier, L. O'Connell, and E. Kelley, "Examining the Diversity of Prosocial Behavior: Helping, Sharing, and Comforting in Infancy," *Infancy* 16 (2011): 227–47.

51 **Or perhaps their helpful acts are performed . . . for the adults' approval:** K. Wynn, "Constraints on Natural Altruism," *British Journal of Psychology* 100 (2009): 481–85.

51 **Alia Martin and Kristina Olson conducted an experiment:** A. Martin and K. R. Olson, "When Kids Know Better: Paternalistic Helping in 3-Year-Old Children," *Developmental Psychology,* forthcoming.

52 **three-year-olds were more likely to help someone who had previously helped someone else:** A. Vaish, M. Carpenter, and M. Tomasello, "Young Children Selectively Avoid Helping People with Harmful Intentions," *Child Development* 81 (2010): 1661–69.

52 **Kristen Dunfield and Valerie Kuhlmeier got similar results:** K. A. Dunfield and V. A. Kuhlmeier, "Intention-Mediated Selective Helping in Infancy," *Psychological Science* 21 (2010): 523–27.

52 **Children begin to spontaneously share:** H. L. Rheingold, D. F. Hay, and M. J. West, "Sharing in the Second Year of Life," *Child Development* 47 (1976): 1148–58; D. F. Hay, "Cooperative Interactions and Sharing Between Very Young Children and Their Parents," *Developmental Psychology* 6 (1979): 647–58; D. F. Hay and P. Murray, "Giving and Requesting: Social Facilitation of Infants' Offers to Adults," *Infant Behavior and Development* 5 (1982): 301–10; Rheingold, Hay, and West, "Sharing in the Second Year."

53 **Celia Brownell and her colleagues:** C. A. Brownell, M. Svetlova, and S. Nichols, "To Share or Not to Share: When Do Toddlers

Respond to Another's Needs?," *Infancy* 14 (2009): 117–30, quote from 125.

54 **Rodolfo Cortez Barragan and Carol Dweck find:** R. C. Barragan and C. Dweck, "Young Children's 'Helpfulness': How Natural Is It?," unpublished manuscript, Stanford University, 2013.

55 **an intimate connection between judging others and judging ourselves:** R. F. Baumeister, A. M. Stillwell, and T. F. Heatherton, "Guilt: An Interpersonal Approach," *Psychological Bulletin* 115 (1994): 243–67. For discussion, see Pinker, *Better Angels.*

55 **Babies in the first year of life show distress when they harm others:** For review, see Hoffman, *Empathy and Moral Development.*

55 **a clever experiment on the elicitation of guilt in children:** Charlotte Buhler, *From Birth to Maturity: An Outline of the Psychological Development of the Child* (London: Kegan Paul, 1935), 66–67, cited in Peter Hobson, *The Cradle of Thought: Exploring the Origins of Thinking* (London: Macmillan, 2002).

57 **the psychological pull of compassion:** Smith, *Theory of Moral Sentiments,* 9.

3. FAIRNESS, STATUS, AND PUNISHMENT

60 **William Damon, in a series of influential studies:** William Damon, *The Social World of the Child* (San Francisco: Jossey-Bass, 1977), 81. The example that I give here is also cited in S. Nichols, "Emotions, Norms, and the Genealogy of Fairness," *Politics, Philosophy and Economics* 9 (2010): 275–96.

61 **the same equality bias in younger children:** K. R. Olson and E. S. Spelke, "Foundations of Cooperation in Preschool Children," *Cognition* 108 (2008): 222–31.

61 **The equality bias is strong:** A. Shaw and K. R. Olson, "Children Discard a Resource to Avoid Inequity," *Journal of Experimental Psychology: General* 141 (2012): 382–95.

63 **the sixteen-month-olds preferred the fair divider:** A. Geraci and L. Surian, "The Developmental Roots of Fairness: Infants' Reactions to Equal and Unequal Distributions of Resources," *Developmental Science* 14 (2011): 1012–20.

63 **the fifteen-month-olds looked longer at the unfair division:** M. F. H. Schmidt and J. A. Sommerville, "Fairness Expectations and Altruistic Sharing in 15-Month-Old Human Infants," *PLoS ONE* 6, no. 10 (2011): e23223.

63 **children can sometimes override their focus on equality:** S. Sloane, R. Baillargeon, and D. Premack, "Do Infants Have a Sense of Fairness?," *Psychological Science* 23 (2012): 196–204.

63 **children are smart about what to do with the extra resources:** Shaw and Olson, "Children Discard a Resource"; K. R. Olson and E. S. Spelke, "Foundations of Cooperation in Preschool Children," *Cognition* 108 (2008): 222–31.

64 **Some experiments that I've done:** K. McCrink, P. Bloom, and L. Santos, "Children's and Adults' Judgments of Equitable Resource Distributions," *Developmental Science* 13 (2010): 37–45.

64 **And other studies find that . . . develops even through adolescence:** I. Almas, A. W. Cappelen, E. O. Sorensen, and B. Tungodden, "Fairness and the Development of Inequality Acceptance," *Science* 328 (2010): 1176–78.

64 **we are natural-born egalitarians:** Frans De Waal, *The Age of Empathy: Nature's Lessons for a Kinder Society* (New York: Random House, 2009), 200.

65 **Aleksandr Solzhenitsyn tells an unnerving story:** Aleksandr Solzhenitsyn, *The Gulag Archipelago, 1918–1956: An Experiment in Literary Investigation* (New York, Harper, 1974), 69–70.

67 **the anthropologist Christopher Boehm addressed this issue:** Christopher Boehm, *Hierarchy in the Forest: The Evolution of Egalitarian Behavior* (Cambridge, MA: Harvard University Press, 1999).

67 **Hunter-gatherer societies are hyperviolent:** Boehm, *Hierarchy in the Forest.* For review, see Steven Pinker, *The Better Angels of Our Nature: Why Violence Has Declined* (New York: Viking, 2011).

68 **" 'insulting the meat' ":** N. Angier, "Thirst for Fairness May Have Helped Us Survive," *New York Times*, July 5, 2011.

69 **"Among the Hadza . . . his efforts amused them":** Boehm, *Hierarchy in the Forest,* 75.

69 **And there are more serious penalties:** Boehm, *Hierarchy in the Forest,* 121, 82.

69 **"a bizarre type of political hierarchy":** Boehm, *Hierarchy in the Forest*, 3.

70 **the Ultimatum Game:** W. Güth, R. Schmittberger, and B. Schwarze, "An Experimental Analysis of Ultimatum Bargaining," *Journal of Economic Behavior and Organization* 3 (1982): 367–88.

72 **According to the behavioral economist Dan Ariely:** Dan Ariely, *The Upside of Irrationality: The Unexpected Benefits of Defying Logic at Work and at Home* (New York: Harper, 2010). See also J. R. Carter and M. D. Irons, "Are Economists Different, and If So, Why?," *Journal of Economic Perspectives* 5 (1991): 171–77.

72 **our minds were not adapted for one-shot anonymous interactions:** A. W. Delton, M. M. Krasnow, J. Tooby, and L. Cosmides, "The Evolution of Direct Reciprocity Under Uncertainty Can Explain Human Generosity in One-Shot Encounters," *Proceedings of the National Academy of Sciences* 108 (2011): 13335–40.

72 **You can see this in the recipients' faces:** H. A. Chapman, D. A. Kim, J. M. Susskind, and A. K. Anderson, "In Bad Taste: Evidence for the Oral Origins of Moral Disgust," *Science* 5918 (2009): 1222–26.

72 **and in their brains:** A. G. Sanfey, J. K. Rilling, J. A. Aronson, L. E. Nystrom, and J. D. Cohen, "The Neural Basis of Economic Decision-Making in the Ultimatum Game," *Science* 300 (2003): 1755–58.

72 **In one study, where recipients were allowed to send anonymous messages:** E. Xiao and D. Houser, "Emotion Expression in Human Punishment Behavior," *Proceedings of the National Academy of Sciences* 102 (2005): 7398–7401. For discussion, see Nichols, "Emotions, Norms."

73 **What, precisely, is so annoying about being lowballed?:** Nichols, "Emotions, Norms," 289.

73 **the Dictator Game:** D. Kahneman, J. Knetsch, and R. H. Thaler, "Fairness and the Assumptions of Economics," *Journal of Business* 59 (1986): 285–300.

73 **Plainly, a self-interested agent would give nothing. But this is not what people do:** C. Engel, "Dictator Games: A Meta Study," *Experimental Economics* 14 (2011): 583–610.

74 **We are often generous, but not in this sort of indiscriminate way:** S. D. Levitt and J. A. List, "What Do Laboratory Experiments Measuring Social Preferences Reveal About the Real World," *Journal of Economic Perspectives* 21 (2007): 153–74.

75 **the more observable one's choice is, the more one gives:** Steven D. Levitt and Stephen J. Dubner, *Superfreakonomics* (New York: William Morrow, 2009); E. Hoffman, K. McCabe, K. Shachat, and V. Smith, "Preferences, Property Rights, and Anonymity in Bargaining Games," *Games and Economic Behavior* 7 (1994): 346–80; A. Franzen and S. Pointner, "Anonymity in the Dictator Game Revisited," *Journal of Economic Behavior and Organization* 81 (2012): 74–81.

75 **Even pictures of eyes on the wall or on the computer screen make people kinder:** K. Haley and D. Fessler, "Nobody's Watching? Subtle Cues Affect Generosity in an Anonymous Economic Game," *Evolution and Human Behavior* 26 (2005): 245–56; M. Bateson, D. Nettle, and G. Roberts, "Cues of Being Watched Enhance Cooperation in a Real-World Setting," *Biology Letters* 12 (2006): 412–14.

75 **Tom Lehrer, in his song about the Boy Scouts:** Quoted in Martin A. Nowak and Roger Highfield, *SuperCooperators: Altruism Evolution and Why We Need Each Other to Succeed* (New York: Free Press, 2011).

76 **the psychologist Jason Dana and his colleagues tweaked the standard Dictator Game:** J. Dana, M. C. Daylian, and R. M. Dawes, "What You Don't Know Won't Hurt Me: Costly (but Quiet) Exit in Dictator Games," *Organizational Behavior and Human Decision Processes* 100 (2006): 193–201.

76 **The second set of experiments was done by the economist John List:** J. List, "On the Interpretation of Giving in Dictator Games," *Journal of Political Economy* 115 (2007): 482–94.

77 **The economist Ernst Fehr and his colleagues:** E. Fehr, H. Bernhard, and B. Rockenbach, "Egalitarianism in Young Children," *Nature* 454 (2008): 1079–83.

78 **more recent research on the Dictator Game in different countries:** P. Rochat, M. D. G. Dias, G. Liping, T. Broesch, C. Passos-Ferreira, A. Winning, and B. Berg, "Fairness in Distributive Justice

in 3- and 5-Year-Olds Across Seven Cultures," *Journal of Cross-Cultural Psychology* 40 (2009): 416–42.

79 **The psychologist Vanessa LoBue and her colleagues:** V. LoBue, T. Nishida, C. Chiong, J. S. DeLoache, and J. Haidt, "When Getting Something Good Is Bad: Even Three-Year-Olds React to Inequality," *Social Development* 20 (2011): 154–70.

80 **In this regard, they are similar to monkeys, chimpanzees, and dogs:** S. F. Brosnan and F. B. M. de Waal, "Monkeys Reject Unequal Pay," *Nature* 425 (2003): 297–99; S. F. Brosnan, H. C. Schiff, and F. B. M. de Waal, "Tolerance for Inequity May Increase with Social Closeness in Chimpanzees," *Proceedings of the Royal Society B* 1560 (2005): 253–58; F. Range, L. Horn, Z. Viranyi, and L. Huber, "The Absence of Reward Induces Inequity Aversion in Dogs," *Proceedings of the National Academy of Sciences* 106 (2008): 340–45.

80 **Children can also be spiteful in their preferences:** P. R. Blake and K. McAuliffe, " 'I Had So Much It Didn't Seem Fair': Eight-Year-Olds Reject Two Forms of Inequity," *Cognition* 120 (2011): 215–24.

81 **Further evidence of children's spiteful natures:** M. Sheskin, K. Wynn, and P. Bloom, "Anti-equality: Social Comparison in Young Children," under review.

82 **a medieval Jewish folktale about an envious man:** Thanks to Shira Telushkin.

82 **"We are born of risen apes, not fallen angels":** Quoted in A. J. Jacobs, *The Know-It-All: One Man's Humble Quest to Become the Smartest Person in the World* (New York: Simon & Schuster, 2004).

82 **some scholars . . . view moral outrage as more important to morality than empathy:** Jesse Prinz, "Is Empathy Necessary for Morality?," in *Empathy: Philosophical and Psychological Perspectives,* ed. Amy Coplan and Peter Goldie (New York: Oxford University Press, 2010).

82 **Let us start with revenge:** For a review, see M. E. McCullough, R. Kurzban, and B. A. Tabak, "Cognitive Systems for Revenge and Forgiveness," *Behavioral and Brain Sciences* 36 (2013): 1–15.

83 **Adam Smith describes our feelings toward a man who has murdered someone we love:** Adam Smith, *The Theory of Moral Sentiments* (1759; repr., Lawrence, KS: Digireads.com, 2011), 50.

83 **"Prepare to die!":** These famous lines are from the book by William Goldman, but the scene where he explains this to the man in black is only in the movie (1987, directed by Rob Reiner). See William Goldman, *The Princess Bride: S. Morgenstern's Classic Tale of True Love and High Adventure* (New York: Harcourt, 2007).

83 **"A past wrong against you . . . that such treatment is acceptable":** P. Hieronymi, "Articulating an Uncompromising Forgiveness," *Philosophy and Phenomenological Research* 62 (2001): 546, quoted in A. Martin, "Owning Up and Lowering Down: The Power of Apology," *Journal of Philosophy* 107 (2010): 534–53.

84 **cultures of honor:** Richard E. Nisbett and Dov Cohen, *Culture of Honor: The Psychology of Violence in the South* (Denver, CO: Westview Press, 1996).

84 **Steven Pinker argues:** Pinker, *Better Angels.*

85 **The theme of payback shows up over and over in fiction:** John Kerrigan, *Revenge Tragedy: From Aeschylus to Armageddon* (Oxford: Oxford University Press, 1994); William Flesch, *Comeuppance: Costly Signaling, Altruistic Punishment, and Other Biological Components of Fiction* (Cambridge, MA: Harvard University Press, 2007).

85 **"human flesh search engines":** T. Downey, "China's Cyberposse," *New York Times Magazine,* March 7, 2010.

86 **the Public Goods Game:** G. Hardin, "The Tragedy of the Commons," *Science* 162 (1968): 1243–48; D. G. Rand, A. Dreber, T. Ellingsen, D. Fudenberg, and M. A. Nowak, "Positive Interactions Promote Public Cooperation," *Science* 325 (2009): 1272–75.

88 **inevitably some participants succumb to temptation:** E. Fehr and S. Gächter, "Altruistic Punishment in Humans," *Nature* 415 (2002): 137–40.

89 **Ernst Fehr and the economist Simon Gächter explored this idea:** Fehr and Gächter, "Altruistic Punishment in Humans."

90 **it's vexingly hard to explain how such behavior could evolve through natural selection:** See, for example, A. Dreber, D. G. Rand, D. Fudenberg, and M. A. Nowak, "Winners Don't Punish," *Nature* 452 (2008): 348–51.

90 **Perhaps altruistic punishment could have evolved through some sort of group selection:** R. Boyd, H. Gintis, S. Bowles, and P. J. Richerson, "The Evolution of Altruistic Punishment,"

Proceedings of the National Academy of Sciences 100 (2003): 3531–35.

90 **perhaps punishers thrive because other individuals like them and prefer to interact with them:** H. Gintis, E. A. Smith, and S. Bowles, "Costly Signaling and Cooperation," *Journal of Theoretical Biology* 213 (2001): 103–19.

91 **altruistic punishment is rare—or even nonexistent—in the small-scale societies of the real world:** F. Guala, "Reciprocity: Weak or Strong? What Punishment Experiments Do (and Do Not) Demonstrate," *Behavioral and Brain Sciences* 35 (2012): 1–59.

91 **"antisocial punishment":** B. Herrmann, C. Thoni, and S. Gächter, "Antisocial Punishment Across Societies," *Science* 319 (2008): 1362–67.

92 **Adam Smith's view:** Smith, *Theory of Moral Sentiments,* 52.

92 **Consistent with the idea . . . the person harming the victim:** Thanks to Jonathan Phillips for discussing this with me.

93 **Even young children have some appreciation of the logic of third-party punishment:** D. Pietraszewski and T. German, "Coalitional Psychology on the Playground: Reasoning About Indirect Social Consequences in Preschoolers and Adults," *Cognition* 126 (2013): 352–63.

93 **some of the odder features of our punitive sentiments:** J. M. Darley, K. M. Carlsmith, and P. H. Robinson, "Incapacitation and Just Deserts as Motives for Punishment," *Law and Human Behavior* 24 (2000): 659–83; C. R. Sunstein, "Moral Heuristics," *Behavioral and Brain Sciences* 28 (2005): 531–43; J. Baron and I. Ritov, "Intuitions About Penalties and Compensation in the Context of Tort Law," *Journal of Risk and Uncertainty* 7 (1993): 17–33.

94 **"He must be made to repent . . .":** Smith, *Theory of Moral Sentiments,* 50.

94 **"All men, even the most stupid and unthinking . . .":** Smith, *Theory of Moral Sentiments,* 66.

94 **Young children are highly aggressive . . . it peaks at about age two:** S. Côté, T. Vaillancourt, J. C. LeBlanc, D. S. Nagin, and R. E. Tremblay, "The Development of Physical Aggression from Toddlerhood to Pre-adolescence: A Nationwide Longitudinal Study of Canadian Children," *Journal of Abnormal Child Psychology* 34 (2006): 71–85.

95 **Children tattle . . . the children would spontaneously complain to adults:** H. Rakoczy, F. Warneken, and M. Tomasello, "The Sources of Normativity: Young Children's Awareness of the Normative Structure of Games," *Developmental Psychology* 44 (2008): 875–81.

95 **In studies of siblings . . . they were not making things up:** I. M. Den Bak and H. S. Ross, " 'I'm Telling!' The Content, Context, and Consequences of Children's Tattling on Their Siblings," *Social Development* 5 (1996): 292–309; H. S. Ross and I. M. Den Bak-Lammers, "Consistency and Change in Children's Tattling on Their Siblings: Children's Perspectives on the Moral Rules and Procedures of Family Life," *Social Development* 7 (1998): 275–300.

95 **Gordon Ingram and Jesse Bering explored tattling by children in an inner-city school:** G. P. D. Ingram and J. M. Bering, "Children's Tattling: The Reporting of Everyday Norm Violations in Preschool Settings," *Child Development* 81 (2010): 945–57.

96 **Children also don't tattle about insignificant things:** A. Vaish, M. Missana, and M. Tomasello, "Three-Year-Old Children Intervene in Third-Party Moral Transgressions," *British Journal of Developmental Psychology* 29 (2011): 124–30.

97 **a variant of the good guy/bad guy experiments:** J. K. Hamlin, K. Wynn, P. Bloom, and N. Mahajan, "How Infants and Toddlers React to Antisocial Others," *Proceedings of the National Academy of Sciences* 108 (2011): 19931–36.

99 **an influential theory of moral development:** L. Kohlberg, "Stage and Sequence: The Cognitive-Developmental Approach to Socialization," in *Handbook of Socialization Theory and Research*, ed. David A. Goslin (Chicago: Rand McNally, 1969), 347–480; Jean Piaget, *The Moral Judgement of the Child*, trans. Marjorie Gabain (New York: Free Press, 1965). For review and discussion, see John C. Gibbs, *Moral Development and Reality: Beyond the Theories of Kohlberg and Hoffman* (New York: Sage, 2003).

100 **"hodgepodge morality":** D. A. Pizarro, "Hodgepodge Morality," in *What Is Your Dangerous Idea?* ed. John Brockman (New York: HarperCollins, 2007), 63.

4. OTHERS

101 **Good Samaritan:** Luke 10:30–35 (King James Version).

102 **"Never mind ethnicity, community, or traditional categories of neighbor-ness":** J. Waldron, "Who Is My Neighbor? Humanity and Proximity," *Monist* 86 (2003): 343.

103 **"to venture out of one's territory to meet [other] humans . . . was equivalent to suicide":** Jared Diamond, *The Third Chimpanzee: The Evolution and Future of the Human Animal* (New York: HarperCollins, 1992), 229.

103 **"Most primitive tribes feel . . . the most appropriate thing to do is bludgeon him to death":** Interview quoted in Howard Bloom, *The Lucifer Principle: A Scientific Expedition into the Forces of History* (New York: Atlantic Monthly Press, 1997), 74.

103 **Jane Goodall describes what happens:** Jane Goodall, *The Chimpanzees of Gombe: Patterns of Behavior* (Cambridge, MA: Harvard University Press, 1986).

104 **Newborn babies prefer to look at their mother's face:** T. M. Field, D. Cohen, R. Garcia, and R. Greenberg, "Mother-Stranger Face Discrimination by the Newborn," *Infant Behavior and Development* 7 (1984): 19–25.

104 **they prefer their mother's smell:** A. MacFarlane, "Olfaction in the Development of Social Preferences in the Human Neonate," in *Parent-Infant Interaction, Ciba Foundation Symposium* 33 (New York: Elsevier, 1975), 103–13.

104 **they prefer her voice:** A. J. Decasper and W. P. Fifer, "Of Human Bonding: Newborns Prefer Their Mother's Voice," *Science* 208 (1980): 1174–76.

105 **babies who are raised by a woman look longer at women:** P. Quinn, J. Yahr, A. Kuhn, A. Slater, and O. Pascalis, "Representation of the Gender of Human Faces by Infants: A Preference for Females," *Perception* 31 (2002): 1109–21.

105 **Caucasian babies prefer to look at Caucasian faces:** D. J. Kelly, P. C. Quinn, A. M. Slater, K. Lee, A. Gibson, M. Smith, L. Ge, and O. Pascalis, "Three-Month-Olds, but Not Newborns, Prefer Own-Race Faces," *Developmental Science* 8 (2005): 31–36; Y. Bar-Haim, T. Ziv, D. Lamy, and R. M. Hodes, "Nature and Nurture in Own-Race Face Processing," *Psychological Science* 17 (2006):

159–63; D. J. Kelly, S. Liu, L. Ge, P. C. Quinn, A. M. Slater, K. Lee, Q. Liu, and O. Pascalis, "Cross-Race Preferences for Same-Race Faces Extend Beyond the African Versus Caucasian Contrast in 3-Month-Old Infants," *Infancy* 11 (2007): 87–95.

106 **adults automatically encode three pieces of information when we meet a new person:** For review, see D. Messick and D. Mackie, "Intergroup Relations," *Annual Review of Psychology* 40 (1989): 45–81.

106 **there is something strange about this triad:** R. Kurzban, J. Tooby, and L. Cosmides, "Can Race Be Erased? Coalitional Computation and Social Categorization," *Proceedings of the National Academy of Sciences* 98 (2001): 15387–92.

107 **our hominid ancestors may have regularly encountered other hominid species:** D. Fessler, "Twelve Lessons (Most of Which I Learned the Hard Way) for Evolutionary Psychologists," International Cognition and Culture Institute, Daniel Fessler's Blog, January 20, 2012, www.cognitionandculture.net/home/blog/74 -daniel-fesslers-blog/2344-twelve-lessons-most-of-which-i-learned -the-hard-way-for-evolutionary-psychologists.

107 **our tendency to *biologize* race:** Lawrence A. Hirschfeld, *Race in the Making: Cognition, Culture, and the Child's Construction of Human Kinds* (Cambridge, MA: MIT Press, 1996).

108 **the "mere exposure" effect:** R. B. Zajonc, "Mere Exposure: A Gateway to the Subliminal," *Current Directions in Psychological Science* 10 (2001): 224–28.

108 **the memory-confusion paradigm:** S. E. Taylor, S. T. Fiske, N. L. Etcoff, and A. J. Ruderman, "Categorical and Contextual Bases of Person Memory and Stereotyping," *Journal of Personality and Social Psychology* 36 (1978): 778–93.

109 **age, sex, and a third, variable category:** Jim Sidanius and Felicia Pratto, *Social Dominance: An Intergroup Theory of Social Hierarchy and Oppression* (New York: Cambridge University Press, 1999); F. Pratto, J. Sidanius, and S. Levin, "Social Dominance Theory and the Dynamics of Intergroup Relations: Taking Stock and Looking Forward," *European Review of Social Psychology* 17 (2006): 271–320.

110 ***shibboleth:*** Judges 12:5–6, cited in Steven Pinker, *The Better Angels of Our Nature: Why Violence Has Declined* (New York: Viking, 2011).

110 **Lollapalooza:** Guillermo C. Jimenez, *Red Genes, Blue Genes: Exposing Political Irrationality* (New York: Autonomedia, 2009).

110 **babies can recognize the language that they have been exposed to, and they prefer it to other languages:** F. Ramus, "Language Discrimination by Newborns: Teasing Apart Phonotactic, Rhythmic, and Intonational Cues," *Annual Review of Language Acquisition* 2 (2002): 85–115.

111 **In one experiment, they tested ten-month-olds in Boston and Paris:** K. D. Kinzler, E. Dupoux, and E. S. Spelke, "The Native Language of Social Cognition," *Proceedings of the National Academy of Sciences* 104 (2007): 12577–80.

111 **twelve-month-olds would rather take food from a stranger who speaks their language:** K. Shutts, K. D. Kinzler, C. B. McKee, and E. S. Spelke, "Social Information Guides Infants' Selection of Foods," *Journal of Cognition and Development* 10 (2009): 1–17.

111 **two-year-olds prefer to give a gift to a speaker of their language:** K. D. Kinzler, E. Dupoux, and E. S. Spelke, "'Native' Objects and Collaborators: Infants' Object Choices and Acts of Giving Reflect Favor for Native over Foreign Speakers," *Journal of Cognition and Development,* forthcoming.

111 **five-year-olds prefer a child who speaks their own language as a friend:** K. D. Kinzler, K. Shutts, J. De Jesus, and E. S. Spelke, "Accent Trumps Race in Guiding Children's Social Preferences," *Social Cognition* 27 (2009): 623–34.

111 **Babies prefer to look at a speaker without an accent:** Kinzler, Dupoux, and Spelke, "Native Language of Social Cognition."

111 **When choosing friends, five-year-olds are more likely to choose children who speak American English:** Kinzler, Shutts, De Jesus, and Spelke, "Accent Trumps Race."

111 **four- and five-year-olds trust a native speaker more than an accented speaker:** K. D. Kinzler, K. H. Corriveau, and P. L. Harris, "Children's Selective Trust in Native-Accented Speakers," *Developmental Science* 14 (2011): 106–11.

112 **research into the development of racial bias in children:** For review, see Frances E. Aboud, *Children and Prejudice* (London: Blackwell, 1988).

112 **The psychologist Frances Aboud:** Aboud, *Children and Prejudice,* especially 10.

113 **But better-designed experimental methods . . . are established by the age of six:** H. McGlothlin and M. Killen, "Intergroup Attitudes of European American Children Attending Ethnically Homogeneous Schools," *Child Development* 77 (2006): 1375–86; H. McGlothlin, M. Killen, and C. Edmonds, "European-American Children's Intergroup Attitudes About Peer Relationships," *British Journal of Developmental Psychology* 23 (2005): 227–49.

113 **Other studies find . . . but again this holds mostly in racially homogeneous schools:** J. A. Graham and R. Cohen, "Race and Sex as Factors in Children's Sociometric Ratings and Friendship Choices," *Social Development* 6 (1997): 355–72.

113 **When the studies are run in heterogeneous schools, children don't care about race:** J. Moody, "Race, School Integration, and Friendship Segregation in America," *American Journal of Sociology* 107 (2001): 679–716.

114 **the "contact hypothesis":** Gordon W. Allport, *The Nature of Prejudice* (Reading, MA: Addison-Wesley, 1954); T. E. Pettigrew, "Intergroup Contact Theory," *Annual Review of Psychology* 49 (1998): 65–85.

114 **Studies with three-year-olds find that . . . gender matters:** K. Shutts, M. R. Banaji, and E. S. Spelke, "Social Categories Guide Young Children's Preferences for Novel Objects," *Developmental Science* 13 (2010): 599–610.

114 **But race doesn't matter for the three-year-olds:** K. D. Kinzler and E. S. Spelke, "Do Infants Show Social Preferences for People Differing in Race?," *Cognition* 119 (2011): 1–9.

114 **even for the older children who do take race into account, it's not as important as language:** Kinzler, Shutts, DeJesus, and Spelke, "Accent Trumps Race."

115 **Sherif and Tajfel were both interested in what it takes to form an Us that clashes with a Them:** David Berreby, *Us and Them: The Science of Identity* (Chicago: University of Chicago Press, 2008).

117 **The Robbers Cave experiment:** Muzafer Sherif, O. J. Harvey, B. Jack White, William R. Hood, and Carolyn W. Sherif, *Intergroup Conflict and Cooperation: The Robbers Cave Experiment* (Norman: University of Oklahoma Book Exchange, 1961). For review and discussion, see Berreby, *Us and Them.*

117 **This was Tajfel's question. He did a simple experiment:** H. Tajfel, M. G. Billig, R. P. Bundy, and C. Flament, "Social Categorization and Intergroup Behaviour," *European Journal of Social Psychology* 1 (1971): 149–78.

117 **These findings have been replicated many times:** B. Mullen, R. Brown, and C. Smith, "Ingroup Bias as a Function of Salience, Relevance, and Status: An Integration," *European Journal of Social Psychology* 22 (1992): 103–22.

117 **Such "minimal-group" studies have been done with children as well:** R. S. Bigler, L. C. Jones, and D. B. Lobliner, "Social Categorization and the Formation of Intergroup Attitudes in Children," *Child Development* 68 (1997): 530–43; M. M. Patterson and R. S. Bigler, "Preschool Children's Attention to Environmental Messages About Groups: Social Categorization and the Origins of Intergroup Bias," *Child Development* 77 (2006): 847–60.

118 **Other researchers found that explicit cues from a teacher weren't even necessary:** Y. Dunham, A. S. Baron, and S. Carey, "Consequences of 'Minimal' Group Affiliations in Children," *Child Development* 82 (2011): 793–811.

119 **The science writer David Berreby begins his book:** Berreby, *Us and Them*, xi.

119 **Jews make up . . . 4 percent of the population in New Haven:** We know this from survey data gathered by Ira Sheskin, father of Mark Sheskin, who worked with Karen Wynn and me on some of the inequity studies discussed in the last chapter; see A. Appel, "Survey: Region Has 23,000 Jews," *New Haven Independent*, February 4, 2011, www.newhavenindependent.org/index.php/archives/entry/jews_23000.

120 **teachers sorted the children into groups by astrological sign:** Berreby, *Us and Them*, 208.

120 **children born in 1976, which was a Dragon year, actually do turn out to be better educated:** N. D. Johnson and J. V. C. Nye, "Does Fortune Favor Dragons?," *Journal of Economic Behavior and Organization* 78 (2011): 85–97.

121 **we "must think with the aid of categories . . .":** Allport, *Nature of Prejudice*, 20.

122 **stereotypes of racial and ethnic groups tend to be accurate:** Lee

Jussim, *Social Perception and Social Reality: Why Accuracy Dominates Bias and Self-Fulfilling Prophecy* (New York: Oxford University Press, 2012).

123 **After World War II started, Americans switched their attitudes about the Chinese and the Japanese:** Berreby, *Us and Them.*

123 **adults tend to rate individuals with certain non-native accents as less competent:** A. Gluszek and J. F. Dovidio, "The Way They Speak: A Social Psychological Perspective on the Stigma of Nonnative Accents in Communication," *Personality and Social Psychology Review* 14 (2010): 214–37.

123 **we are prone to think of members of highly unfamiliar outgroups as lacking emotions that are seen as uniquely human:** S. Loughnan, N. Haslam, T. Murnane, J. Vaes, C. Reynolds, and C. Suitner, "Objectification Leads to Depersonalization: The Denial of Mind and Moral Concern to Objectified Others," *European Journal of Social Psychology* 40 (2010): 709–17; J. Ph. Leyens, M. P. Paladino, R. T. Rodriguez, J. Vaes, S. Demoulin, A. P. Rodriguez, and R. Gaunt, "The Emotional Side of Prejudice: The Attribution of Secondary Emotions to Ingroups and Outgroups," *Personality and Social Psychology Review* 4 (2000): 186–97.

123 **The typical participants in a psychology experiment . . . may well be the least racist people in the world:** A. R. Pearson, J. F. Dovidio, and S. L. Gaertner, "The Nature of Contemporary Prejudice: Insights from Aversive Racism," *Social and Personality Psychology Compass* 3 (2009): 314–38.

124 **Children don't start off seeing race as taboo:** E. P. Apfelbaum, K. Pauker, N. Ambady, S. R. Sommers, and M. I. Norton, "Learning (Not) to Talk About Race: When Older Children Underperform in Social Categorization," *Developmental Psychology* 44 (2008): 1513–18.

124 **a pressing anxiety about appearing racist:** Pearson, Dovidio, and Gaertner, "Nature of Contemporary Prejudice."

125 **even the least racist people in the world have unconscious racial biases:** For review, see M. R. Banaji and L. Heiphetz, "Attitudes," in *Handbook of Social Psychology,* ed. Susan T. Fiske, Daniel T. Gilbert, and Gardner Lindzey (New York: Wiley, 2010), 348–88.

125 **The worst example I ever saw was during an episode of the**

television show *Lie to Me:* From *Lie to Me,* Fox, Season 1, Episode 5 ("Unchained").

126 some critics have argued that such findings tell us little about stereotyping and prejudice in the real world: H. Arkes and P. E. Tetlock, "Attributions of Implicit Prejudice, or 'Would Jesse Jackson Fail the Implicit Association Test?'," *Psychological Inquiry* 15 (2004): 257–78.

126 these measures correlate with considerations that really matter: A. G. Greenwald, A. Poehlman, E. Uhlmann, and M. R. Banaji, "Understanding and Interpreting the Implicit Association Test III: Meta-analysis of Predictive Validity," *Journal of Personality and Social Psychology* 97 (2009): 17–41; Banaji and Heiphetz, "Attitudes"; Pearson, Dovidio, and Gaertner, "Nature of Contemporary Prejudice."

126 Asian applicants to universities have higher-than-average SAT scores: Thomas. J. Espenshade and Alexandria W. Radford, *No Longer Separate, Not Yet Equal: Race and Class in Elite College Admission and Campus Life* (Princeton: Princeton University Press, 2009).

127 As the psychologist Francisco Gil-White points out . . . it's a statement about the ethnicities of their ancestors: F. Gil-White, "Are Ethnic Groups Biological 'Species' to the Human Brain? Essentialism in Our Cognition of Some Social Categories," *Current Anthropology* 42 (2001): 515–54.

129 "one of the natural founts of human imagination and creative pleasure": Berreby, *Us and Them,* xiv.

129 The philosopher Kwame Anthony Appiah: Kwame Anthony Appiah, *Cosmopolitanism: Ethics in a World of Strangers* (New York: Norton, 2006), 98.

129 Appiah cites Cicero on this point: Appiah, *Cosmopolitanism,* xviii.

5. BODIES

131 Primo Levi tells how the Nazis denied Jewish prisoners access to toilets: Primo Levi, *The Drowned and the Saved* (London: Abacus, 1988), 70–71.

132 "a being disgustingly soft and porous . . .": Martha C. Nussbaum,

Upheavals of Thought: The Intelligence of the Emotions (New York: Cambridge University Press, 2001), 347.

132 **George Orwell is eloquent about the role of disgust in class divisions:** George Orwell, *The Road to Wigan Pier* (London: Penguin, 1937), 79.

133 **Certain objects, substances, and experiences:** For reviews, see P. Rozin, J. Haidt, and C. R. McCauley, "Disgust," in *Handbook of Emotions*, 3rd ed., ed. Michael Lewis, Jeannette M. Haviland-Jones, and Lisa F. Barrett (New York: Guilford Press), 757–76; Paul Bloom, *Descartes' Baby: How the Science of Child Development Explains What Makes Us Human* (New York: Basic Books, 2004); Daniel Kelly, *Yuck! The Nature and Moral Significance of Disgust* (Cambridge, MA: MIT Press, 2011); Rachel Herz, *That's Disgusting: Unraveling the Mysteries of Repulsion* (New York: Norton, 2012); William Ian Miller, *The Anatomy of Disgust* (Cambridge, MA: Harvard University Press, 1997).

133 **a scale to measure people's "disgust sensitivity":** J. Haidt, C. McCauley, and P. Rozin, "Individual-Differences in Sensitivity to Disgust: A Scale Sampling 7 Domains of Disgust Elicitors," *Personality and Individual Differences* 16 (1994): 701–13. For a modified version, see B. O. Olatunji, N. L. Williams, D. F. Tolin, C. N. Sawchuck, J. S. Abramowitz, J. M. Lohr, and L. S. Elwood, "The Disgust Scale: Item Analysis, Factor Structure, and Suggestions for Refinement," *Psychological Assessment* 19 (2007): 281–97.

134 **people's disgust sensitivity ratings predict how willing they are to actually engage in disgusting activities:** P. Rozin, J. Haidt, C. McCauley, L. Dunlop, and M. Ashmore, "Individual Differences in Disgust Sensitivity: Comparisons and Evaluations of Paper-and-Pencil Versus Behavioral Measures," *Journal of Research in Personality* 33 (1999): 330–51.

135 **William Ian Miller's explanation . . . tears lack the physical properties of disgusting substances:** Miller, *The Anatomy of Disgust*, 90.

135 **"The excreta arouse no disgust in children":** Sigmund Freud, *Civilization and Its Discontents* (New York: Norton, 1961), 54.

135 **young children will touch and even eat all manner of disgusting things:** P. Rozin, L. Hammer, H. Oster, T. Horowitz, and V. Marmora, "The Child's Conception of Food: Differentiation of

Categories of Rejected Substances in the 1.4 to 5 Year Range," *Appetite* 7 (1986): 141–51.

136 ***Don't try to make the child share your adult disgust at feces:*** Penelope Leach, *Your Baby and Child: From Birth to Age Five* (New York: Knopf, 1989), 317.

136 **everything else in this passage is mistaken:** See also Bloom, *Descartes' Baby.*

137 **disgust evolved to ward us away from eating bad foods:** Rozin, Haidt, and McCauley, "Disgust."

138 **"It is remarkable how readily and instantly retching or actual vomiting is induced":** Charles Darwin, *The Expression of the Emotions in Man and Animals* (1872; repr., Oxford: Oxford University Press, 1998), 257.

138 **pregnant women are exceptionally disgust-sensitive:** D. M. T. Fessler, S. J. Eng, and C. D. Navarrete, "Elevated Disgust Sensitivity in the First Trimester of Pregnancy: Evidence Supporting the Compensatory Prophylaxis Hypothesis," *Evolution and Human Behavior* 26 (2005): 344–51.

138 **the anterior insular cortex . . . becomes active when people are shown disgusting pictures:** B. Wicker, C. Keysers, J. Plailly, J. P. Royet, V. Gallese, and G. Rizzolatti, "Both of Us Disgusted in My Insula: The Common Neural Basis of Seeing and Feeling Disgust," *Neuron* 40 (2003): 655–64; P. Wright, G. He, N. A. Shapira, W. K. Goodman, and Y. Liu, "Disgust and the Insula: fMRI Responses to Pictures of Mutilation and Contamination," *Neuroreport* 15 (2004): 2347–51.

138 **Some have argued that the food-based theory is incomplete:** For discussion, see Kelly, *Yuck!*

138 **disgust has evolved to warn us away from pathogens and parasites more generally:** V. Curtis, R. Aunger, and T. Rabie, "Evidence That Disgust Evolved to Protect from Risk of Disease," *Proceedings of the Royal Society B* 271 (2004): 131–33. For review, see V. Curtis, M. DeBarra, and R. Aunger, "Disgust as an Adaptive System for Disease Avoidance Behaviour," *Philosophical Transactions of the Royal Society B: Biological Sciences* 366 (2011): 389–401.

139 **"a native touched with his finger some cold preserved meat . . .":** Darwin, *Expression of the Emotions*, 255.

140 **Thalia Wheatley and Jonathan Haidt hypnotized participants to feel a flash of disgust:** T. Wheatley and J. Haidt, "Hypnotic Disgust Makes Moral Judgments More Severe," *Psychological Science* 16 (2005): 780–84.

140 **In other experiments, participants were asked to make judgments . . . after . . . a disgusting experience:** S. Schnall, J. Haidt, G. L. Clore, and A. H. Jordan, "Disgust as Embodied Moral Judgment," *Personality and Social Psychology Bulletin* 34 (2008): 1096–1109.

140 **Even eating a bitter food, which evokes a sensation akin to physical disgust, makes people harsher:** K. Eskine, N. Kacinik, and J. Prinz, "A Bad Taste in the Mouth: Gustatory Disgust Influences Moral Judgment," *Psychological Science* 22 (2011): 295–99.

141 **individuals with high disgust sensitivity have harsher attitudes toward certain other people:** G. Hodson and K. Costello, "Interpersonal Disgust, Ideological Orientations, and Dehumanization as Predictors of Intergroup Attitudes," *Psychological Science* 18 (2007): 691–98.

142 **The mystery for moral psychologists . . . [is] why we should be so concerned with the sex that other people are having:** See also P. DeScioli and R. Kurzban, "Mysteries of Morality," *Cognition* 112 (2009): 281–99.

143 **a recent poll:** L. Saad, "U.S. Acceptance of Gay/Lesbian Relations Is the New Normal," May 14, 2012, www.gallup.com/poll/154634 /Acceptance-Gay-Lesbian-Relations-New-Normal.aspx.

143 **Jefferson proposed the following law:** Robert M. Pallitto, *Torture and State Violence in the United States: A Short Documentary History* (Baltimore: Johns Hopkins University Press, 2011).

144 **"What, you would like to marry your sister?":** Margaret Mead, *Sex and Temperament in Three Primitive Societies* (New York: William Morrow, 1935), 79.

145 **As the psychologist Steven Pinker points out:** Steven Pinker, *How the Mind Works* (New York: Norton, 1997).

145 **Co-residence during childhood is one of the cues:** D. Lieberman, J. Tooby, and L. Cosmides, "Does Morality Have a Biological Basis? An Empirical Test of the Factors Governing Moral Sentiments Relating to Incest," *Proceedings of the Royal Society B: Biological Sciences* 270 (2003): 819–26.

145 **a stepfather who enters the family when the daughter is past a certain age:** Martin Daly and Margo Wilson, *The Truth About Cinderella* (London: Weidenfeld, 1998).

146 **a well-known hypothetical:** J. Haidt, "The Emotional Dog and Its Rational Tail: A Social Intuitionist Approach to Moral Judgment," *Psychological Review* 108 (2001): 814–34. See also Jonathan Haidt, *The Righteous Mind: Why Good People Are Divided by Politics and Religion* (New York: Pantheon, 2012).

147 **"third-degree incest":** W. Saletan, "Incest Is Cancer," *Slate*, December 14, 2010.

148 **viewing disgusting images led to more negative implicit attitudes toward homosexuality:** N. Dasgupta, D. A. DeSteno, L. Williams, and M. Hunsinger, "Fanning the Flames of Prejudice: The Influence of Specific Incidental Emotions on Implicit Prejudice," *Emotion* 9 (2009): 585–91.

148 **exposing people to a bad smell—a fart spray—made them report less warmth toward gay men:** Y. Inbar, D. A. Pizarro, and P. Bloom, "Disgusting Smells Cause Decreased Liking of Gay Men," *Emotion* 12 (2009): 23–27.

148 **greater sensitivity was associated with more conservative attitudes:** Y. Inbar, D. A. Pizarro, and P. Bloom, "Conservatives Are More Easily Disgusted Than Liberals," *Cognition and Emotion* 23 (2009): 714–25.

148 **students' disgust sensitivity scores correlated with their implicit attitudes about homosexuals:** Y. Inbar, D. A. Pizarro, J. Knobe, and P. Bloom, "Disgust Sensitivity Predicts Intuitive Disapproval of Gays," *Emotion* 9 (2009): 435–39.

149 **We are now disgusted by anything that threatens our self-image . . . and reminds us that we are animals:** P. Rozin, J. Haidt, and C. McCauley, "Disgust," in *Handbook of Emotions*, 2nd ed., ed. Michael Lewis and Jeannette M. Haviland (New York: Guilford Press, 2000), 642.

149 **"a stratagem adopted to cordon off the dominant group":** Martha C. Nussbaum, *Hiding from Humanity: Sexual Orientation and Constitutional Law* (Princeton: Princeton University Press, 2004), 16.

150 **Physical cleansing is part of the rituals of many religions:** For a review, see S. W. S. Lee and N. Schwarz, "Wiping the Slate Clean:

Psychological Consequences of Physical Cleansing," *Current Directions in Psychological Science* 20 (2011): 307–11.

150 **We see this connection as well in language:** Bloom, *Descartes' Baby*. For discussion of how children use the language of disgust, see J. Danovitch and P. Bloom, "Children's Extension of Disgust to Physical and Moral Events," *Emotion* 9 (2009): 107–12.

150 **the Macbeth effect:** C.-B. Zhong and K. Liljenquist, "Washing Away Your Sins: Threatened Morality and Physical Cleansing," *Science* 5792 (2006): 1451–52.

151 **a follow-up study:** S. W. S. Lee and N. Schwarz, "Dirty Hands and Dirty Mouths: Embodiment of the Moral-Purity Metaphor Is Specific to the Motor Modality Involved in Moral Transgression," *Psychological Science* 21 (2010): 1423–25.

151 **And this cleaning actually did help to alleviate guilt and shame:** Lee and Schwarz, "Wiping the Slate Clean."

151 **reminders of cleanliness make subjects more disapproving toward acts like watching pornography:** C.-B. Zhong , B. Strejcek, and N. Sivanathan, "A Clean Self Can Render Harsh Moral Judgment," *Journal of Experimental Social Psychology* 46 (2010): 859–62.

152 **In comparison to those who didn't get purity reminders, these subjects rated themselves as more politically conservative:** E. Helzer and D. A. Pizarro, "Dirty Liberals: Reminders of Cleanliness Promote Conservative Political and Moral Attitudes," *Psychological Science* 22 (2011): 517–22.

152 **an ethics of divinity:** R. A. Shweder, N. C. Much, M. Mahapatra, and L. Park, "The 'Big Three' of Morality (Autonomy, Community, Divinity), and the 'Big Three' Explanations of Suffering," in *Morality and Health*, ed. Allan M. Brandt and Paul Rozin (New York: Routledge, 1997), 138.

153 **Elliot Turiel defines morality:** Elliot Turiel, *The Development of Social Knowledge: Morality and Convention* (Cambridge: Cambridge University Press, 1983), 3.

153 **Jonathan Haidt defines it:** Haidt, *Righteous Mind*, 270.

155 **a poetic plea for kindness to the handicapped:** Lev. 19:14 (King James Version).

155 **"the wisdom of repugnance":** Leon Kass, "The Wisdom of Repugnance," *New Republic*, June 2, 1977, 20.

155 **My own view is different:** See also Bloom, *Descartes' Baby*; Nussbaum, *Hiding from Humanity*.

6. FAMILY MATTERS

159 **Family Matters:** A very preliminary version of this chapter was published as P. Bloom, "Family, Community, Trolley Problems, and the Crisis in Moral Psychology," *Yale Review* 99 (2011): 26–43.

159 **mother and son:** Alison Gopnik, *The Philosophical Baby: What Children's Minds Tell Us About Truth, Love, and the Meaning of Life* (New York: Farrar, Straus and Giroux, 2009).

160 **Our best theories of adult moral psychology have little to say:** John Doris and the Moral Psychology Research Group, eds., *The Moral Psychology Handbook* (New York: Oxford University Press, 2010).

161 **Philosophers in this area are split into two main camps:** For an accessible summary, see Michael Sandel, *Justice: What's the Right Thing to Do?* (New York: Farrar, Straus and Giroux, 2009).

162 **"reflective equilibrium":** John Rawls, *A Theory of Justice* (New York: Oxford University Press, 1971).

163 **The philosopher Peter Unger offers a scenario:** Peter K. Unger, *Living High and Letting Die: Our Illusion of Innocence* (New York: Oxford University Press, 1996), cited in Peter Singer, "The Singer Solution to World Poverty," *New York Times Magazine,* September 5, 1999.

165 **a runaway trolley case:** P. Foot, "The Problem of Abortion and the Doctrine of the Double Effect" [1967], in *Virtues and Vices,* ed. Philippa Foot (Oxford: Basil Blackwell, 1978); J. J. Thompson, "Killing, Letting Die, and the Trolley Problem," *Monist* 59 (1976): 204–17.

165 **most people intuitively feel that these cases are different:** For review, see G. Miller, "The Roots of Morality," *Science* 320 (2008): 734–37.

166 **the Doctrine of Double Effect:** A. McIntyre, "Doctrine of Double Effect," in *The Stanford Encyclopedia of Philosophy* (Fall 2011 Edition), ed. E. N. Zalta, http://plato.stanford.edu/archives/fall2011/entries/double-effect.

167 **the work of the psychologist Lewis Petrinovich and his colleagues:** P. O'Neill and L. Petrinovich, "A Preliminary Cross-Cultural Study of Moral Intuitions," *Evolution and Human Behavior* 19, no. 6 (1998): 349–67.

167 **John Mikhail did a series of studies:** The dissertation was published as John Mikhail, *Elements of Moral Cognition: Rawls' Linguistic Analogy and the Cognitive Science of Moral and Legal Judgment* (Cambridge: Cambridge University Press, 2010).

167 **a paper in *Science* that used brain-imaging techniques:** J. D. Greene, R. B. Sommerville, L. E. Nystrom, J. M. Darley, and J. D. Cohen, "An fMRI Investigation of Emotional Engagement in Moral Judgment," *Science* 293 (2001): 2105–8.

167 **a wave of trolley-problem research:** For review, see G. Miller, "The Roots of Morality," *Science* 320 (2008): 734–37.

167 **all neurologically normal people . . . between the switch case and the bridge case:** F. Cushman, L. Young, and M. Hauser, "The Role of Conscious Reasoning and Intuition in Moral Judgments: Testing Three Principles of Harm," *Psychological Science* 17 (2006): 1082–89; Mikhail, *Elements of Moral Cognition*.

167 **Even three-year-olds . . . will tend to say that throwing the switch is the right thing to do:** S. Pellizzoni, M. Siegal, and L. Surian, "The Contact Principle and Utilitarian Moral Judgments in Young Children," *Developmental Science* 13 (2010): 265–70.

168 **a universal moral faculty analogous to the universal grammar:** Mikhail, *Elements of Moral Cognition*; Marc Hauser, *Moral Minds: How Nature Designed Our Universal Sense of Right and Wrong* (New York: HarperCollins, 2006).

168 **language and morality differ quite sharply:** P. Bloom and I. Jarudi, "The Chomsky of Morality?," review of *Moral Minds: How Nature Designed Our Universal Sense of Right and Wrong*, by Marc Hauser, *Nature* 443 (2006): 909–10.

168 **Greene and his colleagues:** J. D. Greene, F. A. Cushman, L. E. Stewart, K. Lowenberg, L. E. Nystrom, and J. D. Cohen, "Pushing Moral Buttons: The Interaction Between Personal Force and Intention in Moral Judgment," *Cognition* 111 (2009): 364–71.

169 **One clever study looked at effects of cues as to the race of the characters:** E. L. Uhlmann, D. A. Pizarro, D. Tannenbaum, and

P. H. Ditto, "The Motivated Use of Moral Principles," *Judgment and Decision Making* 4 (2009): 476–91.

169 **In another study, people were given trolley problems after seeing a humorous clip:** P. Valdesolo and D. DeSteno, "Manipulations of Emotional Context Shape Moral Judgment," *Psychological Science* 17 (2006): 476–77.

169 **the dense trolley literature "makes the Talmud look like Cliff Notes":** Kwame Anthony Appiah, *Experiments in Ethics* (Cambridge, MA: Harvard University Press, 2008), 91.

170 **fruit flies of the moral mind:** J. D. Greene, "Fruit Flies of the Moral Mind," in *What's Next: Dispatches from the Future of Science,* ed. Max Brockman (New York: Vintage, 2009).

170 **Adam Smith makes this point well:** Adam Smith, *The Theory of Moral Sentiments* (1759; repr., Lawrence, KS: Digireads.com, 2011), 61.

172 **The natural history of morality began with small groups of people in families and tribes:** W. D. Hamilton, "The Genetical Evolution of Social Behavior, Parts 1 and 2," *Journal of Theoretical Biology* 7 (1964): 1–52; R. L. Trivers, "The Evolution of Reciprocal Altruism," *Quarterly Review of Biology* 46 (1971): 35–57; R. L. Trivers, "Parental Investment and Sexual Selection," In *Sexual Selection and the Descent of Man,* ed. B. Campbell (Chicago: Aldine, 1972).

172 **Others argue for a two-stage account:** Peter J. Richerson and Robert Boyd, *Not by Genes Alone: How Culture Transformed Human Evolution* (Chicago: University of Chicago Press, 2005).

173 **debates over whether group selection . . . plays a role in the origin of morality:** For a recent defense, see E. O. Wilson, *The Social Conquest of Earth* (New York: Liveright, 2012).

173 **Darwin's own speculation about the origin of our moral capacities:** Charles Darwin, *The Descent of Man* (1871; repr., London: Penguin, 2004), 121 (emphasis added).

174 **altruism as emerging from the care we give to our helpless offspring:** C. Daniel Batson, *Altruism in Humans* (New York: Oxford University Press, 2011); Paul Zak, *The Moral Molecule: The Source of Love and Prosperity* (New York: Dutton, 2012); Patricia Churchland, *Braintrust: What Neuroscience Tells Us About Morality* (Princeton: Princeton University Press, 2011).

174 **people dosed with the hormone become more trusting and more generous:** M. Kosfeld, M. Heinrichs, P. J. Zak, U. Fischbacher, and E. Fehr, "Oxytocin Increases Trust in Humans," *Nature* 435 (2005): 673–76; T. Baumgartner, M. Heinrichs, A. Vonlanthen, U. Fischbacher, and E. Fehr, "Oxytocin Shapes the Neural Circuitry of Trust and Trust Adaptation in Humans," *Neuron* 58 (2008): 639–50; P. J. Zak, A. A. Stanton, S. Ahmadi, and S. Brosnan, "Oxytocin Increases Generosity in Humans," *PLoS ONE* 2 (2007): e1128.

174 **more empathetic and less susceptible to stress:** S. M. Rodrigues, L. R. Saslow, N. Garcia, O. P. John, and D. Keltner, "Oxytocin Receptor Genetic Variation Relates to Empathy and Stress Reactivity in Humans," *Proceedings of the National Academy of Sciences* 106 (2009): 21437–41.

174 **the response that oxytocin generates is itself morally complex:** C. K. W. De Dreu, L. L. Greer, G. A. Van Kleef, S. Shalvi, and M. J. J. Handgraaf, "Oxytocin Promotes Human Ethnocentrism," *Proceedings of the National Academy of Sciences USA* 108 (2011): 1262–66.

175 **a trinity of moral foundations:** R. A. Shweder, N. C. Much, M. Mahapatra, and L. Park, "The 'Big Three' of Morality (Autonomy, Community, Divinity), and the 'Big Three' Explanations of Suffering," in *Morality and Health,* ed. Allan M. Brandt and Paul Rozin (New York: Routledge, 1997), 119–69.

175 **a sextuplet of distinct moral foundations:** This was originally developed in collaboration with Craig Joseph, in J. Haidt and C. Joseph, "Intuitive Ethics: How Innately Prepared Intuitions Generate Culturally Variable Virtues," *Daedalus* 133 (Fall 2004): 55–66. For a recent summary, see Jonathan Haidt, *The Righteous Mind: Why Good People Are Divided by Politics and Religion* (New York: Pantheon, 2012).

177 **betrayal is a sin—and a very serious one:** Haidt, *Righteous Mind.*

177 **In the Gospels, Christ is explicit that he is there to replace the family:** Matt. 10:34–37 (King James Version).

177 **One sees the same preference in the Hebrew Bible:** Deut. 13:6, 9, 10 (King James Version).

178 **no dedicated brain system for reasoning about zero:** K. Wynn,

"Infants Possess a System of Numerical Knowledge," *Current Directions in Psychological Science* 4 (1995): 172–77.

179 **we really are more likely to help others when we see their faces and hear their names:** P. Slovic, "'If I Look at the Mass I Will Never Act': Psychic Numbing and Genocide," *Judgment and Decision Making* 2 (2007): 79–95. For a review, see Dan Ariely, *The Upside of Irrationality: The Unexpected Benefits of Defying Logic at Work and at Home* (New York: Harper, 2010).

180 **Rachel Aviv reports on the lives of homeless gay teenagers:** Rachel Aviv, "Netherland," *New Yorker,* December 10, 2012, 64.

180 **William Godwin . . . once asked his readers:** Peter Singer, *The Expanding Circle: Ethics and Sociobiology* (New York: Farrar, Straus and Giroux, 1981).

180 **As Adam Smith observed:** Adam Smith, *The Theory of Moral Sentiments* (1759; repr., Lawrence, KS: Digireads.com), 60.

181 **we might treat the dilemma as little more than a math problem:** R. A. Shweder, "A Great Moral Legend from Orissa," *Orissa Society of Americas Souvenir,* 40th Annual Convention of the Orissa Society of the Americas, July 2009.

181 **a trolley scenario with teacups:** S. Nichols and R. Mallon, "Moral Rules and Moral Dilemmas," *Cognition* 100 (2006): 530–42.

182 **One study asked one group of subjects to donate money.:** T. Kogut and I. Ritov, "The 'Identified Victim' Effect: An Identified Group, or Just a Single Individual?," *Journal of Behavioral Decision Making* 18 (2005): 157–67; Slovic, "If I Look."

183 **Individuals with damage to the ventromedial prefrontal cortex . . . treat the bridge case just like the switch case:** M. Koenigs, L. Young, R. Adolphs, D. Tranel, F. Cushman, M. Hauser, and A. Damasio, "Damage to the Prefrontal Cortex Increases Utilitarian Moral Judgments," *Nature* 446 (2007): 908–11.

183 **tweaking the consequentialists:** D. Bartels and D. A. Pizarro, "The Mismeasure of Morals: Antisocial Personality Traits Predict Utilitarian Responses to Moral Dilemmas," *Cognition* 121 (2011): 154–61.

184 **I agree with Joshua Greene:** J. D. Greene, R. B. Sommerville, L. E. Nystrom, J. M. Darley, and J. D. Cohen, "An fMRI Investigation of Emotional Engagement in Moral Judgment," *Science* 293 (2001): 2105–8.

184   **we are often nice to strangers, particularly those whom we can visualize as distinct individuals:** Kogut and Ritov, " 'Identified Victim' Effect."

7. HOW TO BE GOOD

187   **charitable giving is the perfect way to advertise one's wealth and status:** Thorstein Veblen, *The Theory of the Leisure Class: An Economic Study of Institutions* (New York: Random House, 1899).

187   **a good way to attract sexual and romantic partners:** G. F. Miller, "Sexual Selection for Moral Virtues," *Quarterly Review of Biology* 82 (2007): 97–125.

188   **he scattered stamped, addressed letters all over New Haven:** S. Milgram, L. Mann, and S. Harter, "The Lost-Letter Technique: A Tool for Social Research," *Public Opinion Quarterly* 29 (1965): 437–38.

188   **Our goodness is evident in other ways as well:** For an extended review, see Steven Pinker, *The Better Angels of Our Nature: Why Violence Has Declined* (New York: Viking, 2011).

188   **Thomas Jefferson's proposal:** Robert M. Pallitto, *Torture and State Violence in the United States: A Short Documentary History* (Baltimore: Johns Hopkins University Press, 2011).

188   **Some see our goodness as evidence for divine intervention:** Francis Collins, *The Language of God: A Scientist Presents Evidence for Belief* (New York: Free Press, 2006); Dinesh D'Souza, *What's So Great About Christianity* (New York: Regnery, 2007), 237. The Wallace quote comes from his review of Charles Lyell's *Principles of Geology* and is cited in Robert J. Richards, *Darwin and the Emergence of Evolutionary Theories of Mind and Behavior* (Chicago: University of Chicago Press, 1989).

191   **this kindness turned into reflex:** Thanks to David Rand for discussion on this point. For discussion of how moral judgment can turn into moral reflex, see also D. A. Pizarro and P. Bloom, "The Intelligence of Moral Intuitions: Comment on Haidt," *Psychological Review* 110 (2001): 197–198.

192   **Herodotus's story:** Herodotus, *The Histories,* rev. ed., trans. Aubrey de Selincourt (New York: Penguin, 2003), 3:38.

193   **how children . . . behave after observing the charitable acts of**

strangers: For a review, see Natalie Henrich and Joseph Henrich, *Why Humans Cooperate: A Cultural and Evolutionary Explanation* (New York: Oxford University Press, 2007).

193 **a recent set of experiments by the psychologist Peter Blake:** P. R. Blake, T. C. Callaghan, J. Corbit, and F. Warneken, "Altruism, Fairness and Social Learning: A Cross-Cultural Approach to Imitative Altruism," paper presented at the Central European University Conference on Cognitive Development, Budapest, Hungary, January 2012.

194 **"the moral circle":** Peter Singer, *The Expanding Circle: Ethics and Sociobiology* (New York: Farrar, Straus and Giroux, 1981); W. E. H. Lecky, *History of European Morals from Augustus to Charlemagne,* vol. 1 (New York: George Braziller, 1955), 103.

195 **our sympathies "became more tender and widely diffused . . .":** Charles Darwin, *The Descent of Man* (1871; repr., London: Penguin, 2004), 149.

195 **the power of personal contact:** Gordon W. Allport, *The Nature of Prejudice* (Reading, MA: Addison-Wesley, 1954). For a review, see T. E. Pettigrew, "Intergroup Contact Theory," *Annual Review of Psychology* 49 (1998): 65–85.

196 **exposure to stories:** M. Nussbaum, "Exactly and Responsibly: A Defense of Ethical Criticism," *Philosophy and Literature* 22 (1998): 354.

197 **the plight of prisoners in solitary confinement:** A. Gawande, "Hellhole," *New Yorker,* March 30, 2009, 36–45.

197 **"Exposure to worlds that can be seen only through the eyes of a foreigner . . .":** Pinker, *Better Angels,* 175.

197 **"treating fictions as moral pep-pills . . .":** H. Vendler, "The Booby Trap," *New Republic,* October 7, 1996, 34, 37.

197 **many of the great stories express terrible values:** R. Posner, "Against Ethical Criticism," *Philosophy and Literature* 21 (1997): 5.

197 **Joseph Goebbels was said to love Greek tragedy:** M. Beard, "Do the Classics Have a Future?," *New York Review of Books,* January 12, 2012.

197 **people who read more fiction have somewhat higher social skills:** R. A. Mar, K. Oatley, J. Hirsh, J. de la Paz, and J. B. Peterson, "Bookworms Versus Nerds: Exposure to Fiction versus Non-fiction, Divergent Associations with Social Ability, and the

Simulation of Fictional Social Worlds," *Journal of Research in Personality* 40 (2006): 694–712.

198 **adults who suffer from mild forms of autism, and hence who are socially impaired, are less interested in fiction:** J. L. Barnes, "Fiction, Imagination, and Social Cognition: Insights from Autism," *Poetics* 40 (2012): 299–316.

198 **the right fiction at the right time can have an effect:** See also Paul Bloom, *Descartes' Baby: How the Science of Child Development Explains What Makes Us Human* (New York: Basic Books, 2004); Pinker, *Better Angels.*

199 **when rural Indian villages start to get cable television . . . there is a decrease in the preference for sons over daughters:** R. Jensen and E. Oster, "The Power of TV: Cable Television and Women's Status in India," *Quarterly Journal of Economics* 124 (August 2009): 1057–94.

200 **they think you cannot be good without believing in God:** P. Bloom, "Religion, Morality, Evolution," *Annual Review of Psychology* 63 (2012): 179–99.

200 **They are seen as self-interested and immoral . . . elitists:** P. Edgell, J. Gerteis, and D. Hartmann, "Atheists as 'Other': Moral Boundaries and Cultural Membership in American Society," *American Sociological Review* 71 (2006): 211–34.

200 **"Challenging the limited altruism . . . a condition of one's recognition of Him":** J. Waldron, "Secularism and the Limits of Community," NYU School Law, Public Law Research Paper No. 10-88, http://papers.ssrn.com/sol3/papers.cfm?abstract_id=1722780, 10. For similar arguments, see D'Souza, *What's So Great About Christianity.*

201 **religion is "violent, irrational, intolerant . . .":** Christopher Hitchens, *God Is Not Great: How Religion Poisons Everything* (New York: Twelve Books, 2007), 56.

201 **some of the most horrific atrocities in history have been motivated by religious faith:** Matthew White, *The Great Big Book of Horrible Things: The Definitive Chronicle of History's 100 Worst Atrocities* (New York: Norton, 2011).

201 **how "little children" teased the prophet Elisha about his baldness:** Kings 2:23–25 (King James Version).

202 **Are the religious individuals in a society more moral than the secular ones?:** For a review, see P. Bloom, "Religion, Morality, Evolution," *Annual Review of Psychology* 63 (2012): 179–99.

203 **"Once we know how observant a person is . . . not religious believing":** Robert D. Putnam and David E. Campbell, *American Grace: How Religion Divides and Unites Us* (New York: Simon & Schuster, 2010), 467, 473.

204 **a strong relationship between religiosity and support for suicide bombing:** J. Ginges, I. Hansen, and A. Norenzayan, "Religion and Support for Suicide Attacks," *Psychological Science* 20 (2009): 224–30.

204 **someone who believes that God wants them to kill infidels is going to be a lot more enthusiastic about killing infidels:** Richard Dawkins, *The God Delusion* (New York: Bantam, 2006), 348.

204 **religious belief does not cause moral belief—it reflects it:** Robert Wright, *Evolution of God* (New York: Little, Brown, 2009), 410.

206 **a bigger moral circle isn't always a better one:** For an earlier exploration of some of the ideas here, see Bloom, *Descartes' Baby*.

206 **lowering a cat onto a fire was considered an acceptable form of public entertainment:** Norman Davies, cited in Pinker, *Better Angels*, 145.

207 **David Brooks provides an articulate defense of this trend:** David Brooks, *The Social Animal: The Hidden Sources of Love, Character, and Achievement* (New York: Random House, 2011), x, xiii.

207 **a classic 2001 paper:** J. Haidt, "The Emotional Dog and Its Rational Tail: A Social Intuitionist Approach to Moral Judgment," *Psychological Review* 108 (2001): 814–34, quotes from 814 and 830.

208 **one whose rallying cry comes from David Hume:** David Hume, *A Treatise of Human Nature* (New York: Oxford University Press, 1978), 415.

208 **Washing our hands (a reminder of purity) makes us more morally disapproving . . . fart spray:** S. Schnall, J. Haidt, G. L. Clore, and A. H. Jordan, "Disgust as Embodied Moral Judgment," *Personality and Social Psychology Bulletin* 34 (2008): 1096–1109; E. Helzer and D. A. Pizarro, "Dirty Liberals: Reminders of Cleanliness Promote Conservative Political and Moral Attitudes," *Psychological Science* 22 (2011): 517–22.

208 **We are more willing to help others if there is the smell of fresh bread in the air or if we have just found a small sum of money:** R. A. Baron and J. Thomley, "A Whiff of Reality: Positive Affect as a Potential Mediator of the Effects of Pleasant Fragrances on Task Performance and Helping," *Environment and Behavior* 26 (1994): 766–84; A. M. Isen and P. F. Levin, "The Effect of Feeling Good on Helping: Cookies and Kindness," *Journal of Personality and Social Psychology* 21 (1972): 384–88.

209 **the struggles faced by black and white children in the American South during the civil rights movement:** Robert Coles, *The Moral Life of Children: How Children Struggle with Questions of Moral Choice in the United States and Elsewhere* (Boston: Houghton Mifflin, 1986).

209 **young women deciding whether to get an abortion:** Carol Gilligan, *In a Different Voice: Psychological Theory and Women's Development* (Cambridge, MA: Harvard University Press, 1982).

209 **individuals who are vegetarians for moral reasons have little problem articulating the rationale for their decision:** Paul R. Amato and Sonia A. Partridge, *The New Vegetarians: Promoting Health and Protecting Life* (New York: Plenum Press, 1989), quotes from 36–37.

209 **six- to ten-year-olds who became vegetarians:** K. M. Hussar and P. L. Harris, "Children Who Choose Not to Eat Meat: A Study of Early Moral Decision-Making," *Social Development* 19 (2010): 627–41.

211 **explicit statements of impartiality:** Peter Singer, *The Expanding Circle: Ethics and Sociobiology* (New York: Farrar, Straus and Giroux, 1981).

213 **"As soon as you try . . . you're sucked into a commitment to the avoidance of harm as a general goal":** Pinker, *Better Angels,* 648.

214 **Empathy and impartiality are often mutually reinforcing:** D. A. Pizarro and P. Bloom, "The Intelligence of Moral Intuitions: Comment on Haidt," *Psychological Review* 110 (2001): 197–98; Martin L. Hoffman, *Empathy and Moral Development: Implications for Caring and Justice* (New York: Cambridge University Press, 2000).

214 **parental behaviors that psychologist Martin Hoffman calls *inductions:*** Hoffman, *Empathy and Moral Development.*

215 **they captured this process of moral persuasion:** Melanie Killen and Adam Rutland, *Children and Social Exclusion: Morality, Prejudice, and Group Identity* (New York: Wiley/Blackwell, 2011), 20–21.

217 **"Look, I'm no good at being noble . . .":** The example of *Casablanca* is noted by Singer as well, in *Expanding Circle*, 340.

INDEX

Abortion, 148, 170, 209
Aboud, Frances, 112
Allport, Gordon, 121
Altruism, 77–79
    biological evolution of, 18,
        189–90
    empathy and, 43, 133
    as evidence of a moral code, 1
    influence of parental care in
        infancy and, 174
    punishment and, 89–91
    self-interest and, 187–88
    sharing and, 52–54;
    toward strangers, 178, 189–90
    Western religion and, 200–201
Altruistic punishment, 89–91
Anger, 31, 72, 99, 154
Angier, Natalie, 68
Animality, 149
Antisocial punishment, 91
Apologies: purpose of, 83–84
Appiah, Kwame Anthony, 129, 169

Aquinas, Thomas, 166
Ardrey, Robert, 82
Ariely, Daniel, 72
Aristotle, 192
Atheism, 200, 202, 203
Augustine of Hippo, Saint, 139
Autonomy, ethics of, 175
Aviv, Rachel, 180

Babies
    ability to distinguish
        languages, 110
    difficulties in studying, 18–20
    disgust in, 135
    empathy and compassion in,
        47–49
    evaluation of fair/unfair
        distributions by, 62–63
    evaluation of good/bad
        characters by, 27–30
    evaluation of just/unjust
        punishers by, 98–99

Babies *(continued):*
  everyday experience of, 21
  looking-time methods and
    study of, 20–22, 26, 27, 105
  moral limitations of, 5–6, 8, 54,
    56, 211, 218
  morality of, 7–8, 27–30, 30–31,
    36–37, 56, 62–63, 96–100
  numerical understanding,
    21–23, 178
  physical understanding, 22
  preference for familiar people,
    104–6
  preference for individuals of
    the same race, 105–6
  reaching methods and study of,
    27, 28
  reward and punishment of,
    96–97
  social understanding of, 23–26
*Baby Laughing Hysterically at
  Ripping Paper* (video), 40
Baillargeon, Renee, 24, 63
Bale, Mary, 3, 86
Barnes, Jennifer, 198
Barragan, Rodolfo Cortez, 54
Batson, C. Daniel, 46–47
Bentham, Jeremy, 163, 181, 183,
  212
Bering, Jesse, 95
Berreby, David, 119, 120, 129
Bestiality, 12, 153, 155
Bigler, Rebecca, 117
Bigotry, 6, 100, 107, 201
  See also Racism
"Biographical Sketch of an
  Infant, A" (Darwin), 36–37
Birth of a Nation (movie), 200

Blake, Peter, 80, 193
Bloch, Maurice, 15
Boehm, Christopher, 67–69
Brain-imaging methods, 19–20,
  167
Brooks, David, 207–8
Brownell, Celia, 53
Buhler, Charlotte, 55
Bundy, Ted, 35

Campbell, David, 203
Cannibalism, 12, 155
Casablanca (movie), 217
Cash, David, Jr., 11, 86
Casino Royale (movie), 40
Categorical imperative, 34
Charitable giving, 187, 203
Children
  bias toward equal distributions
    in, 60–64
  disgust in, 135–37
  empathy and compassion in,
    50–54
  generosity of, 77–82, 193–94
  helping by, 13, 50–52
  moral limitations of, 54, 56,
    77–82, 99–100, 211, 218
  moral reasoning by, 214–17
  moral self-evaluation by, 55–56
  preference for those in their
    social group, 111–19
  preference for those of the same
    race, 112–14, 116, 124
  preference for those who speak
    the same language, 111–12,
    114
  reaction to strangers, 53–54
  retribution by, 94–96

sharing by, 52–54
  spiteful natures of, 80–83
  understanding of appropriate
    conditions for punishment,
    93
Chimpanzees of Gombe, The
  (Goodall), 103
Chomsky, Noam, 168
Cicero, Marcus Tullius, 129
Civil rights movement, 201, 209
Civilization and Its Discontents
  (Freud), 135
Clark, Kenneth, 112
Clark, Mamie, 112
Cleanliness
  and morality, 150–52
Coalitions, 106–17, 127
Coles, Robert, 209
Collateral damage, 166
Collins, Francis, 1–3, 188–90
Community, ethics of, 175
Compassion, 5, 7, 31, 42, 48,
    56–57, 133, 140, 153, 157, 168,
    218
  in babies and toddlers, 48–54
  distinguished from empathy,
    39–40, 43–46, 178
  gender and, 49
  helping and, 50–52
  morality and, 46–47
  sharing and, 52
Confucius, 212
Conscience, 4, 37
Consequentialism, 161–62, 165,
    170–71, 181, 183
Contact hypothesis, 114, 195–96
Cosby Show, The (television
  show), 199

Cosmides, Leda, 106–9
Crying, 47–48
Curtis, Valerie, 138

Damon, William, 34–35, 60
Dana, Jason, 76
Dante Aligheri, 177
Darius, King of Persia, 14, 192
Darwin, Charles, 16–18, 36–37,
    56, 137–39, 173, 195, 205
Darwin, William, 36–37, 47,
    55
Dasgupta, Nilanjana, 148
Dawkins, Richard, 17, 204
De Waal, Frans, 49, 65
Dehumanization, 131–33
Deontology, 161–63
Descent of Man, The (Darwin),
  195
Diamond, Jared, 102–3
Dickens, Charles, 197–98
Dickinson, Emily, 101
Dictator Game, 73–78
Disgust, 6, 72, 103, 131–57, 168,
    178, 200, 208
  animality and, 149
  babies and, 135
  children and, 135–37
  evolution of, 137–39, 141–45,
    148–49, 153–56
  facial expression of, 133, 137
  morality and, 131–35, 139–41,
    147–50, 153–57
  theories of, 135–39
Divinity, ethics of, 175
Doctrine of Double Effect (DDE),
  166, 169
D'Souza, Dinesh, 189–90

Dunfield, Kristen, 52
Dweck, Carol, 54

Economics games, 70–82, 86–89, 174
Egalitarianism, 64–69, 74, 77
Einstein, Albert, 42
Embarrassment, 56
    See also Shame
Empathy, 1, 5, 92, 99, 133, 140, 214, 218
    in babies, 47–49
    distinguished from compassion, 39–40, 43–46, 178
    gender and, 49
    in nonhuman animals, 48
    mirror neurons and, 41–43
    reason and, 213–15
Enlightenment, 4
Equality, 60–65, 67, 68, 78
Ethnic cleansing, 152
    See also Genocide
Euthanasia, 12
Evolution of God, The (Wright), 204–5
Expanding Circle, The (Singer), 194

Fairness, sense of, 5, 59–64, 68, 70, 75, 78–82, 99, 153, 217, 218
Family, 6, 16–17, 108, 127, 170, 171, 173–74, 176, 177, 179–81, 185
Fear, 38–39, 56
Fehr, Ernst, 77–78, 89
Fernyhough, Charles, 19
Fictive kin, 179–80
Flavell, John, 19

Foot, Philippa, 170
Free riders, 88–91
Freud, Sigmund, 135

Gächter, Simon, 89
Gay marriage, 148
Gay men. *See* Homosexuality
Generosity, 64, 75, 76–78
Genocide, 6, 132, 179, 201
Geraci, Alessandra, 62
German, Tamsin, 93
Gil-White, Francisco, 127
Gilligan, Carol, 209
Gilmore, Gary, 35
Ginges, Jeremy, 204
Glover, Jonathan, 45
God, 2, 188–89, 200, 203, 204
Godwin, William, 180
Golden Rule, 211–12
Good Samaritan, 101–2, 185
Goodall, Jane, 103
Gopnik, Alison, 20–21, 160
Greene, Joshua, 167–70, 184
Group selection, 18, 90, 173
Guala, Francesco, 91
Guilt, 31, 39, 54–56, 154
    See also Shame

Habituation (looking-time method), 20
Haidt, Jonathan, 140, 146, 153, 175, 207–8
Haldane, J. B. S., 16
Hamlin, Kiley, 27, 30, 97
Harris, Paul, 209–10
Hebrew Bible, 154–55, 177
Helping behavior, 13, 25–31, 50–52, 54, 179

Helzer, Erik, 151
Herodotus, 14, 15, 192–93, 197
Hierarchy in the Forest (Boehm), 67
Hieronymi, Pamela, 83
"High altruism," 189
  See also Altruism
Hillel the Elder, Rabbi, 212
Histories (Herodotus), 14
Hitchens, Christopher, 201
Hobbes, Thomas, 5
Hoffman, Martin, 49, 214
Holocaust, 2, 129
  See also Genocide
Homosexuality, 12, 142–44, 148, 153–55, 180
Honor, culture of, 84, 94
Hotel Rwanda (movie), 198
Human flesh search engines *(renrou sousuo yinqing)*, 85–86, 96
Human waste, 124, 131, 133, 134, 136, 137, 139, 140, 149
Hume, David, 161, 208, 213
Hunter-gatherer societies, 67–70
Hussar, Karen, 209–10

Impartial spectator, 34, 212
Impartiality, 211–14, 216, 217
Implicit Association Test (IAT), 125
Inbar, Yoel, 148
Incest, 12, 13, 144–47, 153, 155
Inductions (parental behaviors), 214
Ingram, Gordon, 95

Jarudi, Izzat, 168
Jefferson, Thomas, ix, 4, 5, 143, 188
Jensen, Robert, 199
Jews, 129, 131–32, 156, 179
Johnson, Samuel, 56
Judaism. *See* Religion
Justice, sense of, 5, 96–99, 218

Kahneman, Daniel, 73
Kant, Immanuel, 34, 161, 163, 212
Kass, Leon, 155
Killen, Melanie, 113, 214–15
Kindness, 16–17, 75, 78, 176, 187–88
Kinship bonds. *See* Family
Kinzler, Katherine, 111
Knobe, Joshua, 148
Kohlberg, Lawrence, 99–100
Kuhlmeier, Valerie, 25, 29, 52
Kurzban, Robert, 106–9

Language, 192
  acquisition of, 41
  coalition and, 109–110
  as compared to moral knowledge, 168
  preferences of children and, 110–11, 114, 123
Leach, Penelope, 136
Lecky, William, 194–95, 205
Lee, Spike, 151
Lesbians. *See* Homosexuality
Levi, Primo, 131
Lewis, C. S., 189
Lie to Me (television show), 125
Lifeboat problems, 167
Liljenquist, Katie, 150

List, John, 76
LoBue, Vanessa, 79
Looking-time method, 20–22, 26, 27, 105
Louis C. K., 19, 59, 60
Loyalty, 177

Macbeth effect, 150, 151
Mafia, 84
Mahajan, Neha, 97
Marsh, Abigail, 38–39
Martin, Alia, 51–52
Martin, Thomas, 8
McAuliffe, Katherine, 80
McCrink, Koleen, 64
McGlothlin, Heidi, 113
Mead, Margaret, 103, 144
Memory-confusion paradigm, 108–9
Mencius, 44
Mere exposure effect, 108
Mikhail, John, 10, 167
Milgram, Stanley, 187–88
Mill, John Stuart, 181, 183
Miller, William Ian, 135
Mimicry, 47, 194
Minimal-group studies, 117–18, 127
Mirror neurons, 41–43
Moral circle, 194–96, 199–200, 205–6
Moral Psychology Handbook, 160
Moral sense, 31, 56
Morality
    analogy with language and, 168
    analogy with numbers and, 178
    babies and, 7–8, 27–31, 36–37, 56–57, 62–63, 96–100
    brain regions associated with, 21, 125, 183
    children and, 54–56, 60–64, 77–82, 99–100, 211, 214–18
    cultural variation in, 13–15, 91, 188, 194
    custom and, 191–94
    developmental differences in, 99–100, 211
    different ways to explore, 3–4
    disgust and, 133, 139–41, 147–50, 153–57
    distinguished from compassion, 46–47
    evolution of, 2, 4, 5, 8, 15–18, 38, 48, 153–56, 171–73, 174–79, 184, 188–90, 218
    fairness and, 59–60, 211–14
    family and, 160–61, 176–77, 179–81
    oxytocin and, 174–75
    parochial biases and, 5–6, 101–4, 128–29
    punishment and, 82, 87–90
    purity and, 150–52
    religion and, 200–205
    revenge and, 82–85
    scope of, 8–13, 18, 153–57
    self-evaluation and, 54–56
    sex and, 3, 12, 141–50, 153–56
    stories and, 196–200
    strangers and, 5–6, 53–54, 101–4, 177–79, 181–85
    universals of, 15–16
Mortality, relation to disgust of, 149, 150
Mother-child relationship, 159–160, 173–175

Natural selection, 15–18, 38, 90, 107, 137, 172, 173, 176, 189, 190
See also Morality: evolution of
Nazis, 129, 131–32, 156, 179, 197, 198
Negativity bias, 29
Nicholls, Shaun, 73
Nussbaum, Martha, 149–50, 196, 198

Oliver Twist (Dickens), 198
Olson, Kristina, 51–52, 61, 62
On the Nature of Prejudice (Allport), 121
Onishi, Kristine, 24
Orwell, George, 132–33
Oster, Emily, 199
Oxytocin, 174

Parochialism, 6, 100–130, 176–181
Pedophilia, 12, 154
Petrinovich, Lewis, 167
Philosophical Baby, The (Gopnik), 160
Pietraszewski, David, 93
Pinker, Steven, 45, 84, 145, 197, 213
Pizarro, David, 100, 148, 151
Popular culture, effect on moral beliefs of, 196–200
Posner, Richard, 197–98
Postrel, Virginia, 1
Pratto, Felicia, 109
Premack, Ann, 25
Premack, David, 25, 63
Pride, 31, 55, 56

Primates, 41, 42, 47, 49, 53, 103
Princess Bride, The (movie), 83
Prinz, Jesse, 82
Prosocial Game, 78
Psychopathy, 4, 33–35, 38–40, 183
Public Goods Game, 86–89
Punishment, 3, 15, 37–38, 82–85, 88–99, 153, 154, 173, 188
Purity, 149–152, 208
Putnam, Robert, 203

Racism, 14, 196
coalitional theory of, 106–9
developmental origins of, 105–9, 112–16, 119, 124
Rape, 143, 154, 155, 188, 201
Rawls, John, 34, 162, 212
Reason
empathy and, 213–15
importance to morality, 100, 129–30, 157, 206–18
Reflective equilibrium, 162
Religion, 150, 152–53, 200–205, 211
Revenge, 82–85, 91–93, 173
Robbers Cave experiment, 115–17
Robin Hood theory, 65, 68, 71, 73, 74
Rozin, Paul, 133–35, 138, 141, 148, 150
Rusesabagina, Paul, 217
Rutland, Adam, 214–15
Rwanda, 129, 179, 217

Sadism, 46
Santos, Laurie, 64

Satel, Sally, 1
Schadenfreude, 46
Schindler, Oskar, 217
Schmidt, Marco, 63
Schwarz, Norbert, 151
Self-evaluation, moral, 55
Serial killers, 35, 38
Sex. *See* Morality: sex and
Shakespeare, William, 8, 85, 151, 197
Shame, 39, 56, 154, 168
   See also Guilt
Sharing, 52–54, 179
Shaw, Alex, 61–62
Sherif, Muzafer, 115–16
Sheskin, Mark, 81
Shibboleth, 110
Shweder, Richard, 14–15, 152, 175, 181
Sidanius, Jim, 109
Sidgwick, Henry, 212
Singer, Peter, 44, 164, 170–71, 194, 211–13, 216
Slavery, 190, 194, 198, 201, 207
Sloane, Stephanie, 63
Smith, Adam, 4–5, 13, 17, 31, 34, 40, 41, 57, 83, 92, 94, 161, 170, 180–81, 212
Social Animal, The (Brooks), 207
Social groups, evolution of, 66–67, 88–91, 107–8
Social understanding, 24–30
Solzhenitsyn, Aleksandr, 65–66, 198
Sommerville, Jessica, 63
Soothing, 49, 51, 179
Spelke, Elizabeth, 61

Spite, 80–81
Stalin, Joseph, 65–66, 70
Social status, 65, 67–68, 70, 83–84, 141
Stepparents, 145–46
Stereotypes, 121–23, 126
   accuracy of, 119–20, 122, 126–27
   learning of, 121–22,
   origins of, 120
   problems with, 122–23, 129
   unconscious, 125–26
Stowe, Harriet Beecher, 198
Strangers, 6, 53, 54, 101–5, 111, 171, 172, 177–79, 181–85, 190
Strohmeyer, Jeremy, 11
Sucking behavior, use in infant research of, 104
Suicide bombing, 204
Surian, Luca, 62

Tajfel, Henri, 115, 117
Tattling, 95–96
Theology, 2, 3, 188–91
Theory of Moral Sentiments, The (Smith), 4–5, 57
Tipping, 191
Toilet training, 136–37
Tomasello, Michael, 13
Tooby, John, 106–9
Torture, 161–62
Tradition, morality and, 191–94
Trainspotting (movie), 140
Trolley problem, 165–70, 175, 181–85
   bridge version, 165–69, 183–84

switch version, 165–69, 181–83, 185
Turiel, Elliot, 153

Ultimatum Game, 70–74
Uncle Tom's Cabin (Stowe), 198, 200
Unconscious cueing, 27
Unconscious racial bias, 125
Unger, Peter, 163–64
Updike, John, 40
Us and Them (Berreby), 119, 120
Utilitarian philosophy, 34, 180–81

Vaish, Amrisha, 52
Veblen, Thorstein, 187
Vegetarianism, 209–10
Veil of ignorance (John Rawls), 34
Vendler, Helen, 197
Victimless acts and moral outrage, 12
Voltaire, 131–32

Waldron, Jeremy, 102, 200–201
Wallace, Alfred Russel, 189–90
Warneken, Felix, 13
Wealth of Nations, An Inquiry into the Nature and Cause of the (Smith), 4–5, 57
Wheatley, Thalia, 140
Will and Grace (television show), 199
Woodcock, Peter, 35–36
Woodward, Amanda, 23
World War II, 110, 123
Wright, Robert, 204–5
Wynn, Karen, 19, 22, 25, 30, 81, 97, 178

Yale Infant Cognition Center, 24–25
Yamaguchi, Mariko, 29

Zahn-Wexler, Carolyn, 48
Zhong, Chen-Bo, 150–51

About the Author

PAUL BLOOM is the Brooks and Suzanne Ragen Professor of Psychology at Yale University. He is the author or editor of six other books, including the acclaimed *How Pleasure Works*. He has won numerous awards for his research and teaching, and his scientific popular articles have appeared in *The New York Times Magazine, Nature,* the *New Yorker,* the *Atlantic, Science, Slate, The Best American Science Writing,* and many other publications. He lives in New Haven with his wife and two sons. Visit his website at paulbloomatyale.com and follow @paulbloomatyale on Twitter.